CHUCK KLOSTERMAN
IV

ALSO BY CHUCK KLOSTERMAN

Fargo Rock City:
A Heavy Metal Odyssey in Rural Nörth Daköta

Sex, Drugs, and Cocoa Puffs:
A Low Culture Manifesto

Killing Yourself to Live:
85% of a True Story

CHUCK KLOSTERMAN IV

A Decade of Curious People and Dangerous Ideas

faber and faber

First published in 2006 in the USA
by Scribner
First published in Great Britain in 2007 by
Faber and Faber Limited
3 Queen Square London WC1N 3AU

Printed in England by Mackays of Chatham, plc

The right of Chuck Klosterman to be identified as author of this work
has been asserted in accordance with Section 77 of the Copyright,
Designs and Patents Act 1988

Portions of this work reprinted with permission from SPIN magazine
and the Akron Beacon Journal, all rights reserved. Portions of this
work originally appeared in Esquire, The Forum of Fargo-Moorhead
and The New York Times Magazine. "Mannequin Appropriation Project" first appeared in the April 2005 issue of The Believer magazine.

A CIP record for this book
is available from the British Library

ISBN 978–0–571–23399–1

2 4 6 8 10 9 7 5 3 1

CONTENTS

THINGS THAT ARE TRUE

THINGS THAT MIGHT BE TRUE

SOMETHING THAT ISN'T TRUE AT ALL

CHUCK KLOSTERMAN
IV

"Can I tell you something weird?" he asked. This probably isn't a valid question, because one can never say no to such an inquiry. But this is what he asked me.

"Of course," I said in response. "Always."

"Okay, well . . . great. That's great."

He collected his thoughts for fourteen seconds.

"Something is happening to me," he said. "I keep thinking about something that happened to me a long time ago. Years ago. Like, this thing happened to me in eighth fucking grade. This is a situation I hadn't even thought about for probably ten or fifteen years. But then I saw a documentary that reexamined the *Challenger* explosion, and this particular event had happened around that same time. And what's disturbing is that—now—I find myself thinking about this particular afternoon *constantly*. I have dreams about it. Every time I get drunk or stoned, I inevitably find myself sitting in a dark room, replaying the sequence of the events in my mind, over and over again. And the details I remember from this 1986 afternoon are unfathomably intense. Nothing is missing and nothing is muddled. And I'm starting to believe—and this, I suppose, is the weird part—that maybe this day was the most important day of my entire life, and that everything significant about my personality was created on this one particular afternoon. I'm starting to suspect that this memory is not merely about a certain day of my life; this memory is about *the* day, if you get my meaning."

"I think I do," I said. "Obviously, I'm intrigued."

"I thought you would be," he replied. "In fact, that's why I specifically wanted to talk to you about this problem. Because the story itself isn't amazing. It's not like my best friend died

1

on this particular day. It's not like a wolf showed up at my school and mauled a bunch of teachers. It's not a sad story, and it's not even a funny story. It's about a junior-high basketball game."

"A junior-high basketball game."

"Yes."

"The most important day in your life was a junior-high basketball game."

"Yes."

"And you're realizing this now, as a thirty-three-year-old chemical engineer with two children."

"Yes."

I attempted to arch my eyebrows to suggest skepticism, but the sentiment did not translate.

"Obviously, this story isn't *really* about basketball," he said. "I suppose it's *kind of* about basketball, because I was playing a basketball game on this particular afternoon. However, I have a feeling that the game itself is secondary."

"It always is," I said.

"Exactly. So, here's the situation: when I was in eighth grade, our basketball team was kind of terrible. You only play a ten-game schedule when you're in eighth grade, and we lost four of our first six games, a few of them by wide margins. I was probably the best player on the team, and I sucked. We were bad. We knew we were bad. And on the specific afternoon I'm recalling, we were playing the Fairmount Pheasants. We had played Fairmount in the first game of the year, and they beat us by twenty-two points. Fairmount only had three hundred people in their whole goddamn town, but they had the best eighth-grade basketball team in rural southeast North Dakota that winter."

"That's tremendous," I said.

"They had a power forward named Tyler RaGoose. He was the single most unstoppable Pheasant. He was wiry and swarthy and strong, and he almost had a mustache; every great eighth-grade basketball player *almost* has a mustache. The rumor was that he could dunk a volleyball and that he

2

had already fucked two girls, one of whom was a sophomore. It seemed plausible. They also had a precocious, flashy seventh grader who played point guard—I think his name was Trevor Monroe. He was one of those kids who was just naturally good at everything: he played point guard in the winter, short-stop in the summer, and quarterback in the fall. I'm not sure if Fairmount had a golf course, but I assume he was the best chipper in town if they did. They had this guy named Kenwood Dotzenrod who always looked sleepy, but he could get fouled whenever he felt like it. That was his gift—he knew how to get fouled. Do you remember Adrian Dantley? That stoic dude who played for the Utah Jazz and the Detroit Pistons with a really powerful ass? Kenwood Dotzenrod was like a white, thirteen-year-old Adrian Dantley. It seemed like he shot twelve free throws every night. These were just perfect, flawless Pheasants. And it's hard to understand how that happened, because—once those kids got into high school—Fairmount defined mediocrity. They were never better than a .500 club. But as junior-high kids, they were a potato sack full of wolver-ines. They were going to humiliate us, and everybody in my school seemed to know this.

"Because we were junior-high kids, the game started right after school. It was scheduled for 4:15 P.M. That school day was interminable. I was wearing a gray acrylic sweater and cargo pants, because our coach didn't let us wear jeans on game days. It was a different era, I suppose—no rap music. I remember walking around the school in those idiotic cargo pants, eating corndogs at lunch, pretending to care about earth science, and just *longing* for 4:15. Because I had this irrefutable, unexplainable premonition that we were going to play great that day. I didn't think we would necessarily *win*, because Fairmount was better and they had the mustache dude, and we were lazy, underfed losers. But I still had a vague sense that we would not humiliate ourselves. We would execute and hustle, and the game would be close. This feeling was almost spiritual. And I was not the kind of kid who looked on the bright side of *anything*; I was never optimistic about any element of my eighth-grade life. But something made me certain that good things were on the horizon. We started warming up for the game at 3:55, and I can recall standing in the lay-up line and looking at the Pheasants at the other end of the court. Half of their team had spiky rat-tail haircuts, which was the style of the time. It was a different era, I suppose—Don Johnson and David Lee Roth defined masculinity. The gym felt especially hot and especially dry. I couldn't make myself sweat. I remember thinking, *Our school needs a humidifier.* Our cheerleaders weren't even paying attention to us. They were probably looking at Tyler RaGoose's potential mustache."

"So did your team play well?" I asked. "Was your intuition correct?"

"Fuck, yeah," he responded immediately. "We couldn't have played any better than we did. I mean, remember: we were junior-high kids. We were just little guys—half our squad weighed less than one hundred pounds. I still didn't have pubic hair. But we played like basketball geniuses. Fairmount scored on the first possession of the game, we scored on the second possession, and it just went back and forth like that for the entire first half. Nobody on either team seemed to miss. Do you recall when Villanova upset Georgetown in the 1985 NCAA championship game? It was like we were all possessed by the spirit of Villanova. This was unlike any junior-high game I've ever witnessed, before or since. It was better than half of the shit they show on ESPN2. That Trevor Monroe kid—this spiky-haired little elf who was maybe five feet tall—knocked down three twenty-one-foot jump shots in a row. My memories of this are all so goddamn vivid. It actually freaks me out, because I barely remember anything else from that winter; I barely remember anything else from that entire school year. But I somehow recall that the score was 35 to 33 in Fairmount's favor with ten seconds left in the first half, and somebody from our team dribbled the ball off his own foot. Trevor Monroe rushed the rock up the court and threw a blind bounce pass to a kid named Billy Barnaby in the right

4

corner; Barnaby was a 4.00 student, and he was probably the only fourteen-year-old boy in Fairmount who actively liked poetry. Girls felt safe around him—he looked like Topher Grace. I jumped in his direction, but Barnaby threw in a fadeaway jumper at the buzzer, pushing Fairmount's halftime lead to four points. When the rock nestled in the net, Barnaby awkwardly clapped his hands and sprinted into the visitors' locker room with one fist in the air. It was like he had just blown up a federal building with the White Panthers. It was intense.

"Now, the second half was more like a standard junior-high basketball game. There was less scoring, and we behaved like normal eighth graders. Players would fuck up on occasion. But every possession was still akin to the Bataan death march. I don't think I have ever wanted anything as much as I wanted to win that game. I mean, what else in my life did I care about? I was fourteen. What else mattered to me? Nothing. There was nothing I cared about as much as playing basketball against other eighth graders. I had no perspective. I suppose I liked my bedroom, and I liked girls who owned Def Leppard cassettes, and I liked being Catholic. I liked eating gravy. But this game felt considerably more important than all of those things. If I were to play in a Super Bowl or the World Series tomorrow night, it wouldn't feel as monumental as this event felt twenty years ago. I could not comprehend any valuable existence beyond this specific basketball game; my eighth-grade worldview was profoundly telescopic. I suspect this depth of emotion can only happen when you're that particular age."

"And I assume this realization is what you were referring to earlier," I said. "I assume this realization is why that afternoon was the most important afternoon of your life: it was the cognition of your deepest desire."

"No," he said. "That's not it. That's not even close. The thing is, it started to look like this game was going to go into overtime. It was 48 to 48. Fairmount had the ball, and the semi-mustachioed RaGoose drove the baseline and scored with maybe twenty seconds remaining. We could not contain his machismo. So now we were behind, 50 to 48. Still, I believed we would somehow tie things up. I was certain we would score; for the whole game, we had always managed to score when we truly needed to score. But this time, we didn't. We turned it over. We were trying to feed our post player, and the ball ricocheted off his paw. So now the Pheasants had the ball with a two-point lead, and I had to intentionally foul Kenwood Dotzenrod with five seconds remaining. It was the only way to stop the clock. It was an act of desperation. I was desperate. It was the most desperate thing I've ever done."

"So . . . you lost," I said. "And I gather that this must be one of those stories about dealing with heartache: this was when you realized that losing can be more meaningful than winning."

"No," he said. "We ended up winning this game. Kenwood Dotzenrod missed his free throw. He shot a line drive at the front of the iron and the ball bounced straight into my hands; I called time-out while I was catching it. Our coach designed a play that didn't work, but that aforementioned post player—Cubby Jones, a semi-fundamentalist Christian who's now a high-school math teacher—got fouled at midcourt with one second remaining. One of the lesser Pheasants stupidly went for the steal—remember, we were just eighth graders. We were all stupid. So now Cubby Jones had to make both of these free throws with one second on the clock, which is an insane amount of pressure to put on a fourteen-year-old named Cubby. But he rattled in the first shot and swished the second, and the game went into overtime. And—not to brag or anything, because this is just what happened—I ended up hitting a sixteen-foot jump shot at the buzzer at the end of OT. We won 56 to 54. It was the greatest night of my life, at least up to that point. So I suppose I am technically the hero of this particular anecdote."

We both finished our beverages.

"Curious," I said. "Don't take this the wrong way, but I'm a little disappointed. This story is far more conventional than I anticipated. I would never have assumed that the biggest moment of your existence would be making a jump shot before you had pubic hair. To be frank, this is kind of a rip-off. You've made dozens of confessions that were far more consequential than this."

"But I still haven't told you the part that I remember most," he said. "Winning the game, making the shot . . . I remember those things, yes. They made me happy at the time. They are positive memories. But the moment I remember more than any other—the moment that is more than just a nostalgic imprint—is the feeling that came after desperately fouling Kenwood Dotzenrod. Because when that happened, I was certain we had lost. Everything felt hopeless. It seemed unlikely that Kenwood would miss, implausible that we would get a reasonable opportunity to score if such a miss occurred, and impossible that such an opportunity would result in any degree of success. And I had invested so much energy into the previous twenty-three minutes and fifty-five seconds of this eighth-grade basketball game. I had—at some point, probably late in the third quarter—unconsciously decided that losing this game would be no different than being alone forever. It would be the same as being buried alive. Everything else became trivial. So when I desperately slapped Kenwood Dotzenrod on the wrist and I heard the referee's whistle, I felt the life drain from my blood. My bones softened. I felt this . . . this . . . this kind of *predepression*. Like, I knew I couldn't be depressed *yet*, because the game was still in progress. I still had to try to win, because that is what you do whenever you play any game. You try to win. You aren't allowed to give up, even philosophically. I still had to pretend that those final five seconds had meaning, and I could not outwardly express fear or sadness or disappointment. But I instantly knew how terrible I would feel when I went to bed that evening. I could visualize my future sadness. And because I was an eighth-grader—because I had no fucking perspective on anything—I assumed this would bother me for the rest of my life. It seemed like something that would never go away. So I stood on the edge of the free-throw lane, tugging on the bottom of my

7

shorts, vocally reminding my teammates to box out, mentally preparing myself for a sadness that would last forever."

"Interesting," I said. "It seems that you are describing how it feels to be doomed."

"Yes!"

"And this sense of doom is why an eighth-grade basketball game remains the most important moment of your life?"

"Maybe," he said. "Actually, yes."

"But you weren't doomed," I said. "You won the game. That one guy, the white Adrian Dantley . . . what was his name again?"

"Kenwood Dotzenrod."

"Right. Kenwood Dotzenrod did, in fact, miss. Your team did, in fact, get an opportunity to score, and Cubby Jones did, in fact, make his free throws. You were never doomed. And even if this scenario had ended differently—even if Kenwood Dotzenrod had made one of his free throws, or if Cubby had missed one of his—your adolescent sadness would have been fleeting. You would have been sad for a week, or a month, or maybe even a year. But those things fade. This is just something specific that you happen to remember, and—because you seem to be actively dwelling upon its alleged significance—you unconsciously re-create all the other details you've forgotten. That's why it seems so vivid: you're *making* it vivid, just by talking about it. I mean, come on: everybody has a basketball game they remember, or a girl they kissed during *Pretty in Pink,* or some alcoholic cousin who died in a hunting accident. Or whatever. You know what I mean? It all seems so arbitrary, and—at least in this case—completely backward. *You're disturbed about something meaningless that worked out exactly the way you wanted.* It's not just that I don't understand what this metaphor signifies; I honestly don't know if this story involves any metaphor at all. Where is the conflict? What is the problem? I mean, you said it yourself: technically, you are the hero of this story."

"Yes," he said in response. "Technically, I am. But isn't that always the problem?"

THINGS
THAT ARE
TRUE

SOUTHERN-FRIED
SEX KITTEN

Britney Spears is the most famous person I've ever interviewed. She was also the weirdest. I assume this is not a coincidence.

The main thing I remember about this interview is that I spent (what seemed like) twelve thousand years waiting for her photo shoot to end. There was minor chaos during the shoot, because—at the last minute—Britney decided she did not want to be photographed pantless, and that specific pantless image was (in truth) the main reason *Esquire* wanted to do a story on her. They needed a pantless Britney on the cover of their magazine. Her refusal created an intense dichotomy among her handlers: Britney's family members didn't want her to do anything overtly sexy, but her publicity team (whom she later fired) *only* wanted her to do things that were overtly sexy. She eventually agreed with her publicist. The singular upside to the photo shoot was the cookies; someone was responsible for providing Britney with warm chocolate chip cookies at all times, and they were fucking awesome.

After I spent my time with Spears, people kept asking me, "What is she *really* like?" My answer was usually, "I don't know, and I don't think she does, either." And that's not sarcasm; I honestly believe Britney Spears was so insulated from the public (and so exhaustively governed by the people trying to control her image) that she became unable to differentiate between (a) the person who was famous and (b) the person she actually was. I suspect this is why she kept making so many strange decisions in the wake of this interview (i.e., getting married in Las Vegas to someone she barely liked, wearing T-shirts that said things like "MILF in Training," constantly being photographed barefoot in public, etc.). Her management team directed so much emphasis toward turning her into an unsophisticated semi-redneck that she now has no idea what is normal and what is marketing. I suppose her life is exciting, but I suspect it's a pretty terrible way to live; I don't think she has any idea what's really happening to her.

That said, I did notice that her Southern accent always seemed to mysteriously disappear whenever she became annoyed with my questions. Maybe she's the blond Machiavelli.

Because the photos that ran with this story were pretty hot, *Esquire* cut about seven hundred words out of my profile to create more space for the pictures. This is the original draft.

BENDING SPOONS
WITH BRITNEY SPEARS
(NOVEMBER 2003)

Twenty feet away from me, Britney Spears is pantless. Her sculpted hair makes her look like Marilyn Monroe on a date with DiMaggio, assuming they're going to Manhattan's finest pantless restaurant. She's wearing a sweater that probably costs more than my parents' house, and her white heels add five inches to her five-foot-four pantless frame. Oh, and did I mention she's pantless? She's not wearing any pants.

This is a hard detail to ignore.

This is a hard detail to ignore because the number of men who have seen a pantless Britney belong to a highly select fraternity: it's Justin Timberlake, her gynecologist, the photographer who's doing this particular photo shoot, and (maybe) the frontman for a fourth-rate rap-metal outfit from Jacksonville, Florida. That's more or less everybody. And— perhaps stupidly—I actually thought I was about to rush this semi-pathetic frat; I honestly believed the reason I was invited to this Manhattan photo shoot was to glimpse Britney's vagina and write about its cultural significance. Somehow, that seemed like the only logical explanation as to why Britney's naked ass was being unleashed on the cover of this magazine; this whole affair must be an aggressive, self-conscious reinvention. I mean, why else would I have been invited here? Why else would Spears have just released the (ahem) "news" that she lost her virginity at the age of eighteen (a story that surfaced only thirty-six hours before this very photo session)? Isn't this how the modern media operates? Isn't everything wholly overt?

Actually, no.

Britney's secret garden will not be seen this afternoon, or at least not seen by me. All her pictures are ultimately shot behind a fifteen-foot-high opaque partition, and nary a heterosexual man is allowed behind its wall. Apparently, the reason I am here is to be reminded that the essence of Britney Spears's rawest sexuality is something *I will never see*, even though I know it's there. This is why I am a metaphor for America, and this is also why Britney Spears is a metaphor for the American Dream. Culturally, there is nothing more trenchant than the fact that Britney Spears will never give it up, even though she already has.

Over the next ninety minutes, I will sit on a couch next to an ostensibly fully clothed Britney and ask her a battery of questions. She will not really answer any of them. Interviewing Britney Spears is like conducting a deposition hearing with Bill Clinton: regardless of the evidence, she does not waiver. "Why do you dress so provocatively?" I ask. She says she doesn't dress provocatively. "But look what you're wearing right now," I say, and I have a point, because I ask this while looking at three inches of her inner thigh, her entire abdomen, and enough cleavage to choke a musk ox. "This is just a shirt and a skirt," she responds. I ask her questions about her iconography, and she acts as though she has no idea what the word *iconography* even means. It is not that Britney Spears denies that she is a sexual icon, or that she disagrees with the assertion that she embodies the "madonna/whore" dichotomy more than any human in history, or that she feels her success says nothing about what our society fantasizes about. She doesn't disagree with any of that stuff, because she swears *she*

13

has never even thought about it. Not even once. When I ask her to theorize about why American men are so fascinated with the concept of the wet-hot virgin, she legitimately acts as if it is the first time anyone has ever brought that query to her attention.

"That's just a weird question," she says. "I don't even want to think about that. That's strange, and I don't think about things like that, and I don't want to think about things like that. Why should I? I don't have to deal with those people. I'm concerned with the kids out there. I'm concerned with the next generation of people. I'm not worried about some guy who's a perv and wants to meet a freaking virgin."

And suddenly, something becomes painfully clear: either Britney Spears is the least self-aware person I've ever met, or she's way, *way* savvier than I shall ever be.

Or maybe both.

Britney smells excellent. She smells like fruit (kiwi in particular). Like many celebrities, she seems smaller in real life than she appears on television, but Spears also looks a little *harder*—sometimes brittle, sometimes fragile. As I ask her questions, I can tell she isn't comfortable (at one point she gets up and walks away, but stops after five steps and returns to apologize). And the more I badger her, the more I find myself feeling sorry for dragging her through this process. For whatever the reason, I really want to love this person.

Compared to the depletion of the ozone layer or the war in Liberia, I concede that the existence of Britney Spears is light-years beyond trivial. But if you're remotely interested in the cylinders that drive pop culture, it's hard to overestimate her significance. She is not so much a person as she is an *idea,* and the idea is this: you can want everything, so long as you get nothing. The Western world has always been fixated with the eroticism of purity; that was how Brooke Shields sold Calvin Kleins, and that was how Annette Funicello sold the beach. But no one has ever packaged that schism like Britney Spears. She is the naughtiest good girl of all time. However, this philosophical chasm is not what makes her important; the chasm merely makes her rich. What makes Spears different is her abject unwillingness to recognize that this paradox exists *at all*. She never winks, she never cracks, and she never relents from her abject naïveté.

I realize this does not seem possible; it did not seem possible to me, either. But this is the crux of her genius. Over and over and over again, I interrogate Spears about the motivations behind her career arc, starting with the first video she ever made, ". . . Baby One More Time." Arguably the last transcendent clip MTV ever aired, the sexual overtones of ". . . Baby One More Time" seem almost stupidly symbolic. Yet when I tell this to Britney, she finds the suggestion ridiculous.

"I was wearing a freaking Catholic school girl's outfit!" she exclaims, which is (of course) exactly why everyone else in the universe views it as the hyperdriven exploitation of an unabashed taboo. But there is no subtext in Britney World. "I was just dancing and doing what I love. To me, that's truly sexy. In so many videos these days, you see girls with their bras on, and they're just hoochie mamas. *Men don't like that!* Well, maybe some men do—the kind of men I'm not attracted to. But real people just want to see someone having a good time. They want to see someone shine."

This is what makes Britney so different: she refuses to deconstruct herself. That falls in stark contrast with the previous generation of blond icons, most notably Madonna (who makes it clear that she controls every extension of her existence) and Pam Anderson (who refuses to take her own Barbie Doll bombast seriously). Madonna would never claim an outfit was merely "a skirt and a shirt." Pam would never deny that her stardom is founded on strangers wanting to sleep with her. Both of those women know exactly what they're doing, and they want you to realize that, too. But Spears wants everything to look like an accident, and this is crucial. If Britney were to forfeit anything—if she were to even *casually* admit that she *occasionally* uses her body as a commercial weapon—all of this would be over. She would immediately become like everybody else. But this will never happen. What keeps Britney perfect—what *makes* Britney perfect—is that she can produce a video where people lick the sweat off her body (as they did in 2001's "I'm a Slave 4 U") and still effortlessly insist the song has no relationship to sex whatsoever. ("It's just about being a slave to the music," she tells me.) On the day of our interview, Britney took another photograph for this magazine wearing only panties and pearls, and she pulled down the elastic of her underwear with her thumbs; if she would have pulled two inches more, *Esquire* would have become *Hustler*. But that reality does not affect *her* reality, which is that this picture has nothing to do with sex.

> **Britney:** Haven't you ever seen girls on the covers of magazines before? Did you see the J-Lo cover? She was wearing a bikini. Did you see the cover with Cameron Diaz on it?
>
> **CK:** Yes I did. And why do you think those women did those photo shoots?
>
> **Britney:** Because it's the freaking cover of *Esquire* magazine! Why not? You get to look beautiful. It's not that deep.
>
> **CK:** So why exactly do you think the magazine puts women like that on its cover?
>
> **Britney:** I don't know. Maybe because those people are pretty and appealing, and they work their asses off, and they believe in themselves.
>
> **CK:** Do you honestly believe that?
>
> **Britney:** Well, some people might say it's just to make money off of them and to sell magazines. But another reason—a better reason, and the one I choose—is that they do it to inspire people.

Britney is like the little kid who freaks out Keanu Reeves in *The Matrix*: You say you want to bend a spoon? Well, the first thing you need to realize is that *there is no spoon*.

• • •

I'm not supposed to ask Britney about Justin Timberlake. This rule is made very clear to me the moment I arrive at the photo shoot. Granted, everyone knows that Spears and the former 'N Sync member used to live together, and everyone knows about their breakup, and everyone knows they (evidently) had sex when Spears was eighteen. But her handlers still request that I don't ask any questions about their relationship. When I eventually ask Spears about this anyway, her response is extraordinarily innocuous. "The bottom line—and I hate talking about this, but whatever—is that we were both too young to be that serious with each other." However, she does say that the alleged postbreakup "dance-off" at the L.A. club Lounge never happened, and she admits that she and Justin don't speak anymore, even though she considers him a "creative genius."

Viewed retrospectively, there's no doubt the Justin-Britney romance helped Timberlake's career more than hers—especially since Spears always insisted she was a virgin, even when they were living together. Optimistic thirteen-year-old girls could imagine Justin as the ultimate gentleman, perfectly content to keep his paws to himself while the foxiest girl on the planet sat around the house in her underwear, sucking on Popsicles and telling him to wait until she was ready. They were, in a sense, Virgin Royalty: super-rich, *über*-clean pop stars who epitomized just how wonderful teenage Americans could still be.

This is why it was so jarring to hear Fred Durst on *The Howard Stern Show* in February, graphically discussing his alleged sexual dalliances with Spears. Her encounter with the Limp Bizkit vocalist—regardless of its truth—publicly cemented Spears's fall from grace; Durst is universally perceived as rock's sleaziest baboon. Yet the moment Britney "explains" what happened, the gravity of the situation deflates. Here again, Spears's persona becomes weirdly Clintonesque: deny, deny, deny . . . and then classify everything as old news.

"That was my fault for hanging out with people like that," she says of Durst. "Fred was a very great guy. He was a nice

17

guy. And at the time he was trying to come on to me, I wasn't in the right frame of mind to have a relationship with anybody. So maybe I did hurt his ego, and [going on the radio] was his way of dealing with that. But I learned my lesson. And at the time, I was kind of confused, because my tour had just ended. Me and my girlfriends went out one night, and I was feeling like a free bird. But I really don't want to talk about this."

I have no idea what those last two statements are supposed to mean; either she obviously slept with him, or she obviously didn't. The odds are 50–50. And this is a balance Britney either (a) consciously strives for, or (b) sustains without even trying. Cliché as it may sound, she is truly all things to all people: a twelve-year-old girl thinks she's a hero; that girl's older brother thinks she's a stripper; that older brother's girl-friend thinks she's an example of why women hate themselves; that girlfriend's father secretly wishes his own twelve-year-old daughter would invite Britney over for a slumber party. As long as she never dictates her character—as long as Spears never overtly says "This is who I am"—everyone gets to inject their own meaning. Subconsciously, we all get to rebrand Britney Spears.

"The public knows when someone is being honest," she says. "The people know what's real. This might be a weird analogy, but it's like watching *Friends* on the TV. You just get what those people are talking about. It's funny to you, and you're drawn into them."

Here again, we see the brilliance of Britney: on the surface, this statement is insane. Anyone who watches *Friends* would never argue it's successful because of its authenticity, nor would it seem like those characters have conversations that reflect any kind of tangible normalcy.[1] But every single week,

---

1. In retrospect, I might be wrong on this point. I think the evolution of *Friends* over its ten seasons makes my argument seem reasonable, because—after about 1998—the show had completely transgressed into a vehicle for the on-screen personalities of its six stars. By its conclusion, none of the characters on *Friends* seemed even semi-real and all the dia-

twenty million people watch *Friends*. They see something in Chandler Bing and Phoebe Buffay that makes them happy. And what those twenty million people see is something that Britney sees—and perhaps Britney *understands*—in a way that most of us do not.

"Had I not went into music," she tells me, "I probably would have gone to college and became a schoolteacher. That was my dream, because I love kids. Either that, or an entertainment lawyer." For a moment, I think this is a joke. But it's not a joke. But it's brilliant. Schoolteacher, entertainment lawyer, pop star, African warlord—what's the fucking difference? "I'm famous," she concedes, "but I'm not famous like freaking Brad Pitt or Jennifer Aniston. But in my weird little head, I just think we're all here to inspire each other. We're all equal. We just bounce off of each other and show the world what we can do."

Logic would suggest that Spears's upcoming fourth album will be a reinvention, and that she will try to attract a more mature audience (much like Christina Aguilera did with her album *Dirrty* and a freshly conceived "Gothic Hooker" image). Britney says nay. "Actually, the record label wanted me to do certain kinds of songs, and I was like, 'Look, if you want me to be some kind of sex thing, that's not me.' I will never do that. I'm still doing what I love to do."

So that settles it. Don't be fooled by the photos that accompany this story, true believers: Britney Spears is not going to

---

logue sounded like skit comedy. But when the program was conceived in 1994, most of the action was built around relatively plausible problems; I recall one episode from the second season where three of the characters (Chandler, Ross, and Monica) had decent jobs while the other three were essentially unemployed, and that economic disparity created a class issue among people who normally perceived themselves as peers (and which manifested itself through a Hootie and the Blowfish concert). This is a common problem for young people who enter the job market immediately after college, as many of their collegiate friends are left eating ramen noodles while they earn actual money. This, I suppose, would suggest that *Friends* did illustrate "authenticity" and "normalcy." Britney is like Max Weber.

become "some kind of sex thing." She is still the person you want to imagine. She always will be. And she is making that decision; you are not.

"I was just talking about sexuality with my makeup artist," she tells me a mere ten minutes into our conversation, "and I was explaining to her that—when I was thirteen years old—I used to walk around my house completely naked. And my dad would say, 'Britney, put some clothes on, we have people over.' My family just always walked around the house naked. We were earthy people. I've never been ashamed of my body. We were very free people."

True. And I'm sure this has no freaking significance whatsoever.

(THIS HAPPENED IN)
OCTOBER

U2 is the most self-aware rock band in history. This generally works to their advantage.

There are myriad reasons why U2 has been successful, but the quality I found most relevant was the depth of their inwardly focused consciousness. They are not an inauthentic band, but they are also not an organic band; nothing about U2 is accidental. ABC sports broadcaster Al Michaels likes to tell an anecdote about Howard Cosell: Michaels claims he once watched Cosell break up a fistfight between a couple of anonymous thugs. After it was over, Michaels asked Cosell how he found the guts to get involved in a random street brawl between two hyperaggressive maniacs, both of whom could have killed him. "I know who I am," Cosell said in response. Bono is the same way; Bono knows who he is.

What Bono can see (and what so many other groups tend to miss) is the relationship between capitalism and freedom. U2 never had to worry about Island Records interfering with their musical vision because the band understands a very basic equation: as long as they make everyone money, they will be allowed to do whatever they want. It's assumed that any time an entity becomes corporate, that entity loses its autonomy; this was not the case with U2. As U2 grew larger and larger, they actually became more free. When I met them in fall of 2004, they had a limitless kind of autonomy that surpassed any indie band on any independent label. I've never met a rock group more satisfied with the condition of their career.

Because Bono always behaves like he's being filmed for a documentary, he gave me bushels of material. I think I was able to type this entire piece in less than an hour. However, the rest of the experience sucked. Dublin was cold and wet, and the pubs were filled with American tourists who didn't understand how to be drunk in public. All my friends at *SPIN* told me that I would love Ireland and that complete strangers would want to make conversation at every bar I stumbled into; this only happened once, and the guy turned out to be a Norwegian white supremacist. I had one good meal, and it was at a Hard Rock Cafe. I should never go anywhere.

MYSTERIOUS DAYS
(DECEMBER 2004)

"The job of art is to chase away ugliness," Bono tells me as he twists the ignition key of his Maserati Quattroporte. "So let's start with the roads. Cars are so ugly. America is supposedly the country that brought us the love of the automobile, yet they haven't produced a beautiful car in decades. Americans used to make feminine cars with a sense of humor, but now it's all SUVs. The Germans kind of picked up the slack for a while, but the Italians ultimately were the ones that took them on. But the Italians pick such arrogant names. Do you know what *Quattroporte* means? Four-door. It means four-door."

Bono laughs, and I pretend to understand why this is funny. I'm not sure why an expository word like *quattroporte* would seem pretentious, but I certainly can't disagree with his core argument: this is not an ugly car. This is, in fact, the nicest automobile I've ever touched; I've never even had a dream that included a vehicle like this. Sitting in the passenger seat is like being inside a spaceship. I have just spent the last two hours interviewing Bono about the new U2 album, *How to Dismantle an Atomic Bomb*, their tenth career album and their first release in over four years. He is about to drive me back to the Clarence Hotel in Dublin's Temple Bar area, a hotel that Bono co-owns with guitarist the Edge (and which includes a restaurant where Bono plans to have supper with an eighty-two-year-old Irish painter). Our conversation (conducted on the ground floor of U2's headquarters and recording studio) touched on numerous questions, some about music but mostly about politics and celebrity and the meaning of freedom. However, there is only one question about U2 that actually matters, and I'm still trying to figure it out while this four-door Maserati backs out of the studio's garage: is Bono for real, or is Bono full of shit?

We begin driving away from the studio, a faceless two-story building nestled along the canal in Dublin's most relentlessly industrial neighborhood. Suddenly, Bono—who is wearing sunglasses to spite the darkness—spots four teenagers sitting on a bench in the dark, huddled next to some U2 graffiti and bundled in sweaters (it's fifty degrees outside, but it feels colder). Two of the girls are from Belgium, one girl is from Austria, and one guy is Irish. They have been sitting there for seven hours, hoping to see anything that vaguely resembles a transcendent rock band. "I'm going to talk to these kids," Bono says as he stops the Maserati and jumps out. I can see him signing autographs in the rearview mirror. This strikes me as quaint, and I begin jotting down the event in my notebook. But then Bono opens the trunk and throws the teenagers' bags inside. Suddenly, there are four pale kids climbing into the backseat of this car. I guess we're lucky this is a Quattroporte.

"We're gonna give these kids a ride," says Bono. I look over my right shoulder at the girl from Austria, and I am able to see what it looks like when someone's mind is blown out of her skull; I can almost see her brains and blood splattered across the rear window. The car takes off; Bono drives recklessly, accelerating and braking at random intervals. "Do you want to hear the new album?" he asks the glassy-eyed teenagers. This was over a month before *How to Dismantle an Atomic Bomb* would be released. They say yes. Bono punches up track four, "Love and Peace or Else." He hits the play button, and it's loud; it sounds like someone dropping the throttle on a Harrier jump jet. Bono starts singing along, harmonizing with himself. He's playing air drums while he drives. The music changes, and he exclaims, "This is the Gary Glitter part!" The music changes again. "This is the Brian Wilson moment!" The teenagers aren't even talking; they're just kind of looking at one another, almost like they're afraid this is some Celtic version of *Punk'd*. One of the kids specifically asks to hear "Miracle Drug," which makes Bono nervous; he is worried that the album may have leaked to the Internet. But he plays it anyway, still singing along, and he turns the volume even higher when we get to the lyrics "Freedom has a scent / Like the top of a newborn baby's head." He calls these two lines the best on the album. This behavior is incredibly charming, and a little embarrassing, and amazingly weird. But we eventually get to the hotel, and Bono drives up on the sidewalk. He unloads the kids' bags, and they walk away like zombies. The two of us amble into the Clarence. We shake hands in the lobby, and then Bono disappears into the restaurant to meet some aging painter I've never heard of. And I find myself thinking, *Did this really just happen? Am I supposed to believe he does this kind of thing all the time, even when he doesn't have a reporter in the front seat of his car? And does that even matter? Was that car ride the greatest moment in those four kids' lives? Was this whole thing a specific performance, or is Bono's entire life a performance? And if your entire life is a performance, does that make everything you do inherently authentic? Is this guy for real, or is this guy completely full of shit?*

Which is kind of how our conversation had started two hours ago.

Two hours before I sat in his Maserati with some freaked-out Belgian teenagers, Bono and I began our dialogue about rock 'n' roll by discussing a computer company. I had already interviewed bassist Adam Clayton two days before, and he was fine (he was smart and sarcastic, and he has very large hands). I had interviewed the Edge earlier that afternoon, and he was equally fine (serious and soft-spoken and wearing that stupid skullcap). I'll talk to drummer Larry Mullen next week over the telephone, and he will be likewise affable. They are all quotable people, and—within the context of the band—they are all equally important. Their longtime producer Brian Eno once said U2 was "the only real group" he'd ever met, because their music is so dependent on the interlocking, democratic nature of the songwriting. But from a cultural perspective—from the perspective of someone who is interested in what U2 is supposed to *mean*—Bono is pretty much the whole band. He's probably the least musical member of U2, but he talks more than the other three members combined—I have never met anyone who likes being interviewed more than Bono.[1] He can talk about anything. And the first thing he talks about is the kind of thing rock singers rarely talk about; the first thing he talks about is Steve Jobs.

"The company that best exemplifies the marriage of technology and pop culture is Apple," Bono says as he paces the floor. "They understand music. They like music. They like the art object. The iPod is probably the greatest pop object since the electric guitar. We—as a band—feel strongly about the iPod. We—as a band—talked about the idea for an iPod years ago. We—as a band—are fans of Apple."

We are in a room with a telephone. Bono points to the telephone.

"We have just now—ten minutes ago—made a partnership with Apple, right on that very phone," he continues. "We want to work with them. The Edge wants to work with their scientists. We want to play with their design team. We want to be in

---

1. This, however, is a little deceptive: I just received a copy of *Bono: In Conversation with Michka Assayas*. The book is essentially a one-person oral history; it's a transcript of several dialogues between Bono and Assayas, a French journalist and longtime U2 fanatic. Many of the seemingly off-the-cuff remarks Bono made to me in October of 2004 were identical to things he said to Assayas during an interview they'd conducted two years earlier, all the way down to the specific words Bono stressed for emphasis. Like I said, nothing about U2 is accidental. But—then again—Assayas and I asked a lot of the same questions; I suppose it would actually be more troubling if he had said things that were completely different.

their commercial. We will do a commercial with Apple for our album, and no money will change hands—which is important, because we have been offered boatloads of money from many other people. But we will make an Apple commercial that's as good as any video. And next year, you will be able to go to a U2 show and download the concert onto your iPod. We're going to make a digital box set, where you can get every U2 album and every U2 B-side and every U2 lyric, all at once. We want to do this because we like their company. It's art, commerce, and technology colliding."

It strikes me that Bono is talking about Apple the same way he talks about Rwandan genocide. He is nothing if not charismatic; if he worked in advertising, we would probably say he has a strong "force of personality." But it also feels a little odd to hear the leader of a rock band talking about how awesome it's going to be to make a commercial for a computer company. I ask him if this partnership will require some kind of compromise, or if this move could somehow bring U2's credibility into question.

"I'm very fond of Steve [Jobs] personally," he responds. "I'm a fan of his company. And you know, we already operate within this kind of corporate structure. We've all been whining about how white rock 'n' roll has its head in the sand on a lot of these issues and how hip-hop has a much more honest approach. Russell Simmons laughs at all those middle-class college kids who are preoccupied with the fear of selling out. I've never been afraid of commerce. I've never been afraid of people who run music companies. There is this cliché that artists are pure and businesspeople can't be trusted. Well, in my life I've met a lot of artists who were real assholes, and I've met a lot of businessmen who walk their dogs. So these things aren't true. We need new thinking."

"New thinking" is one of Bono's critical buzzwords: he wants the world to think differently about many, many things. He wants people to realize the war against AIDS is much more significant than the war against Iraq. He wants American taxpayers to believe that forgiving third world nations of their debt is more beneficial to the world than forcing them to pay it back. These are the causes he has embraced, and not without success; Bono is the most tangibly successful rock 'n' roll activist of all time (he's certainly the only rock star who has been taken seriously by United Nations Secretary General Kofi Annan, ultra-right-wing North Carolina senator Jesse Helms, and former U.S. Treasury Secretary Paul O'Neill). This is the man who prompted *Time* magazine to rhetorically ask whether or not he could "save the world." So when one considers how much power Bono actually wields, and when one considers the state of the planet, and when one considers that U2 is metaphorically using words like *dismantle* and *bomb* in the context of an album title, one might assume that this U2 album will be the most overtly political album of 2004.

Which it is not.

How to Dismantle an Atomic Bomb is not political at all; it's a wholly personal album, and many of the songs were inspired by the death of Bono's father, Bob Hewson, who succumbed to cancer in August 2001. The songwriting process worked as it normally does for the band: the Edge brought in guitar demos, the band collaborated on the sonic skeletons and turned them into U2 songs, and Bono added the lyrics at the end. And though Bono fully intended these songs to be political, it just didn't happen.

"When we make a record, it's not a contrived process," explains the Edge in his signature monotone. "It's not like we sit down and say, 'We're going to write about this.' I don't think any of us thought, *Let's make a political record.* But we certainly thought that was going to be part of it. I am a little bit surprised that it's so personal. I was expecting it to be a *little* more political, but it hasn't gone that way."

What's most interesting about Edge's sentiment is how hard the band openly worked toward that goal. The album's first single, "Vertigo" (which oddly resembles the Supremes' "You Keep Me Hanging On") was originally titled "Native Son," and every single lyric was different; originally, it was

27

completely a political track. But it felt forced; this was not a rebel song. What Bono ultimately realized is that you cannot be political just because other people assume it's your job. No matter how many times he appears on *The O'Reilly Factor*, he's still more of an artist than a politician.

"I write feelings, not thoughts," Bono says while lying on a leather couch, the caricature of a therapy patient. "Feelings are much stronger than thoughts. We are all led by instinct, and our intellect catches up later.[2] This album proves that point. I would have certainly preferred to take on the issues that I deal with politically, but what came out of me were the other things in my life I wasn't tending to: my family, the hypocrisy of my own heart, and my father's death. I mean, why aren't I spending more time with my kids? Why am I trying to save other people's kids instead? How can I sing about love when I'm never at home? There are a lot of things that need to be addressed in the world. But those other things just came pouring out of me."

By the time you read this, the United States either has the same president it had a few weeks ago or it has a new president who is taller. That was not the case when I spoke to U2; during the week of our interviews, it was still September. Not surprisingly, we talked about the impending election (even less surprising, the Irish are far more interested in America than Americans are interested in Ireland). The Edge was open about his support for John Kerry, but Bono—supremely aware that he will have to work with whomever wins—remained staunchly nonpartisan. "I have forsaken my ability to talk about this issue," he said, and I find it hilarious that he actually used the word *forsaken*. For the past twenty-five years, countless people have referred to Bono as "messianic." Now he actually talks like Jesus.

---

2. This sentence is probably the best description of U2's career I've ever heard.

Bono's nonpartisanship has been the catalyst for everything he and his band have accomplished; it's why he can work with legitimate political figures in a meaningful way, and it's why U2 can become business partners with Apple without giving up on rock 'n' roll. But it does raise a paradox: the reason U2 were (arguably) the most important band of the 1980s was because audiences felt they *always* took a side. What makes "Sunday Bloody Sunday" a powerful song is that something seemed to be at stake, even if you had no idea what happened in Northern Ireland during the winter of 1972. If anything, U2 seemed to care about things too much; there was no middle of the road on the drive toward Joshua Tree. And somewhat surprisingly, the band now expresses mild sheepishness about the 1980s, even though that era made them famous.

"If you had to reduce U2 down to the waving of the white flag, which is a moment from the *War* tour, that would be the worst thing," says Clayton when I ask what he hopes U2 will *not* be remembered for in fifty years. "At the time, I think it was in the spirit of the performance. But we weren't very ironic people back then. We were pretty serious people, and we didn't see that we could have been a little more subtle about things like that. But, hey, as mistakes go, that's probably not a bad one."

Part of that revisionism might have to do with age; U2 have now moved into the ever-expanding idiom of Rock Bands Who Could Have Plausibly Fathered the People Who Now Buy Most of Their Albums (Bono is forty-four; Edge, forty-three; Clayton, forty-four; Mullen, forty-two). Their ironic distance also seems to be a product of the 1997 *Pop* album and its subsequent Pop-Mart tour, two projects that largely failed. "I think what happened with that record was this fusion of electronica and the club world, which was not foreign to us," says Clayton. "But what we should have focused on were tracks that were going to be radio friendly. We presented tracks that sounded—in a European context— absolutely appropriate to what we'd hear on the radio. That whole record did a lot better in Europe. But American programmers wouldn't play it. I think that was where we kind of screwed up."

Still, the decision to tour with a giant lemon was important; it was the point where U2's aesthetic changed completely. And this is still happening today: they are actively trying not to be self-aware, which (by definition) is completely impossible. But they're still trying.

"I don't think anyone who's famous didn't *want* to be famous," says Bono, which might be true for everybody but is certainly true for him. "The people who hide in the shadows and cover their heads with their coats when they're being photographed by the paparazzi probably think being famous is more important than it actually is, and—in a way—probably need fame more than anyone else. I've gotten to the stage where I almost forget I'm in a rock band, which was never the case in the 1980s. And that was annoying, because that wasn't sexy. Self-consciousness is never sexy. I mean, I've watched myself being interviewed on TV, and I just think to myself, *What an asshole*."

While I am in Dublin, Larry Mullen is in New York; when I return to New York, Larry Mullen returns to Dublin. For the past nine years, Mullen has been racked with back pain he credits to having never been taught how to play drums; because he sits behind the kit incorrectly, and because he holds his sticks incorrectly, and because he basically just "enjoys hitting things," his spine has paid the price. He missed our scheduled initial conversation because he had to get medical treatment in the States. One of the things Bono casually mentioned in our interview was that Mullen is "incapable of lying," an interesting quality to employ when describing a coworker. When Mullen telephones a week later, I describe the situation with Bono and his Maserati and the teenagers, and I ask if this was a constructed event or a guileless occurrence.

"Well, it would be very easy for me to just say, 'Yes, it was guileless,' because how would you ever know if I was lying?" Mullen says. "But the truth is that Bono really *does* do stuff like that all the time. He really has this insatiable urge to be all things to all people, even when we try to stop him. Now, does he act differently today than he did twenty-five years ago? Of course. But he has always had this desire to be everything. Bono thinks rock 'n' roll is so shallow, in a way. He has always enjoyed the trappings of fame, but he feels this urge to balance it with something more substantial. He really is a walking contradiction. It's always all or nothing with him. There is almost nothing in the middle."

Like the other members of U2, Mullen—who technically founded the band by pinning a "musicians wanted" note on a school bulletin board as a fifteen-year-old—has slowly come to recognize just how bizarre his life has been. Like most bands, the 1979 incarnation of U2 had impossible dreams: they wanted to become famous, and they wanted to be on the radio constantly. They wanted to change the cultural climate. They wanted to be the Beatles and the Stones of their generation. But unlike 99.9 percent of fledgling rock bands, all of that pretty much happened.

"I think Bono probably did have a clear goal," says Mullen. "But I was fifteen when we started playing. I was just enjoying the experience. And we had to work harder than most bands, because we couldn't play and we didn't understand songwriting at all. The truth is that we all had dreams, and we all wanted to be transcendent, but I don't think anyone really believed any of that would happen."

But here's the thing: I think Bono *did* believe all that would happen. And even if he didn't believe it, he's certainly spent a lot of time thinking about it, because it seems like he's thought about everything. At one point, we talked about the Pixies, one of roughly eighteen thousand artists Bono claims to adore. One of the things Bono loves about the Pixies was that they "invented something." I ask Bono if he thinks U2 invented anything. His answer is like Bill Clinton's speech after the 1995 Oklahoma City bombing[3]—it's somehow completely natural and completely rehearsed (at the exact same time).

"Oh yeah," Bono says, and—as he talks—I can vaguely hear the Edge playing the intro to "I Will Follow" through the walls of the studio. "I wouldn't be holding my head up this high if I didn't think that. If I can use the analogy of the spectrum, I think there are certain colors we absolutely own—certain sounds, certain emotions. We can write songs about God and have them right next to songs about girls. I think we weave God, sex, and politics together in a way that's very unusual in white music. And I'm not saying this is a reason that someone should like our music, or that it proves we're great—but I do think that can be said with some objectivity. I hope that doesn't sound arrogant."

Well, it sort of does. But arrogance doesn't matter if you're right.

---

3. You may have noticed that this is the second time I've compared a musician's oratory style to that of Bill Clinton's. I made a similar analogy between Clinton and Britney Spears (although for very different reasons).

CALL ME "LIZARD KING."
NO . . . REALLY. I INSIST.

When I was leaving Val Kilmer's ranch house, he gave me a present. He found a two-page poem he had written about a melancholy farmer, and he ripped it out of the book it was in (in 1988, Val apparently published a book of free-verse poetry called *My Edens After Burns*). He taped the two pages of poetry onto a piece of cardboard and autographed it, which I did not ask him to do. "This is my gift to you," he said. I still possess this gift. Whenever I stumble across those two pages, I reread Val Kilmer's poem. Its theme is somewhat murky. In fact, I can't even tell if the writing is decent or terrible; I've asked four other people to analyze its merits, and the jury remain polarized. But this is what I will always wonder: Why did Val Kilmer give me *this* poem? Why didn't he just give me the entire book? Was Kilmer trying to tell me something?

The man did not lack confidence.

CRAZY THINGS SEEM NORMAL,
NORMAL THINGS SEEM CRAZY
(JULY 2005)

"I just like looking at them," Val Kilmer tells me as we stare at his bison. "I liked looking at them when I was a kid, and I like looking at them now." The two buffalo are behind a fence, twenty-five feet away. A 1,500-pound bull stares back at us, bored and tired; he stomps his right hoof, turns 180 degrees, and defecates in our general direction. "Obviously,

33

we are not seeing these particular buffalo at their most noble of moments," Kilmer adds, "but I still like looking at them. Maybe it has something to do with the fact that I'm part Cherokee. There was such a relationship between the buffalo and the American Indian—the Indians would eat them, live inside their pelts, use every part of the body. There was almost no separation between the people and the animal."

Val Kilmer tells me he used to own a dozen buffalo, but now he's down to two. Val says he named one of these remaining two ungulates James Brown, because it likes to spin around in circles and looks like the kind of beast who might beat up his wife. I have been talking to Kilmer for approximately three minutes; it's 5:20 P.M. on April Fool's Day. Twenty-four hours ago, I was preparing to fly to Los Angeles to interview Kilmer on the Sunset Strip; this was because Val was supposedly leaving for Switzerland (for four months) on April 3. Late last night, these plans changed entirely: suddenly, Val was not going to be in L.A. Instead, I was instructed to fly to New Mexico, where someone would pick me up at the Albuquerque airport and drive me to his 6,000-acre ranch. However, when I arrived in Albuquerque this afternoon, I received a voicemail on my cell phone; I was now told to rent a car and drive to the ranch myself. Curiously, his ranch is not outside Albuquerque (which I assumed would be the case, particularly since Val himself suggested I fly into the Albuquerque airport). His ranch is actually outside of Santa Fe, which is seventy-three miles away. He's also no longer going to Switzerland; now he's going to London.

The drive to Santa Fe on I-25 is mildly Zen: there are public road signs that say "Gusty Winds May Exist." This seems more like lazy philosophy than travel advice. When I arrive in New Mexico's capital city, I discover that Kilmer's ranch is still another thirty minutes away, and the directions on how to arrive there are a little confusing; it takes at least forty-five minutes before I find the gate to his estate. The gate is closed. There is no one around for miles, the sky is huge, and my cell phone no longer works; this, I suppose, is where the buffalo roam (and where roaming rates apply). I locate an intercom phone outside the green steel gate, but most of the numbers don't work. When an anonymous male voice finally responds to my desperate pleas for service, he is terse. "Who are you meeting?" the voice mechanically barks. "What is this regarding?" I tell him I am a reporter, and that I am there to find Val Kilmer, and that Mr. Kilmer knows I am coming. There is a pause, and then he says something I don't really understand: "Someone will meet you at the bridge!" The gate swings open automatically, and I drive through its opening. I expect the main residence to be near the entrance, but it is not; I drive at least two miles on a gravel road. Eventually, I cross a wooden bridge and park the vehicle. I see a man driving toward me on a camouflaged ATV four-wheeler. The man looks like a cross between Jeff Bridges and Thomas Haden Church, which means that this is the man I am looking for. He parks next to my rental car; I roll down the window. He is smiling, and his teeth are huge. I find myself staring at them.

"Welcome to the West," the teeth say. "I'm Val Kilmer. Would you like to see the buffalo?"

"I've never been that comfortable talking about myself, or about acting," the forty-five-year-old Kilmer says. It's 7:00 P.M. We are now sitting in his lodge, which is more rustic than I anticipated. We are surrounded by unfinished wood and books about trout fishing, and an African kudu head hangs from the wall. There seem to be a lot of hoofed animals on this ranch, and many of them are dead. Kilmer's friendly ranch hand (a fortyish woman named Pam Sawyer) has just given me a plateful of Mexican food I never really wanted, so Val is eating it for me. He is explaining why he almost never gives interviews and why he doesn't like talking about himself, presumably because I am interviewing him and he is about to talk about himself for the next four hours. "For quite a while, I thought that it didn't really matter if I defended myself [to journalists], so a lot of things kind of snowballed when I didn't rebuke them. And I mainly didn't do a lot of interviews

35

because they're hard, and I was sort of super-concerned. When you're young, you're always concerned about how you're being seen and how you're being criticized."

I have not come to New Mexico to criticize Val Kilmer. However, he seems almost disturbingly certain of that fact, which is partially why he invited me here. Several months ago, I wrote a column where I made a passing reference about Kilmer being "Advanced."[1] What this means is that I find Kilmer's persona compelling, and that I think he makes choices other actors would never consider, and that he is probably my favorite working actor. This is all true. However, Kilmer took this column to mean that I am his biggest fan on the planet, and that he can trust me entirely, and that I am among his closest friends. From the moment we look at his buffalo, he is completely relaxed and cooperative; he immediately introduces me to his children, Mercedes (age thirteen) and Jack (age ten). They live with their British mother (Kilmer's ex-wife Joanne Whalley, his costar from *Willow*) in Los Angeles, but they apparently spend a great chunk of time on this ranch; they love it here, despite the fact that it doesn't have a decent television. Along with the bison, the farmstead includes horses, a dog, two cats, and (as of this afternoon) five baby chickens, one of which will be eaten by a cat before the night is over. The Kilmer clan is animal crazy; the house smells like a veterinarian's office. Jack is predominantly consumed with the chicks in the kitchen and the trampoline in the backyard. Mercedes is an artist and a John Lennon fan; she seems a little too smart to be thirteen. When I ask her what her favorite Val Kilmer movie is, she says, "Oh, probably *Batman Forever*, but only because it seems like it was secretly made by Andrew Lloyd Webber."

For the first forty-five minutes I am there, the five of us— Kilmer, his two kids, Pam the ranch hand, and myself—occupy the main room of the ranch house and try to make casual con-

---

1. For a protracted explanation of Advancement, see pages 231–36.

versation, which is kind of like making conversation with friendly strangers in a wooden airport. Mercedes has a lot of questions about why Kilmer is "Advanced," and Val mentions how much he enjoys repeating the word *Advanced* over and over and over again. He tells me about an *Afterschool Special* he made in 1983 called *One Too Many*, where he played a teenage alcoholic alongside Mare Winningham (his first teenage girlfriend) and Michelle Pfeiffer (a woman he would later write poetry for). I mention that he seems to play a lot of roles where he's a drug-addled drunk, and he agrees that this is true. In fact, before I got here, I unconsciously assumed Val would be a drug-addled drunk during this interview, since every story I've ever heard about Kilmer implies that he's completely crazy; he supposedly burned a cameraman with a cigarette on the set of *The Island of Dr. Moreau*. There are a few directors (most notably Joel Schumacher) who continue to paint him as the most egocentric, unreasonable human in Hollywood. As far as I can tell, this cannot possibly be accurate. If I had to describe Kilmer's personality in one word (and if I couldn't use the word *Advanced*), I would have to employ the least incendiary of all potential modifiers: Val Kilmer is *nice*. The worst thing I could say about him is that he's kind of a name-dropper; beyond that, he seems like an affable fellow with a good sense of humor, and he is totally not fucked up.

But he is *weird*.

He's weird in ways that are expected, and he's weird in ways that are not. I anticipated that he might seem a little odd when we talked about the art of acting, mostly because (a) Kilmer is a Method actor, and (b) all Method actors are insane. However, I did not realize how much insanity this process truly required. That started to become clear when I asked him about *The Doors* and *Wonderland*, two movies where Kilmer portrays self-destructive drug addicts with an acute degree of realism; there is a scene late in *Wonderland* where he wordlessly (and desperately) waits for someone to offer him cocaine in a manner that seems painfully authentic. I ask if he ever went through a drug phase for real. He says no. He says he's never freebased cocaine in his life; he was simply interested in "exploring acting," but that he understands the mind-set of addiction. The conversation evolves into a meditation on the emotional toll that acting takes on the artist. To get a more specific example, I ask him about the "toll" that he felt while making the 1993 Western *Tombstone*. He begins telling me about things that tangibly happened to Doc Holliday. I say, "No, no, you must have misunderstood me—I want to know about the toll it took on *you*." He says, "I know, I'm talking about those feelings." And this is the conversation that follows:

    CK: You mean you think you literally had the same experience as Doc Holliday?

    Kilmer: Oh, sure. It's not like I believed that I actually shot somebody, but I absolutely know what it feels like to pull the trigger and take someone's life.

    CK: So you're saying you understand how it feels to shoot someone as much as a person who has actually committed a murder?

    Kilmer: I understand it more. It's an actor's job. A guy who's lived through the horror of Vietnam has not spent his life preparing his mind for it. Most of these guys were borderline criminal or poor, and that's why they got sent to Vietnam. It was all the poor, wretched kids who got beat up by their dads, guys that didn't get on the football team, guys who couldn't finagle a scholarship. They didn't have the emotional equipment to handle that experience. But this is what an actor trains to do. So—standing onstage—I can more effectively represent that kid in Vietnam than a guy who was there.

    CK: I don't question that you can more effectively *represent* that experience, but that's not the same thing. If you were talking to someone who's in prison for murder, and the guy said, "Man, it really fucks you up to kill another person," do you think you could reasonably say, "I completely know what you're talking about"?

Kilmer: Oh yeah. I'd know what he's talking about.

CK: You were in *Top Gun*. Does this mean you completely understand how it feels to be a fighter pilot?

Kilmer: I understand it more. I don't have a fighter pilot's pride. Pilots actually go way past actors' pride, which is pretty high. Way past rock 'n' roll pride, which is even higher. They're in their own class.

CK: Let's say someone made a movie about you—Val Kilmer—and they cast Jude Law[2] in the lead role. By your logic, wouldn't this mean that Jude Law— if he did a successful job—would therefore understand what it means to be Val Kilmer more than you do?

Kilmer: No, because I'm an actor. Those other people that are in those other circumstances don't have the self-knowledge.

CK: Well, what if it was a movie about your young life? What if it was a movie about your teen years?

Kilmer: In that case, I guess I'd have to say yes. No matter what the circumstances are, it's all relative. I think Gandhi had a sense of mission about himself that was spiritual. He found himself in political circumstances, but he became a great man. Most of that story in the film *Gandhi* is about the politics; it's about the man leading his nation to freedom. But I know that Sir Ben Kingsley understood the story of Gandhi to be that personal journey of love. It would be impossible to portray Gandhi as he did—which was perfectly—without having the same experience he put into his body. You can't *act* that.

CK: Okay, so let's assume you had been given the lead

_____

2. I have no idea why I would cast Jude Law in this role, particularly if Heath Ledger were available.

role in *The Passion of the Christ*. Would you understand the feeling of being crucified as much as someone who had been literally crucified as the Messiah?

Kilmer: Well, I just played Moses [in a theatrical version of *The Ten Commandments*]. Of course.

CK: So you understand the experience of being Moses? You understand how it feels to be Moses? Maybe I'm just taking your words too literally.

Kilmer: No, I don't think so. That's what acting is.

I keep asking Kilmer if he is joking, and he swears he is not. However, claiming that he's not joking might be part of the joke. A few weeks after visiting the ranch, I paraphrased the preceding conversation to Academy Award–winning conspiracy theorist Oliver Stone, the man who directed Kilmer in 1991's *The Doors* and 2004's *Alexander*. He did not find our exchange surprising.

"This has always been the issue with Val," Stone said via cell phone as his son drove him around Los Angeles. "He speaks in a way that is propelled from deep inside, and he doesn't always realize how the things he says will sound to other people. But there *is* a carryover effect from acting. You can never really separate yourself from what you do, and Val is ultrasensitive to that process."

Stone says Kilmer has substantially matured over the years, noting that the death of Kilmer's father in 1993 had an immediate impact on his emotional flexibility. "We didn't have the greatest relationship when we made *The Doors*," he says. "I always thought he was a technically brilliant actor, but he was difficult. He can be moody. But when we did *Alexander*, Val was an absolute pleasure to work with. I think part of his problems with *The Doors* was that he just got sick of wearing leather pants every day."

Kilmer and his two kids are playing with the cats. Because there are two of these animals (Ernest and Refrigerator), the living room takes on a *Ghost and the Darkness* motif. While they play with the felines, Val casually mentions he awoke that morning at 4:00 A.M. to work on a screenplay, but that he went back to bed at 6:00 A.M. His schedule is unconventional. A few hours later, I ask him about the movie he's writing.

"Well, it's a woman's story," he says cautiously. "It's about this woman who was just fighting to survive, and everything happened to her."

I ask him if this is a real person; he says she is. "Her first husband died. Her own family took her son away from her. She marries a guy because he promises to help her get the son back, and then he doesn't. The new husband is a dentist, but he won't even fix her teeth. She ends up divorcing him because he gets captured in the Civil War. She meets a homeopathic guy who's probably more of a mesmerist hypnotist. For the first time in her life, at forty-two years old, she's feeling good. But then she slips on the ice and breaks every bone in her body, and the doctor and the priest say she should be dead. But she has this experience while she's praying and she gets up. People literally thought they were seeing a ghost. And then she spent the rest of her life trying to articulate what had happened to her. How was she healed? That's what the story is about: the rest of her life. Because she lived until she was ninety and became the most famous lady in the United States."

His vision for this film is amazingly clear, and he tells me the story with a controlled, measured intensity. I ask him the name of the woman. He says, "Mary Baker Eddy. She died in 1910." We talk a little more about this idea (he'd love to see Cate Blanchette in the lead role), but then the conversation shifts to the subject of *Common Sense* author Thomas Paine, whom Kilmer thinks should be the subject of Oliver Stone's next movie.

It is not until the next morning that I realize Mary Baker Eddy was the founder of *The Christian Science Monitor*, and that Val Kilmer is a Christian Scientist.

"Well, that is what I am trying to be," he says while we sit on his back porch and look at the bubbling blueness of the Pecos River. "It is quite a challenging faith, but I don't think I'm hedging. I just think I am being honest."

There are many facets to Christian Science, but most people only concern themselves with one: Christian Scientists do not take medicine. They believe that healing does not come from internal processes or from the power of the mortal mind; they believe healing comes from the Divine Mind of God. Growing up in Los Angeles, this is how Kilmer was raised by his parents. This belief becomes more complex when you consider the context of the Kilmer family: the son of an engineer and a housewife, Val had two brothers. They lived on the outskirts of L.A., neighbors to the likes of Roy Rogers. Over time, the family splintered. Val's parents divorced, and he remains estranged from his older brother over a business dispute that happened more than ten years ago ("We have a much better relationship not speaking," Val says). His younger brother Wesley died as a teenager; Wesley had an epileptic seizure in a swimming pool (Val was seventeen at the time, about to go to school at Juilliard). I ask him if his brother's epilepsy was untreated at the time of his death.

"Well, this is a complicated answer," he says. "He was treated periodically. There is a big misnomer with Christian Science; I think maybe that misnomer is fading. People used to say, 'Christian Science. Oh, you're the ones that don't believe in doctors,' which is not a true thing. It's just a different way of treating a malady. It could be mental, social, or physical. In my little brother's case, when he was diagnosed, my parents were divorced. My father had him diagnosed and Wesley was given some medical treatment for his epilepsy. When he was in school, they would stop the treatment. Then periodically, he would go back and forth between Christian Science and the medical treatment."

I ask him what seems like an obvious question: Isn't it possible that his brother's death happened when he was being untreated, and that this incident could have been avoided?

"Christian Science isn't responsible for my little brother's death," he says, and I am in no position to disagree.

We're still sitting on his porch, and his daughter walks past us. I ask Val if he would not allow her to take amoxicillin if she had a sore throat; he tells me that—because he's divorced—he doesn't have autonomous control over that type of decision. But he says his first move in such a scenario would be to pray, because most illness comes from fear. We start talking about the cult of Scientology, which he has heard is "basically Christian Science without God." We begin discussing what constitutes the definition of religion; Kilmer thinks an institution cannot be classified as a religion unless God is involved. When I argue that this is not necessarily the case, Val walks into the house and brings out the *Oxford English Dictionary*; I'm not sure how many working actors own their own copy of the OED, but this one does. The print in the OED is minuscule, so he begins scouring the pages like Sherlock Holmes. He pores over the tiny words with a magnifying glass that has an African boar's tusk as a handle. He finds the definition of *religion*, but the OED's answer is unsatisfactory. He decides to check what *Webster's Second Unabridged Dictionary* has to say, since he insists that *Webster's Second* was the last dictionary created without an agenda. We spend the next fifteen minutes looking up various words, including *monastic*.

So this, I suppose, is an illustration of how Val Kilmer is weird in unexpected ways: he's a Christian Scientist, and he owns an inordinate number of reference books.

I ask Val Kilmer if he agrees that his life is crazy. First he says no, but then he (kind of) says yes.

"I make more money than the whole state of New Mexico," he says. "If you do the math, I've probably made as much as six hundred thousand or eight hundred thousand people in this state. And I know that's crazy. You know, I live on a ranch that's larger than Manhattan. That's a weird circumstance." Now, this is something of a hyperbole; the island of

Manhattan is 14,563 acres of real estate, which is more than twice as large as Val's semiarid homestead. But his point is still valid—he's got a big fucking backyard, and that's a weird circumstance. "The thing I'm enjoying more is that there are lots of things that fame has brought me that I can use to my advantage in a quiet way. For example, a friend of mine is an amazing advocate for trees. He's so incredible and selfless. He's planted [something like] twenty million trees in Los Alamos. I actually got to plant the twenty-millionth tree. And we got more attention for doing that simply because I've made some movies and I'm famous."

Kilmer's awareness of his fame seems to partially derive from his familiarity with other famous people. During the two days we spend together, he casually mentions dozens of celebrities he classifies as friends—Robert DeNiro, Nelson Mandela, Steve-O. Val tells me that he passed on the lead role in *The Insider* that eventually went to Russell Crowe; he tells me he dreams of making a comedy with Will Ferrell, whom he considers a genius. At one point, Kilmer does a flawless Marlon Brando impersonation, even adjusting the timbre of his voice to illustrate the subtle difference between the '70s Brando from *Last Tango in Paris* and the '90s Brando from *Don Juan DeMarco*. We talk about his longtime camaraderie with Kevin Spacey, and he says that Spacey is "proof that you can learn how to act. Because he was horrible when he first started, and now he's so good." We talk about the famous women he's dated; the last serious relationship he had was with Darryl Hannah, which ended a year ago. During the 1990s, he was involved with Cindy Crawford, so I ask him what it's like to sleep with the most famous woman in the world. His short answer is that it's awesome. His long answer is that it's complicated.

"Cindy is phenomenally comfortable in the public scene," Kilmer says. "I never accepted that responsibility. If you're the lead in a film, you have a responsibility to the company and the studio. With a great deal of humor, Cindy describes herself as being in advertising. She's an icon in it; we actually talked about her image in relation to the product. And I was uncomfortable with that. We got in a huge fight one night because of a hat she was wearing. The hat advertised a bar, and I used to be so unreasonable about that kind of thing. I had a certain point of view about the guy who owned the bar, and I was just being unreasonable. I mean, she knows what she's doing, and she's comfortable with it. But I knew we were going to go to dinner and that we'd get photographed with this hat, and I was just hard to deal with. It was a really big deal."

This is the kind of insight that makes talking to an established movie star so unorthodox: Kilmer remembers that his girlfriend wearing a certain hat was a big deal, but he doesn't think it was a big deal that the girlfriend was Cindy Crawford. Crazy things seem normal, normal things seem crazy. He mentions that he is almost embarrassed by how cliché his life has become, despite the fact that the manifestation of this cliché includes buffalo ownership. However, there are certain parts of his life that even he knows are strange. This is most evident when—apropos of nothing—he starts talking about Bob Dylan.

"I am a friend of Bob's, as much as Bob has friends," Kilmer says. "Bob is a funny guy. He is the funniest man I know." Apparently, Dylan loved *Tombstone* so much that he decided to spend an afternoon hanging out in Kilmer's hotel room, later inviting Val into the recording studio with Eric Clapton and casting him in the film *Masked and Anonymous*. Much like his ability to mimic Brando, Kilmer is able to impersonate Dylan's voice with detailed exactness and loves re-creating conversations the two of them have had. What he seems to admire most about Dylan is that—more than anything else—Bob Dylan never appears to care what anyone thinks of him. And that is something Val Kilmer still cares about (even though he'd like to argue otherwise).

"I never cultivated a personality," he says, which is something I am skeptical of, but something I cannot disprove. "Almost everyone that is really famous has cultivated a personality. I can safely say that no one who has ever won an Oscar didn't want to win an Oscar. I think that Bob Dylan would have loved to win a Grammy during all those years when he knew he was doing his best work. Advanced or not, he was certainly ahead of his time, and he was more worthy than whoever won . . . Dylan was doing stuff that was so new that everyone hated it. Like when he started playing the electric guitar, for example: he toured for a year, and he was booed every night. Onstage, I could never take three performances in a row and be booed. I just don't think I'm that strong. I think that I would just go to the producers of the play and say, 'Well, we tried, but we failed to entertain here.' But Dylan spent a year being booed. They were throwing bottles at him. And he still can't play it! Forty years later, he is still trying to play the electric guitar. I mean, he has a dedication to an ideal that I can't comprehend."

On the shores of the Pecos River, nothing is as it seems: Kevin Spacey was once a terrible actor, Bob Dylan remains a terrible guitar player, and Val Kilmer is affable and insecure. Crazy things seem normal, normal things seem crazy. Gusty winds may exist.

1,400 MEXICAN MOZ FANS
CAN'T BE (TOTALLY) WRONG

One of the inherent problems with feature writing is that the slant for most stories is decided long before the journalist goes anywhere or talks to anyone. This is nobody's fault; it's just how things work. In order to get a story assigned, either the editor or the writer has to create a *reason* for why said story needs to be written. As a result, the proposed thesis of an article often becomes its ultimate conclusion. And this is (usually) a bad idea, since these presuppositions are (usually) totally wrong.

This is one example where that problem was avoided by accident: no one had any idea what the original thesis was supposed to be. I was living in Akron, and an editor from *SPIN* e-mailed me and said, "Hey, do you want to go to a Smiths convention in Los Angeles and write something about it?" I asked what I should write about. He said, "I have no fucking idea. I'm not sure why we're even doing this story, to be totally honest. Just go there and find some freaks." What neither of us knew, of course, was that the overwhelming majority of hard-core Smiths fans in the L.A. area are Latino teenagers, which still seems bizarre to me. But it made for a nice story that was almost completely unreliant on freaks.

One person at this Smiths convention (who was ultimately cut from the story) was a white dude in his midtwenties. I can't remember his name, but his claim to fame was winning Morrissey look-alike contests. He didn't sing and wasn't a musician, but he claimed he could dance exactly like Morrissey (and he did resemble Mr. Moz, although he was trying pretty hard to make that happen). He had won something like seven or eight of these contests over the past three years. But what was so intriguing about this guy was that he intended to turn his pastime into a full-time job; he hoped to make a living by looking like Morrissey's clone. However, he didn't have much of a strategy for making this a reality. I remember asking him,

47

"How will you earn money by looking like Morrissey, considering that you don't do anything else?" He said, "Oh, I don't know. I'm sure I could do in-store appearances around Los Angeles and San Francisco whenever a new Morrissey album is released." This seemed like a dangerous career move, particularly since Morrissey once went eight years without releasing an album. "That's a good point," he said when I mentioned that fact. "Maybe I'll have to do in-store appearances for Johnny Marr solo albums, too."

VIVA MORRISSEY!
(AUGUST 2002)

People feel nervous around Cruz Rubio. That's unfair, but it's true. He looks like a badass: Dude is twenty years old, he's from East Los Angeles, the sleeves are ripped off his flannel shirt, and he looks like an extra from the movie *Colors*. I have no doubt whatsoever that he could kick the shit out of me on principle. But I am not nervous around Cruz Rubio. I am not nervous, because he is telling me how Morrissey makes him weep.

"Some nights I lay in my bedroom and I listen to 'There Is a Light That Never Goes Out,' and I cry," he tells me. "I cry and cry and cry. I cry like a little bitch, man."

Perhaps you are wondering what a cut-like-marble Latino could possibly see in a quintessentially British, marvelously effeminate white guy best known for reading Oscar Wilde and sporting his espoused asexuality on his sweater sleeve. Frankly, there's no concrete answer to that question. But Cruz Rubio is definitely seeing *something*, because he is not the exception; within the walls of the sixth annual Smiths/Morrissey convention in Hollywood's Palace Theater, he is the rule.

For two days in April, fans of a disbanded Mancunian pop group and its forgotten frontman smoked clove cigarettes, picked over U.K. bootlegs, and danced to "Hairdresser on Fire" like dehydrated Helen Kellers, which is how people at Smiths conventions are supposed to behave. Yet these fans are not the glowering white semi-goths you'd expect to encounter; this scene looks like a 1958 sock hop in Mexico City. To argue that Morrissey's contemporary audience skews Hispanic would be inaccurate; Morrissey's contemporary audience *is* Hispanic, at least in L.A. Of the 1,400 people at this year's convention, at least 75 percent of the ticket buyers—virtually all under twenty—were Latino. For reasons that may never be completely understood, teenage Hispanics tend to be the only people who still care about Manchester's saddest sack. But they care a lot.

"He speaks to us, man. As Latinos. He addresses us personally," Rubio explains. "His music fits our lifestyle. I mean, where was the one place Morrissey always said he was dying to tour? It was Mexico, man. That's where his heart is."

Moments later, twenty-three-year-old construction worker Albert Velazquez expresses a nearly identical sentiment. "The last time I saw him live, he looked into the audience and said, 'I wish I had been born Mexican, but it's too late now.' Those were his exact words. And the crowd just exploded. He loves the Mexican culture, and he understands what we go through."

Velazquez is 235 pounds and six foot five (six foot eight if you include his pompadour). He plans to celebrate Morrissey's birthday on May 22; everybody at this convention seems to know that date. Velazquez also tells me he's going to drink a few Coronas that afternoon, because that's Morrissey's favorite beer. Everyone seems to know that, too.

Morrissey once sang that we must look to Los Angeles for the language we use, because London is dead. And so it is: The question is no longer "How soon is now?"; the question is "*¿Es realmente tan extraño?*"

• • •

The fact that the Smiths have sustained a cult following fifteen years after their demise is understandable. They were a band built for the darkly obsessive. In a decade categorized by excess, the Smiths—and especially their sexually baffling frontman—were introspective, iconoclastic, and alienated. There weren't "casual" Smiths fans in the America of 1986; it was an all-or-nothing equation. Though superstars in the U.K., the Smiths were fringe interlopers in the U.S.—the well-read pop-rock gods for the fey underground. That being the case, it isn't surprising to discover there's been a Smiths/"Moz" convention in Los Angeles every year since 1997. It's easy to imagine thirty-year-old ex-wallflowers digging out their black turtlenecks and reminiscing about how *The Queen Is Dead* convinced them not to hang themselves while everyone else was at the prom. Generally, that's who rock conventions appeal to—aging superfans embracing nostalgia.

That's why this Smiths convention is so startling. Those predictably pasty people don't show up (at least not in significant numbers). For the kids who live between the 5 and 10 highways in East L.A., this is a contemporary event, even though Morrissey hasn't released a solo album in five years. These new Morrissey fans—these Latino "neo-Mozzers"— see him as a completely relevant artist. Moreover, their interest goes against the grain of traditional Caucasian Moz fans; these kids like Morrissey's solo material as much as his work with the Smiths, and almost nobody here gives a damn about Johnny Marr (the guitarist originally perceived as the Smiths' true genius). Nobody even seems to care about Britpop in general. The focus is almost singularly on the forty-three-year-old Steven P. Morrissey and his infinite sadness.

"Morrissey's family emigrated to England from Ireland, and they were kind of socially segregated from the rest of the country," says Gloria Antunez, a twenty-three-year-old junior-high teacher who uses Morrissey lyrics as a teaching tool in her English class, most notably "Reader Meet Author" from 1995's *Southpaw Grammar*. "That's very similar to the

Latino experience here in Los Angeles. We see things within his songs that we can particularly relate to. He sings about loneliness. He sings about solitude. Those are things any minority group can relate to."

The impact of Morrissey's immigration experience is the most widespread hypothesis for why he's been embraced by Mexican Americans, but the theory has flaws. He's never mentioned or implied it in any of his songs, and it seems the majority of Latino neo-Mozzers have never even considered the significance of that connection. "I don't think it has anything to do with immigration," says Kristin Kaiser, a twenty two year old who looks like a bookish Penélope Cruz. "The greasers are into him because they completely associate Morrissey with rockabilly, which pisses off some of the original Smiths fans," explains Kaiser's friend Michelle Perez. "But what pisses me off more is when people try to say the 'pomp' evolved from Morrissey. I don't think so, man."

Perez is referring to the second-most common explanation for the Hispanic Moz revival—that Morrissey's flirtation with rockabilly invokes Latino "greaser" culture, à la the 1950s of James Dean and Ritchie Valens. Morrissey hired rockabilly musicians for 1992's *Your Arsenal*; though it's impossible to quantify, one suspects this movement started in earnest sometime after the release of that album. It's also possible that Morrissey's L.A. address amplifies his local profile, although he's infamously reclusive and never attends these conventions. (Despite repeated attempts, Morrissey couldn't be reached for this piece.) But maybe it's much simpler than that. Maybe it's just that Latino kids still hear what conflicted bookworms heard during the Reagan administration: the soul of a man who's tirelessly romantic, yet perpetually unloved. Assembly-line stars such as Ricky Martin and Enrique Iglesias simply can't touch the authenticity of Morrissey's quiet desperation.

"We're passionate people. He's passionate like us," says Martha Barreras, standing outside the Palace doors with her well-coiffed, tattooed boyfriend. "The music our parents played when we were growing up was always about love and emotion, and it's the same thing with Morrissey."

It's possible this whole "Why do Latinos love Morrissey?" question will haunt us forever. Fortunately, Canadian academics are on the case.

Colin Snowsell is a thirty-one-year-old PhD candidate at Montreal's prestigious McGill University. He couldn't make it to the Smiths convention because he was busy working on his dissertation, an extension of his master's thesis, *Monty, Morrissey, and Mediatized Utopia*. Frankly, Snowsell doesn't know how all this happened, either—but he's certainly thought about this paradox more than most.

"It really seems like Morrissey wouldn't have any career whatsoever if it wasn't for these Latino fans," Snowsell says. "The rest of the world sees him as a has-been, by and large, and it's rare to see Morrissey covered by the media in any way that isn't negative. But maybe Latino kids don't read the Anglo media."

There's no question that Morrissey's persona has been universally hammered over the past decade,[1] especially in the U.K. Though the British weekly *New Musical Express* recently classified the Smiths as the most influential act of the last fifty years, that publication often paints Morrissey as a self-absorbed caricature, fascinated by skinhead culture and bent on alienating his adoring minions.

Meanwhile, there are signs that he's aware of—and enthused by—his new fan base. He dubbed a recent tour *¡Oye Esteban!* and has performed while wearing a Mexico belt buckle. Perhaps more significant, rumors persist that

---

1. Morrissey finally released a new album in 2004 (*You Are the Quarry*), and it was generally well received by critics. He also started doing press again, but it had almost no impact on the commercial success of the record. It seems that the people who remain interested in Morrissey don't really care if he talks about himself or not.

Morrissey wants to serve as the opening act for a Mexican rock group called Jaguares at the Hollywood Bowl, a venue he sold out as a headliner ten years ago.

"If he's trying to get back his old Smiths fans, I don't think opening for a Mexican rock band would be the way to do it," Snowsell says. "I think he relishes being seen as a messianic figure among these young Latino fans, and I think he feels it validates his relevance. Morrissey has really done everything in his power to reject his old fans. I suspect he'd love it if the only people who cared about him were these Hispanic kids. I think he hates the fact that he tried to change the world, but most of those original Smiths fans now see him as no different than Echo and the Bunnymen."

Snowsell's use of the word *messianic* is telling, particularly when applied to someone like nineteen-year-old Carlos Torres, who tells me "Morrissey is like God" and is "immortal." However, when Torres talks about the time he met Morrissey at an in-store record signing, he illustrates the most confusing aspect of neo-Moz culture: just about everybody who's ever seen or heard Morrissey assumes he is gay—except for these Latino kids.

"I kissed Morrissey once," Torres says. "I kissed his hand. I wish I would have kissed him, but his hand was good enough. But I'm not gay or anything. It's just that he's Morrissey, you know? There is sort of a homophobic vibe among some Latinos, and they seem to think, *Well, we like him, so he can't be gay.* But that's stupid."

Torres's take is pretty liberal; a few Latinos at the convention concede that Morrissey might be bisexual, but none would classify him as gay. "People are always asking me if I'm gay because I have a photo of Morrissey hugging Johnny Marr," says Alex Diaz, a sixteen-year-old Smiths fanatic who plans on joining the Marines when he's old enough. "My friends always ask me, 'Why do you like these queers?' But, you know, he's probably just bisexual. His songs aren't all about guys. Look at

'Girlfriend in a Coma'—that's about a girl.[2] I think there probably would be some people who'd hate it if Morrissey ever came out and said he was gay, but, personally, I don't really care. And like I said, he's probably bisexual."

Though it's understandable how a culture that invented the term *machismo* might be uncomfortable lionizing a gay icon, it's ironic that Morrissey has now been adopted by two diametrically opposed subcultures. Fifteen years ago, closeted gay teens loved Morrissey because they thought he shared their secret; today, future Marines try to ignore the fact that their hero might find them foxy.

Young Latinos worship an aging Brit who aspires to live at the YWCA and get hit by a double-decker bus, and that's pretty crazy. But imagine how crazy it seems to the guys in These Charming Men, the tribute band that performed both nights of the convention (Saturday night was mostly Smiths songs; Sunday was mainly solo Moz). These Charming Men are from Dublin, and this is the second year they've made the trip to Hollywood. When they arrived in 2001, they expected to see the same faces that populate the pubs they play in the U.K. What they didn't anticipate was an audience of East L.A. homeboys who mosh when they hear the opening chords of the gingerly raucous "You're Gonna Need Someone on Your Side."

"It was quite shocking when we first came here," recalls vocalist Richard Cullen, his accent thicker than his hair. "My theory is that they picked up on the fashion sense and the visual elements of rockabilly music. And you know, Morrissey is something of an exile, just like a lot of them. I think

---

2. Diaz's point about "Girlfriend in a Coma" is—in a technical sense—true. Of course, it should be noted that this is a song where the protagonist looks at his comatose acquaintance and reminisces about all the times he considered murdering her. It may also be less than coincidental that *Girlfriend in a Coma* is also the name of a novel by author Douglas Coupland, who publicly announced he was gay in 2005.

perhaps they feel like they're living in the present tense with this mysterious character who's just down the road in his mansion."

The performances by These Charming Men were clearly the linchpin of the 2002 convention, and Cullen's attention to detail is remarkable; he's a good singer and a great actor. The band played for two hours each night, expending more energy than Morrissey himself has offered in years. Fans were expected to rush onstage and hug Cullen while he pretended to ignore them, a simulation of every Morrissey concert since the dawn of time. It's very postmodern: the audience becomes a "tribute audience," earnestly simulating hyperkinetic adoration while the band earnestly simulates *Meat Is Murder*.

But not everyone gets what they want.

Mark Hensley Jr. and Flore Barbu refuse to watch These Charming Men, a seemingly odd decision when you consider they each paid thirty dollars to attend a convention where that band was performing twice. These are the prototypical "weird white kids": Hensley appears to be auditioning for Bud Cort's role in a remake of *Harold and Maude,* and Barbu seems like the kind of woman who thinks Sylvia Plath was an underrated humorist. Both are wearing neckties for no apparent reason. These are the people you remember as being Smiths fans. And heaven knows they're miserable now.

"I don't think a true Morrissey fan would want to see a Morrissey cover band," Barbu says without a hint of inflection. "Morrissey would be depressed if he showed up here. He'd cry for a week. Have you seen those people around here wearing T-shirts that say 'Got Morrissey?' instead of 'Got Milk?' It's ridiculous. Morrissey would hate this."

It's obvious that Barbu and Hensley are smart, and they're endlessly, hopelessly sarcastic. There was a time when they would have embodied everything Morrissey seemed to represent. But Moz didn't hang on to his friends. He found new ones who liked him more. It's not that Barbu and Hensley feel their subculture has wound up in the wrong hands; it's just that these neo-Mozzers are too enthusiastic to be properly dour.

"People have actually said to me, 'You like Morrissey? That's weird for a white guy.' And I find that completely bizarre," Hensley tells me, momentarily dropping his veil of irony for a grain of semi-sincere annoyance. "Most of the other people here wouldn't even know who Jarvis Cocker is. They only like Morrissey. We just came here to make fun of people."

But perhaps that joke isn't funny anymore.

CHOMP CHOMP

It took me two years to convince my employers at *The Forum* to let me eat a few hundred Chicken McNuggets as an extension of my job. This was actually one of the first decent ideas I ever had for a newspaper feature; for some reason, I thought it would be an interesting way to write about all the things that happen inside fast-food restaurants when nobody is around to notice. As it turns out, nothing happens inside fast-food restaurants when nobody is around to notice . . . but I was shocked by how fascinated readers were with the premise of eating only one food item for an entire week. I assume people in third world nations do this on a regular basis, but Americans perceive this practice as beyond torturous. After I wrote this piece, people kept asking me, "Will you ever be able to eat McNuggets again?" I think I ordered them four days after the story was published. If something is good today, it will be good tomorrow. Variety is overrated; variety is for philanderers.

I wrote the McNuggets story in 1996. This is made stupidly obvious by my decision to casually cite Oasis vocalist Liam Gallagher as the epitome of decadence. What's curious, though, is how eating at McDonald's somehow became "political" over the eight years that followed. Eric Schlosser's *Fast Food Nation* came out in 2001, and Morgan Spurlock's *Super Size Me* was released in 2004. I interviewed Spurlock for an *Esquire* column about his movie, and I made it clear that (a) I had once done something vaguely similar to his documentary, and (b) I didn't think eating at McDonald's was especially dangerous. I still don't. But I do think it's an interesting coincidence that we both thought of trying to prove some larger idea about life through eating fried foodstuffs.

I suppose this is really a two-part story, written eight years apart.

THE AMAZING McNUGGET DIET
(NOVEMBER 1996)

We are a nation obsessed.

American culture is nothing more than a pastiche of fixations. We are obsessed with health. We are obsessed with pleasure. We are obsessed with speed. We are obsessed with efficiency. In simplest terms, we are obsessed by the desire to accelerate every element of our existence in a futile attempt to experience as much life as we can in the shortest possible time. We have all entered a race to devour the largest volume of gratification before it kills us.

Keeping this in mind, I ate nothing but McDonald's Chicken McNuggets for seven straight days.

One could argue that McDonald's is the vortex of American society. Granted, this would be a horribly weak argument. But McDonald's is the epitome of fast food, and fast food is the epitome of accelerated culture. It is the intersection of obsessions: a media-driven chain restaurant that tries to feed America as fast and as often as possible. For seven consecutive days, I embraced this theory with every fabric of my existence. With the exception of McNuggets and sauce, no solid food entered my body. I ate absolutely nothing else.

In order to document the effects of the McNugget Diet, I had a physical examination before and after the weeklong experience. I also kept a daily diary of my McNugget pilgrimage. The following text is excerpts from my chronicles. Although I was eventually overcome with madness, my journal provides a fascinating (and sometimes deeply inspirational) account of the McNugget Lifestyle . . .

• • •

Day 1: Today I began my journey with a visit to the PRACS, a pharmaceutical research institute in North Fargo. All my vital signs were tested. Despite some initial confusion about my project (I cryptically claimed I was doing "performance testing" on my body), the PRACS staff agreed to assess my condition through a battery of medical procedures. The testing proved I am ridiculously healthy. I am the ideal weight for my height and frame. My resting pulse rate is low and steady. An EKG showed that my heart is absolutely perfect, and my vertical leap measured a whopping thirty-six inches (the vertical leap part is kind of my own personal estimate, but still). It's been two hours since my exam and, as I write this, I'm eating my first serving: twenty McNuggets and a small orange drink. As expected, the virgin meal is going splendidly. As crazy as this sounds, I can't fathom not enjoying sweet 'n' sour sauce. It takes me about twelve minutes to eat twenty nuggets, which (I assume) are roughly equal to a free-range fryer submerged in fat.

To be honest, my primary fear is that this undertaking will be too easy.

Sitting next to me in the restaurant is a grizzled, elderly transient dressed completely in green. He's eating a Happy Meal. A McDonald's employee asks him if he wants a refill of Diet Coke. "No," he replies as he covers the cup with his hand. "I'll finish this Diet Coke now, and then I'll get a refill of regular Coke before I leave here." He glares at the McDonald's employee as if she is insane. Does life make more sense if you're homeless? Perhaps.

Day 2: Last night I swallowed nine more McNuggets at dusk. Today at noon I attacked twenty more. Ironically, I think I'm actually getting healthier. Since the only means of diversity within these meals is the sauces, I've become something of a sauce alchemist. I have learned that covering a nugget in honey and adding a subtle dab of hot mustard is an electrifying combination. Honey also improves the content of the barbecue sauce. On the whole, sweet 'n' sour is the only flavor that holds up well as an independent condiment. This may all seem boring (and it most certainly is), but it has become a critical part of my existence. I have developed a romantic relationship with the process of dipping.

However, the first downside has arisen: I suddenly feel an urge to wash my face every twenty minutes.

Day 3: I'm noticing a strict protocol to the McDonald's hiring process: Every place I go has the same staff. There's always one serious guy in his midtwenties who runs the ship; he has a military haircut and gets to wear the headset, and he scolds the other employees for making shakes incorrectly. There is always an old person who acts too friendly and often appears confused (sometimes she will try to compensate by bribing you with a mint). The rest of the workers are overambitious teens and underambitious college students, some resembling extras from Marilyn Manson videos. They all work harder than me and they all seem exhausted. These meals are soul darkening.

Day 4: This afternoon I tried dipping McNuggets in cocktail sauce, hoping they might taste like fantail shrimp. To my surprise, it kind of worked. Have you ever read about piranhas in an encyclopedia? According to the encyclopedia, a school of piranha can skeletonize a cow in minutes. I've always wondered how cows became the universal measuring stick for skeletonization. Tonight, I shall see how many minutes it will take me to skeletonize a box of McNuggets. Sadly, it seems they have no bones.

You know what's great about McDonald's? It's the last universal place in America. Nobody over the age of six actively aspires to go to McDonald's but—eventually—everyone does. As I sit in my vinyl booth and scribble these notes into a legal pad, I am surrounded by every aspect of society: angst-ridden teenagers, three boring businessmen, a table of grandparents, one depressed drunk guy, and the most beautiful woman I've seen since May of 1993. I wonder if this woman would be impressed if I told her I ate forty McNuggets today?

Sadly, the blond bombshell dumps her tray and walks out of the door . . . and out of my life. My heart is broken. It hurts almost as much as my tummy.

Day 5: You know, fast food really isn't that fast. I went through the drive-through today and—after I paid for my food—they told me I had to park my car and wait. "It will be a few minutes on those McNuggets," they sneered. Doesn't this defeat the whole purpose of using the drive-through? "We'll run them out to you," they said. Oh yeah, I'm sure they'll "run." Those trolls don't give a damn if I live or die.

I can no longer live inside this charade: I'm a little sick. I feel like I've spent an afternoon drinking Jägermeister with Liam Gallagher. I don't blame McDonald's for this (obviously, they did not intend anyone to live on their food), but I'm struggling. Whenever I start to chew, my esophagus contracts and I have to force myself to swallow. It's not that the nuggets taste horrible; they still taste good. But my body craves anything else. "Where are the Cocoa Puffs?" asks my stomach. "Where is the Franco-American ravioli?" inquires my small intestine. My internal organs must assume I'm in a death camp governed by Mayor McCheese's secret police.

Day 6: Today I smoked a pack of Camel cigarettes just so there would be a different taste in my mouth. I've escaped to "flavor country" (or something like that), but things have not improved. This was a stupid idea. I'm an idiot. Do McNuggets have riboflavin? I think I need some riboflavin. I'm having a hard time concentrating. I bet it's my riboflavin deficiency. I wonder if I'll contract rickets? No, that's from a lack of sunlight. What about scurvy? No, that's the disease pirates get. I'm no pirate. At least pirates were allowed to eat fish.

I'm currently sitting in the McDonald's on Main Avenue. Except for me, everyone here has a side order of fries. Boy, they sure look delicious. That would really change the scope of my existence. If I could have a handful of fries, everything would be different. All my problems would disappear. That's the answer! None of these mindless dolts have any idea how lucky they are. They live perfect lives, eating french fries whenever they please, laughing and joking with their perverted condescension. Mark my words—I will spite these fry-gorged gargoyles. The streets will flow with the blood of the nonbelievers!

Day 7: i do not feel very good i think i am dying and although i have not vomited i think it might be fun to do so. my world is crisp and rubbery and dripping with sauce and irony but people are still eating fries. words and their meanings have been swallowed by the deep-fat fryer of social depravity. fast-food culture? ha! there is no such thing. darkness . . . imprisoning me . . . all that i see . . . absolute horror. ronald mcdonald is the harvester of sorrow. actually these nuggets are still pretty decent they taste a lot like chicken.

Epilogue: My week has ended. All in all, the diabolical experiment has proved successful (if "success" can be measured by survival). Man cannot live on bread alone, but he apparently can live on McNuggets. My return to the PRACS Institute for a follow-up exam offered unexpected results: amazingly, both my blood pressure and cholesterol went down. Somehow, I only gained one pound. My vertical leap also improved to forty-one inches.

I'm not completely positive how many chunks of poultry I ate over those seven days; the number would fall somewhere between 230 and 280. People have asked me if I will ever eat McNuggets again. Well, of course I will. McNuggets have been good to me. Even before the final chicken came home to roost, my journey had been more sweet than sour.

McDICULOUS
(MAY 2004)

Staying alive is complicated. It's the single most difficult thing every single person does every single day. There is just so much in this wicked world that can kill us: cancer, avalanches, liver failure, street gangs wearing baseball uniforms, gravity, electric chairs, death squads, hammerhead sharks, werewolves, hemlock, and a boundless cornucopia of other coldhearted entities who solely exist so that we may not. Everything is bad for you. Food is bad for you. Food— something you need in order to stay alive—is killing you right now. Food hates you. But food cannot be held accountable for its diabolical actions, even if Morgan Spurlock thinks otherwise.

Spurlock is the director of the new documentary *Super Size Me.* The film chronicles Spurlock's performance-testing on his own thirty-two-year-old body: For thirty days, he ate nothing but food from McDonald's. If it wasn't on the menu, he did not consume it. (For example, he wouldn't even take aspirin, as McDonald's does not offer pharmaceuticals.) Within the reality of the movie, the results are staggering; Spurlock gains twenty-five pounds, watches his cholesterol spike sixty-two points, shows signs of liver failure, becomes profoundly depressed, and sporadically vomits. The goal of *Super Size Me* is to illustrate how fast-food restaurants contribute to the overall obesity of America. (Currently, 60 percent of U.S. adults are overweight.) You may remember a situation in 2002 where two girls unsuccessfully sued McDonald's, basing their lawsuit on the presupposition that their inability to stop eating was the fault of McDonald's. (One of the plaintiffs was five foot six and weighed 270 pounds.) Perhaps you thought that lawsuit was frivolous. Well, that's because it was. It was

63

completely idiotic, as is the entire philosophical premise for this movie.

Now, before I get into this, I want to be clear about something. *Super Size Me* is not an unwatchable movie. It's generally interesting and always entertaining. Moreover, Spurlock seems like a great guy; he came over to my apartment to screen his documentary on my living-room TV, and he drank four Sierra Nevada beers, and he has a cool-looking Jack McDowell mustache and a vegan girlfriend who vaguely resembles *Brady Bunch* star Eve Plumb. I hope Spurlock makes money from this movie. In fact, I actively want people to see *Super Size Me*, if for no other reason than to consider its two problems.

The first problem is tangible: *Is this movie true?*

I'm not sure. Maybe it is and maybe it isn't.

The second problem is ideological: *Does this movie make a valid point?*

No.

Let me first address the former query. It may seem irrational to question the reality of *Super Size Me*, since the evidence appears on the screen: we see Spurlock go to the doctor, we see him eat a shitload of Big Macs, and then we see him go back to his physician to track his devolution. Around Day 21, a doctor suggests that Spurlock may die if he doesn't change his diet. I question that diagnosis, and here's why: I once did something *very* similar to this. In 1996, I ate only Chicken McNuggets for an entire week. For seven straight days, I consumed nothing else: no fries, no fish sandwiches, no McDonaldland cookies, no nothing. McNuggets were my sole diet, and I ate somewhere between 230 and 280 of them. And you know what happened to me? Nothing. Nothing happened. I gained exactly one pound. In fact, my cholesterol and blood pressure went *down*.

Now, did I feel stellar at the end of that week? Not quite. I felt like I was coated in petroleum jelly, and I consciously exaggerated that discomfort for the benefit of the article. But I've definitely felt far worse at other points in my life; I think

I feel worse right now. It wasn't a big deal. But in this movie, Spurlock starts struggling *immediately*. By the third day of the experiment, he starts to act like a smack junkie. It all seems pretty sketchy.

Certainly, it's possible that I'm especially well suited for this kind of constructed gluttony; for some reason, my body has an unbelievably high tolerance to everything. My organs are indestructible. But I still suspect *Super Size Me* is somewhat exaggerated; if it wasn't, it couldn't exist. You could not sell a movie about eating fast food and feeling fine. Moreover, Spurlock didn't just eat—he gorged himself at every possible turn. He was ramming down five thousand calories a day. He was eating unreasonably on purpose. But when I pointed that out, he implied that I was missing the point.

"Someone else asked me about that," he said. "And they argued that if I ate nothing but broccoli for a month, that would make you sick, too. And that's probably true. But you know what? Nobody is telling you that broccoli is a meal. McDonald's is trying to convince people that their stuff is a legitimate meal, and that you can eat it every day."

Here is where the second problem with *Super Size Me*—the larger, philosophical problem—comes into focus. This is a movie about alleged victimization. The biggest problem with America is not faceless corporate forces; the biggest problem with America is people who blame faceless corporate forces instead of accepting accountability for their own lives.[1] And that's what *Super Size Me* is ultimately about: it's about blaming a chain restaurant for offering a product that people choose to consume.

Early in the documentary, Spurlock poses an important question: he asks us where personal responsibility ends and corporate responsibility begins. *Super Size Me* never answers that question, but I will. Corporate responsibility begins

---

1. Actually, this is more like the second biggest problem in America; the biggest is that in 2000 and 2004, we somehow managed to elect the worst U.S. president since Ulysses S. Grant. But it's tight.

when corporations start breaking the law, and personal responsibility never stops. Spurlock questions the ethics of offering consumers mammoth 64-ounce beverages and massive portions of fries, because people can't help themselves. "It's just human nature to eat what you get, even if you don't need it or want it," Spurlock says. Well, whose fucking fault is that? Why is a restaurant supposed to worry about people who get fat *by eating food they supposedly don't want*?

Don't get me wrong; I don't feel altogether comfortable defending McDonald's. It almost feels like I'm saying, "Hey, man, Darth Vader had every right to build that Death Star. He had all the proper zoning permits." However, the paradigm advocated by *Super Size Me* is wrong. McDonald's is a publicly traded capitalist venture; its function is to earn as much as it can by giving people a product they want. Perhaps you hate that notion. Well, go ahead and hate it. Hate it hard. But your personal distaste for an ideology has nothing to do with your real-world problems.

Spurlock criticizes McDonald's for not being up-front about the lack of nutrition in its food; this reminds me of people who sue tobacco companies because nobody told them that inhaling smoke is less healthy than inhaling oxygen. Spurlock attacks the prevalence of McDonald's advertising campaigns, and he hates the way they target children; this is intriguing, because I remember seeing thousands of "Just Say No" advertisements when I was young, and those didn't exactly take. All those "Got Milk?" ads don't seem to make people crazy for milk, either. Why is it that the only advertising campaigns that work seem to sell all the bad things people actually desire? Isn't that a weird coincidence?

Commercials for McDonald's claim their food is marvelous and that you should eat it constantly. And maybe you believe that. Maybe you need documentary filmmakers to protect you from yourself, because life is dangerous. And life *is* dangerous. Like I said, staying alive is complicated. But I'll take my chances.

MY SECOND-FAVORITE
CANADIAN

I love writing about sports, but athletes are difficult to interview; they generally don't say interesting things. I have a suspicion that Steve Nash is probably an introspective, complex person, but there was just no way he was going to express that introspective complexity to me. I don't think he trusted me, and I'm not sure why. But this was still a natural piece to write, mostly because Nash plays basketball in a deftly metaphoric manner. There always seems to be a deeper meaning to the way he attacks the game.

I briefly considered bringing up the issue of race in this profile; some people felt the reason Nash won the 2005 MVP over Shaquille O'Neal was because Nash was white and the league wanted a "mainstream" superstar (especially in light of that season's much-publicized brawl between members of the Indiana Pacers and a handful of fans in Detroit, a disquieting conflict immediately burdened with a racial component). However, while I was conducting this interview, three people came up to Nash and told him how awesome he was, and all three of them were black guys. I suspect the only people who think that Nash's whiteness is an issue are other liberal white people.

I wrote this story on a laptop computer in Austin, Texas. I was staying in the downtown Omni Hotel, and—after finishing the last paragraph—I went up to the hot tub on the roof and drank a beverage. There were two women with me in the water; they were very athletic, very married dancers from some kind of traveling theatrical troupe passing through east Texas. They ignored me completely, but I wordlessly listened to them have an intense (and completely serious) forty-five-minute conversation about (a) which gay male dancers in their theatrical troupe were most physically and intellectually attractive, and (b) whether it would count as cheating if they somehow convinced any of these gay guys to have casual heterosexual sex.

Weirdly, their conclusion was that it would only qualify as infidelity if the encounter involved *oral* sex, since the gay men might then fantasize that they were actually getting blowjobs from other males (which would thereby make the physical exchange "reciprocal").

Obviously, this has nothing to do with Steve Nash. But it just seems like the kind of information people need to know.

THE KARL MARX
OF THE HARDWOOD
(NOVEMBER 2005)

For seventy-five minutes, I talked to Steve Nash at a restaurant in Lower Manhattan. Neither one of us ate anything; we mostly just watched it rain. I asked him a lot of questions; he politely answered all of them without saying anything remotely incendiary. He was, I suppose, "pointedly guarded" about his personal life, which is what I should have expected from someone paid $63 million to play point guard. Through the process of this experience, I learned only two things, one of which will seem abundantly obvious (but actually isn't) and one of which is probably self-evident (yet will ultimately prove paradoxical and vividly illustrate how Nash can be the best player in the NBA without even being the most dominating member of the Phoenix Suns).

Canadians make everything complex.

Here is the first thing I learned: STEVE NASH IS FAST. This, as stated earlier, probably appears apparent to anyone with access to cable television. You probably think you know how fast Steve Nash is, because he plays basketball at a different speed than everyone who plays against him. However, to truly understand how fast Steve Nash is, you need to watch him buy baby food. At the conclusion of our interview, Nash got a text message from his wife; she told him he needed to buy food for their twin girl infants. We casually shook hands, made some superfluous banter about how the conversation had been friendly, and then—because it was raining—I reached down to get my umbrella off a chair. By the time I returned to an upright position, Steve Nash was already on the other side of the street. It was like someone had taken a laser beam, obliterated every atom in his body, and instantaneously reconstructed his entire anatomy forty feet to the west. This was some Philip K. Dick–*Star Trek*–vampire shit. And it was also somewhat ironic, because we had spent a large portion of our conversation discussing the very concept of human quickness. Nash says Allen Iverson looks slow during the course of a game, but he probably has the best two steps in the league. He says Stephon Marbury's explosiveness is physically palpable when he blows past people; it feels like wind. He says Jason Kidd is the fastest baseline-to-baseline player in the NBA, but that the Spurs' Manu Ginobili has the greatest agility. ("When Manu went left during the playoffs, he was like Michael Jordan," Nash says. "He scored ninety-five percent of the time when he was able to get to his left hand.") However, I think Nash is being humble; I think that within a confined 94 x 50 foot space, he knows he is the fastest man on earth. Granted, I've never watched A.I. shop for baby food, and it's possible that Nash merely hates getting wet. But the bottom line is that Steve Nash can accelerate in a way that you cannot possibly comprehend. Have you ever seen a college pitcher get struck by a line drive that was hit off an aluminum bat? He's like that line drive, except faster.

So Steve Nash is fast.

But here's the second thing I learned, and this matters more: STEVE NASH IS NOT TECHNICALLY A COMMUNIST. Or at least he's not a good one, since (as previously stated) he gets paid $63 million for throwing bounce passes to guys who barely graduated high school. In *practice*, he is a more successful capitalist than Don Lapre. But in *theory*, Nash is the most successful socialist in contemporary athletics.

And socialism works in sports. It doesn't work in a free society, and it certainly didn't work in Russia. But the principles of socialism make the Phoenix Suns almost impossible to defend, and that's due in totality to Nash, a long-haired liberal thriving inside the conservative idiom of sports.

"These things would probably be easier for you to parallel than they are for me," Nash says when I raise the Red flag. "I suppose there are a lot of connections between socialism and basketball, but none of them are conscious when I'm on the court. I don't even like to use the word *philosophy* when describing what I do for a living; I don't want to glorify the idea of playing basketball. But if you give of yourself, you do get things back. Sometimes that's tangible, and sometimes that's intangible. It's more like gambling: when you gamble, you try to give yourself the best possible odds of success. My goal is to increase the odds of success for each player on the floor, but without negating the odds of success for everyone else in the process."

The reason we were talking about political theory is mostly due to a story that ran in *The New York Times* last January. During a midseason interview, Nash casually mentioned that he had been reading *The Communist Manifesto* (as well as the autobiography of Che Guevara) on a road trip. One gets the sense that this is the kind of statement he regrets, simply because (a) it ended up becoming the only thing anyone remembers from that story, and (b) it was immediately (and incorrectly) connected to pacifist statements he had made at the 2003 All-Star Game. "I honestly don't want to say anything controversial to you, because I don't want to deal with the three weeks that always come with that," he says when I remind him of this. What Nash has come to realize is something guys like Terrell Owens and Gary Sheffield will never understand: when you're a pro athlete, there is no upside to being an interesting interview. All it does is make people hate you. "You know, I never came out and trashed George W. Bush or his administration. I just came out and said that I was personally antiwar, and that it was necessary for everybody to go deeper than the mainstream media to understand the situation in Iraq."

In other words, Steve Nash is just as American as you or I, except that he is Canadian. "I still feel like a Canadian living in America, but that doesn't mean anything," he says. "Everyone in the world is kind of an American, because America rules the free world." This is true: despite its current (and seemingly unprecedented) unpopularity, American thought still dominates the planet. But American thought does not dominate team sports. In fact, it tends to work against it. This country's most successful sports league is the NFL, which (not coincidentally) is also the most socialist; Pete Rozelle's enforced revenue-sharing was the best move any sports commissioner has ever made. The NFL's best team is the New England Patriots, a franchise whose elite players have agreed to accept lower salaries so that there's more capital to attract the best second-tier players. The individual bows to the whole. Pro football is inherently communist, and that's why it works.

Which brings us back to Nash. Last season, he won the MVP by averaging 15.5 points per game. He scores less per forty-eight minutes than Lee Nailon of the New Orleans Hornets. Now, the pedestrian way to explain how Nash won the MVP at a sub-Nailon scoring pace would be to say, "Well, he also led the league in assists. He makes his teammates better." But it's more than that. The reason Nash destroys people is because he transmogrifies the Suns' offense; he maximizes the potential of every player on his team, regardless of how much (or how little) raw potential each one possesses. He will consciously create short-term sacrifice if that loss yields long-term social benefit to players who would be mediocre as self-reliant individuals. From each his ability, to each his needs.

"With someone like Amare," he says of brightest Sun, Amare Stoudemire, "I typically want to give him the ball with some space. You can give him the ball on the block in an isolation situation, and he'll usually score. He's very capable. But that makes the entire offense lean on him. If I give him the ball in space and force guys to run at him, we all become

71

impossible to guard. He suddenly has more options, and everyone's odds of success improve."

In 2004–05, Quentin Richardson led the NBA in both three-pointers made and three-pointers attempted. Last summer, he was traded from Phoenix to New York. In all likelihood, he will make (and take) fewer treys this season. It was Nash who made Richardson's limited game an omnipresent weapon. Joe Johnson played so well last year as a Sun (17.1 points, 3.5 assists) that the Atlanta Hawks were willing to give the Suns two future first-round picks[1] for the right to make Johnson the highest-paid player on their roster. Johnson owes Steve Nash money. So does Shawn Marion, who, upon Nash's arrival in Phoenix, managed to score more points while playing fewer minutes. And these were all things Nash did not need to orchestrate. If he didn't feel compelled to appropriate Frederick Engels's game theory on any given 3-on-2 break, he could still get Stoudemire 36 points while getting 30 for himself; his play-off performances against the Spurs proved that his nonscoring is a choice. But then the Suns would go 42–40, and they'd probably get beat by the Denver Nuggets in the first round of the play-offs. If Nash wasn't a little like Karl Marx, he'd lose to the likes of George Karl.

"There is a lot of id in the NBA," says Nash, a sociology major when he attended UC Santa Barbara. "There is a tremendous amount of ego, and there are a lot of economic issues that are predicated on statistical analysis, which is really wrong. The successful teams—San Antonio, Detroit—are the ones who are able to overcome the relationship between personal statistics and financial success. And that's really the goal."

Ultimately, this is what makes Nash the perfect point guard: his aggressively modern, staunchly progressive thinking prompts him to play like a throwback to the 1960s. Over the

---

1. And a player named Boris Diaw. Yes, his name is *Boris*. Nash (or should I say "Nash-tasha") will play in the backcourt with someone named Boris. Boris!

past decade, pro basketball has embraced the idea of the "lead guard"; these are guys like Iverson and Marbury. These are ball-eating guards whose prime objective is scoring. They are self-interested capitalist point guards, and that's why we ended up with the bronze medal at the 2002 Olympics. If Steve Nash had grown up in Michigan instead of British Columbia, we would have won the gold.

Unfortunately, every man has flaws. Every man has a sickness, and Nash's personal cancer was made public during last year's slam dunk contest, when he bounced a lob pass to Stoudemire off his skull. "I watch much more soccer than basketball," he tells me, and I think he might even be wearing indoor soccer shoes when he says this. He apparently plays pickup soccer every night, all summer long. "It's my favorite sport," he insists. And I'm almost certain he was telling the truth, because both his brother and father played soccer professionally. Somehow, this man really, truly likes soccer more than he loves basketball.

So maybe I'm wrong. Maybe Steve Nash is a communist.[2]

---

2. I realize I've driven this anti-soccer thing into the ground. Sorry!

DEEP BLUE SOMETHING

When you're on a cruise ship, you eat supper every night in the same restaurant, at the same table, with the same people. It's assigned seating, so you end up forging this strange little relationship with total strangers. I took a cruise that was not filled to capacity, so my eight-chaired table was half-empty: it was me, my long-distance girlfriend (Melissa), and a middle-aged couple from Florida. I had just started dating my girlfriend semi-seriously; this cruise was the first time we had ever spent more than a weekend together. The Floridian couple, Peter and Linda, were in their early fifties. Peter was this big, blustery gray-haired guy who worked for Clear Channel as a salesman. He was the type of salesman who was *always* a salesman, even when he was asking for more ice water. I think he ate steak every night we were there. Linda was mousy and almost too thin; she was a lawyer who worked in social services. Linda ate salad, logged several hours a day on a treadmill, and did not possess the potential to be unfriendly. They were both divorced, having met on a blind date. The first night we ate together, the conversation was a little uncomfortable: I would estimate that Peter talked 75 percent of the time, I talked 20 percent of the time, Melissa spoke 3 percent of the time, and Linda uttered four sentences. Peter would occasionally talk over Linda, and this annoyed my girlfriend. However, the more time we spent with these two people, the more Melissa and I liked them. They talked about their kids, and about their previous marriages, and about what they had learned about human nature through their respective careers. Peter *really* loved talking about the radio advertising business. He was naturally domineering, but it was clear that he adored Linda, and it was also obvious that Linda found Peter's charismatic filibustering deeply charming. Every night after we excused ourselves from the table, Melissa and I would walk back to our cabin and break down the night's conversation, analyzing the subtext to everything Peter and Linda said. "Did you see Linda raise her eyebrows when Peter mentioned her ex-husband?" Melissa would note. "Indeed I did," I would respond. "But did you notice how Peter keeps going out of his way to remind us that Linda is more educated than he is?" Melissa and I didn't add much personality to these meals; we were more like relationship spectators. It was like being inside a Raymond Carver story.

However, that changed during the last meal we ate with Peter and Linda. Much to our surprise, it seems Peter and Linda found our interaction even more intense than we did theirs; they told Melissa and I that our casual nightly dinners had been "the highlight of the trip." And even more surprising, they suddenly urged Melissa to move from Minneapolis to New York so that the two of us could be together, because they were certain we were deeply in love and that our respective jobs meant nothing when compared to the life we could share together. And this wasn't drunk talk; this was sincere, openhearted, maternal advisement. They seemed to know details about our relationship that we had never told them, and perhaps that we were not even aware of. And what I slowly realized was that— while Melissa and I (half-jokingly) studied Peter and Linda's interaction as some kind of potential, implausible future—Peter and Linda (quite seriously) saw our present existence as a past they could have experienced, had only they met twenty years earlier.

I have no idea whatever happened to those people, but I kind of love them. They also drove us to the airport after we docked in Miami, so that was convenient.

THAT '70s CRUISE
(MARCH 2005)

"Welcome to the most unusual show Styx has ever played!" The man yelling this phrase is dressed like a sailor, except that he's also wearing a T-shirt advocating the defunct Soviet Union beneath a red sports coat. He's dressed, I suppose, a lot like former Styx singer Dennis DeYoung, although I'm not sure if DeYoung was also an ironic communist. The man's name is Lawrence Gowan, whom you've probably never heard of until you read this particular sentence; six hours ago, I hadn't heard of him, either. But Mr. Gowan knows a lot about the history of Styx; he is, in fact, the current lead singer and keyboardist for Styx. He just sang "The Grand Illusion." And even though he's only been a member of the band for one-sixth of its thirty-three-year existence, I suspect Gowan's correct about the degree to which this particular concert is "unusual," since Styx is—in all likelihood—the first classic-rock band ever to perform a concert on a Carnival cruise ship.

The 2004 incarnation of Styx plays on, and they are a heavily goateed band. Guitarist Tommy Shaw, fifty-one, has evolved into a super-furry animal over the past two decades, but his face is still boyish; he's wearing a Hawaiian shirt and a pair of Chuck Taylors, so he looks like what would happen if Jimmy Buffet went through a skater phase. Second guitarist James "JY" Young, fifty-five, is similarly furry and dressed like . . . well, like someone who's playing in a rock band at the age of fifty-five. The unfamous bass player has a cheetah-print shirt and blond highlights; the unfamous drummer looks completely normal and very, very happy to be playing drums. All five band members are being pelted with panties while they jam, but almost all of the lingerie is being thrown by the same woman; she has evidently hauled a duffel bag of women's underwear into the concert venue. I don't think most of these panties belong to her (or—if they do—she hasn't worn them since 1986). The crowd is losing its collective mind. They love it. We love it. And even if we didn't, there's not much we could do: we're a hundred miles from dry land, floating through international waters, listening to an eighteen-song Styx medley that briefly includes "Mr. Roboto." We are watching a rock concert on a boat. Tomorrow, we will watch another, and that group will be REO Speedwagon; on Friday, we will watch Journey. Seven long days, three arcane bands, one deep ocean. This kind of thing has never been done before. However, it will probably be done again, because everyone involved seems to be absolutely ecstatic.

There are elements to seeing Styx (or any artist, probably) on a cruise ship that are vastly unlike the typical concert experience. Sometimes the boat will (very slightly) pitch or roll or yaw, and I can see Tommy Shaw transfer all his weight onto his right leg while his left hand slides down the neck of his axe; it must be hard to rock an audience when you're being involuntarily rocked by water. The band is now playing a song called "Snowblind," which Young prefaced by alluding to a recent football game between the Denver Broncos and the Oakland Raiders. I can think of at least two other hard-rock songs titled "Snowblind," and this seems to be the only one that is not about cocaine. It doesn't matter: the aforementioned panty-packing woman throws a bra at Young, and he hangs it from his guitar. With the possible exception of the 1980 U.S. Olympic hockey team, I have never seen an audience like anything as much as these middle-aged cruise patrons like Styx. And what's even crazier is that I think they like Journey more.

Come sail away, come sail away, come sail away with me . . .

Two days after Thanksgiving, the Carnival ocean liner *Triumph* leaves Miami for seven days, scheduled to loop around Cuba and make one-day stops in Cozumel, the Cayman Islands, and Jamaica. This is a standard cruise itinerary. However, this particular voyage is different; this particular trip includes the presence of three bands who have not been famous since the introduction of New Coke. On Monday afternoon, Styx will conduct a casual "question-and-answer" session in the ship's thousand-seat lounge and then perform that evening in the same intimate location. On Tuesday, REO

Speedwagon will follow suit with their own conversation and concert. A friendly Q&A session with Journey is set for Thursday afternoon, but they're not playing until Friday night, hours before we redock in Florida.

There are over 2,500 people on the *Triumph* (an unofficial figure provided by my Croatian cruise waiter, Zeljko), but—sadly—they will not all be allowed to rock. Only about 1,000 of the 2,500 have purchased the "Rock Cruise" package. The economics of this trip are profoundly confusing: prices for the rock cruise begin at $1,299, which is roughly $700 more than cruising without the rock. Some guests are paying as much as $3,199, which means they get to sleep in a penthouse suite and are granted "platinum status" (which guarantees they'll be able to meet all the bands backstage). However, some of the *Triumph*'s vacationers are getting a mind-blowing bargain; the rock portion of the cruise is being sponsored by media conglomerate Clear Channel, so Clear Channel employees can experience this trip for a scant $249. I am told by a Clear Channel sales rep that this deal is supposed to be a secret, but everyone on the boat seems to be talking about it.

As I board the *Triumph* on Saturday afternoon, I immediately try to deduce which boat patrons view the three rock concerts as "incidental" to the cruising experience and which view them as "integral" to the cruising experience. While my passport is being examined, I casually explain to my traveling companion that some of these bands are now primarily comprised of replacement musicians, and that the current incarnation of Styx only includes two of its original members. "Not really," interjects a bespectacled fortysomething woman waiting behind us in line. "Tommy Shaw didn't officially join Styx until 1975, so there's only one original member. And the drummer died, so you really can't hold that against the rest of the band."

I decide this woman can be safely placed in the "integral" category.

There are three main hurdles involved with the writing and reporting of this story. The first is that the definitive cruise story has already been written by David Foster Wallace, who published the essay "A Supposedly Fun Thing I'll Never Do Again" in 1995; this is evidently the most popular essay ever produced, as roughly six thousand people have mentioned it to me during the forty-eight hours prior to this trip. The second hurdle is my inability to swim, which means this trip could possibly kill me. The third (and strangest) hurdle is that Clear Channel decreed that I cannot interview any of the three musical outfits, nor can I actively participate in any of the Q&A sessions; apparently, the cruise is supposed to be a vacation for the bands, too.

In truth, talking to members of Journey doesn't interest me that much; I much prefer chatting with my Croatian waiter, as he seems to know a great deal about international politics and international heavy metal. He bristles when I tell him I like KISS. "Oof," guffaws Zeljko. "That is only show! 'I was made for loving you'? Oof. That is no rock. AC/DC is rock, but only from Bon Scott era, and maybe on *Back in Black*. Saxon, Judas Priest—these are the rock bands."

Zeljko works on this Carnival cruise line because Serbians bombed his house during the '90s. Now he supports his wife and kids by refilling my glass with ice water and sending his paycheck across the Atlantic. This makes me so depressed that I briefly consider buying some Saxon records.

It's Wednesday afternoon. Ten minutes ago, I was inside a casino. I don't normally gamble, so this was strange. As I walked past the blackjack tables, I nearly collided with REO Speedwagon lead singer Kevin Cronin. I don't normally hang out with REO Speedwagon, so this was likewise strange.

I've now escaped the casino and I'm meandering across the luxury ship's upper deck, which is where I spot a forty-five-year-old man playing an electric guitar as he stares across the almost idiotic blueness of the Caribbean Sea. With the help of a manual called *Heavy Metal Guitar,* he is trying to figure out the introduction to "Stairway to Heaven." His name is John Shipman, and he's a renaissance man: Shipman teaches high-school psychology in South Carolina, he spent the 1980s flying F-111 fighter jets for the Air Force, and—in his spare time— he runs a martial arts school that specializes in a style of street fighting called American kempo. Shipman is a fourth-degree kempo black belt; he tells me he has already become "like the tiger" and aspires to become "like the dragon." This sounds like a good plan, and I hope he doesn't kick me in the neck. Eventually, I ask him why he and his wife decided to spend their unpaid vacation on the "Rock 'n' Roll Holiday Cruise." And this is what he tells me.

"We felt it was a once-in-a-lifetime opportunity," says Shipman. "Styx is real hard-rocking. REO is great, especially in terms of ballads. Journey is more of a heartfelt, emotional band, but, of course, they also have the fantastic guitar work of Neal Schon."

I agree with at least half of those sentiments. However, it still strikes me as strange that someone would want to experience these particular bands on a boat. It feels goofy to take a Caribbean cruise with REO Speedwagon. At risk of sounding reductionist, the whole idea just seems . . . insane. But as Shipman and I chat about the evolution of guitar-driven rock, and as we discuss the mores and affinities of the high-school kids he teaches in South Carolina, I begin to understand why he (and his peers) are willing to sail below the Tropic of Cancer to hear a song like "Separate Ways." The people on this ship do not necessarily reflect the typical classic-rock fan base, nor do they serve as a rare collection of affluent white-trash party animals with archaic taste in music.

What they personify is half of an emerging generation gap.

These Carnival cruise patrons stand on one side of a philo-sophical chasm; demographically, the chasm can be quantified as the aesthetic abyss between (a) people born just before 1960, and (b) people born just after 1980. And what's fasci-nating about this gap is that both sides love the same thing: they both love rock music. This is not a case of the youth embracing a completely new idiom their parents can't fathom, because the idiom is essentially the same; this is a generation gap over *virtuosity*. Quite simply, the people on this cruise don't believe modern bands know how to play, and they're willing to spend $2,500 to see groups who can.

"You hit the nail on the head," Shipman says when I suggest this hypothesis. "I talk to my students about music all the time, and they're all used to Britney Spears and Madonna and Janet Jackson and all those rap guys. That's what they consider normal music. But those people are just talking over a beat and dancing—it has more to do with what they wear. It's not like someone singing and playing guitar and writing all the material and running around the stage while they play it.[1] It seems like kids today are more interested in the culture around music than in the music itself."

There might be some grains of truth in what Shipman says. However, it's possible that kids are more interested in the culture around music simply because that culture is always more interesting, and it always has been.

Or at least it was on this boat.

A little background information on the three bands involved with this cruise:

- Styx: Originally prog rockers who called themselves Tradewinds (and then briefly TW4), Styx broke into prominence with the ballad "Lady" in 1975. Their greatest success came from the concept albums *Paradise Theatre* in 1981 and *Kilroy Was Here* in 1983, the latter being a futuristic narrative about robots. This caused the band to disintegrate. Lead singer DeYoung portrayed Pontius Pilate in a Broadway production of *Jesus Christ Superstar,* guitar messiah Shaw joined Damn Yankees during the early '90s, and the entire posse reunited in '96 for a tour with Kansas. The reunion was short-lived; DeYoung immediately exited

---

1. If Shipman had a blog, many people in the comment section would accuse him of being "rockist."

the band (for a third time, technically) and the remaining members (plus a few replacements) released an album in 2003 called *Cyclorama* with actor Billy Bob Thornton.

- **REO Speedwagon:** Though always seeming vaguely Canadian, REO was actually founded on the University of Illinois campus in 1968. The band made an artistic leap by adding Cronin as vocalist in 1972, whom they immediately fired in 1973. Cronin rejoined the group in '75 and success soon followed, peaking with 1980's *Hi-Infidelity* (which sold over nine million copies). The best-loved REO songs are 1974's "Ridin' the Storm Out," 1980's "Keep On Loving You," 1984's "Can't Fight This Feeling," and a handful of other songs that would prompt you to say things like, "Oh, I know this song, but I had no idea it was REO Speedwagon."

- **Journey:** Christened in 1973 (via a radio contest on KSAN-FM in San Francisco), Journey began as a primarily instrumental jazz collective. Steve Perry joined in 1977; by 1980, they were rich. In that ephemeral era between Fleetwood Mac's *Tusk* and Van Halen's *1984*, it could be argued that Journey was the world's most popular arena rock band. However, Journey is not very good at remaining Journey. Perry left the group twice (once in 1986 and again in 1996) and released solo tracks like "Oh, Sherry." While on hiatus in the mid-'80s, guitarist Neal Schon and keyboardist Gregg Rolie formed a band with John Waite called Bad English. Eight years ago, a re-formed version of Journey added vocalist Steve Augeri, a man who sings like Steve Perry, looks like Steve Perry, talks like Steve Perry, and is (weirdly) even named "Steve."

Journey is, far and away, the most popular band on this cruise ship.

I spot two shirtless guys drinking low-carb Michelob Ultra and listening to Journey through a boom box on the ninth-floor sundeck. One of them, forty-five-year-old mechanical contractor Larry Zuccari, has seen Journey thirty-one times; his wedding song was the Journey ballad "Faithfully." However, his bride is not on this boat.

"Both our wives allow us to have this time to ourselves," Zuccari explains, gesturing to boyhood friend Bill Hagan. "We don't own bass boats. We don't bowl. We don't hang out in bars. We follow Journey. I saw Journey perform at a Wet 'n' Wild amusement park next to a roller coaster in rural Georgia, so seeing them on a boat doesn't seem all that strange, relatively speaking. If you're a true fan of a band, it doesn't matter where that band plays—you just go. At this point, most of the rock shows I see are held in casinos."

Like virtually everyone I talk to on board the *Triumph*,[2] Zuccari misses the day when groups like Journey were omnipresent. He does not, however, seem completely out of touch; his arguments—though unnecessarily slanted against hip-hop—are rational. "Music seems so synthesized now," he says. "If you listen to an obscure Journey song like 'Mother, Father,' you would be amazed by the degree of musicianship. . . . I don't like rap music. It seems like there's a lot of anger and negativity directed toward women in rap music, and that's something I don't understand. And I do like some new bands. I like Gwen Stefani. And as you probably know, the drummer in No Doubt is a huge Journey fan."

Actually, I did not know this.

When the *Triumph* docks in Jamaica on Thursday morning, I decide to take a respite from the classic-rock avalanche and embark on the Bob Marley Bus Adventure, an organized tour that takes *Triumph* passengers to the community of Nine Mile, the location of Marley's birth and grave (the "reggae

---

2. It's really too bad that one of the bands on this cruise wasn't the Canadian power trio Triumph.

Graceland," as it were). The bus leaves at 8:30 A.M., and its riders are offered a complimentary glass of rum punch at 8:29. Upon sipping our breakfast rum, many of the people on the bus sarcastically joke, "Heh heh, if this is the Bob Marley tour, they're probably going to give us pot." Well, it turns out that this is exactly what happens, pretty much for the entirety of the six-hour tour. You have not truly vacationed until you've spent a morning staring at Bob Marley's childhood bed with twenty super-high soccer moms who haven't touched marijuana since Jimmy Carter was president.

If you discount the crime and the poverty and the overabundance of goats, Jamaica is a wonderful place. According to our tour guide, this is what life there is like: "You wake up, you ride a donkey to work, you go home to smoke, and you dance with your wife. Easy livin'!" Such logic is hard to argue with. Consequently, the Zen perfectitude of my Jamaican morning makes the afternoon's question-and-answer session with Journey seem stilted and contrived. The session's second-best question is directed at drummer Dean Castronovo: "You look so much thinner than I remember—what happened?" (Answer: "I lost fifty-two pounds on the Atkins diet!") The best question is directed toward Schon: "I have a friend named Ken Miller in Concord, and he says he jams with you guys once in a while, and I'm wondering if he's telling the truth?" (Answer: "Kevin who?")

The main problem with the Journey Q&A is bassist Ross Valory, a man who once aspired to be a stand-up comedian and is now the most annoying personality alive. No matter how hard he tries, Valory isn't a fraction as amusing as REO Speedwagon keyboardist Neal Doughty, a guy who's legitimately funny (probably because he doesn't try at all). When asked what's different about the REO of today compared to the REO of twenty-five years ago, Doughty says, "Well, as opposed to getting drunk before shows, we actually learn the songs." When asked what will inspire REO over the next twenty-five years, Doughty says, "Viagra."

Though the least popular of the three outfits on board, REO

is generally the sharpest, least embarrassing band involved with the trip. They even cause a fraction of controversy: while performing a new antiwar song called "Hard to Believe," a few audience members boo and chant, "Four more years! Four more years!" (This is somewhat confusing, inasmuch as George W. Bush has already been elected.) REO's political take also differs vastly from that of Styx, whose second guitarist (James Young) asks us to cheer for all the men and women serving in Iraq who "give us the freedom to do things like this." And by "do things like this," I can only assume he means, "go on rock cruises near Jamaica."

"Tommy Shaw is my idol," says Lori Smola, a thirty-eight-year-old EMT from Daytona Beach. Smola is showing me the Styx tattoo on her shoulder. Smola says she has seen Styx in concert more than two hundred times since 1984, and I believe her. "When I was ten years old, my older brother gave me a poster promoting *The Grand Illusion*, and I liked the shorter guy. That shorter guy was Tommy Shaw. When Tommy joined the Damn Yankees, I was right there with him." Smola's e-mail address begins with "tommy1yank." She's intense.

I ask Smola how she feels about Styx today, and she says, "Well, they're classic rock now, unfortunately." Smola wishes Styx were still just rock. On the *Triumph*, this sentiment is not uncommon; remember, this is a boat where punk never happened, hip-hop doesn't exist, and Nirvana never became famous. After the Styx Q&A, I playfully ask a disgruntled Houston construction worker named Glenn Wells why he didn't pose a query to the band, and his response is terse. "I can't think of any question for any of these bands, except one: 'What the hell happened to the music? You guys wrote all those great songs in the '70s, and now you keep trying to make all this modern crap. What happened?'"

In a way, that question is the universally unspoken fear of the Classic Rock Generation: "Why don't new songs by old bands sound like old songs by new bands?" Journey did not arrive on the *Triumph* until Thursday, ostensibly because they were locked in the studio, toiling away on some (allegedly) awesome album that's set for release in 2005. Now, it is possible that the next Journey studio effort will, in fact, be awesome; of course, it is far more likely that it will be released without fanfare, it will sell less than 100,000 copies, and—when the songs are performed live—mature concert audiences will politely sit through the new material while waiting to hear "Don't Stop Believin'" for the four-thousandth time. This is the nature of classic rock in the present tense; if you want to hear the songs you like, you have to pretend the band's contemporary material still matters. It's akin to sitting through a boring conversation with a self-absorbed high-school teacher because you know you're probably going to have sex when they finally shut up.

But there is something else about these bands that makes them relevant to the people who love them; there is a quality within the musicians that prompts people to spend $3,000 to see them on a cruise ship. The quality is normalcy. There was probably a time when the fans on this boat liked these bands because they were cool; now, part of what the fans appreciate is the fact that these bands *aren't* cool. In 2005, the members of Journey are just dudes who used to be on MTV; they are musicians because music is their job. It is how they pay their mortgage. And people fucking love that.

Case in point: Dominick and Georgia Graziano of Long Island, New York. The Grazianos own a bar called Chili Pepper's Pub, but they plan to rename it the Whiskey Witch. Dominick also works construction. As I talk to a sunbathing Georgia about music (she says she likes "everything," which she classifies as "the Eagles to Velvet Revolver to Switchfoot"), she begs her husband to tell his Journey story. "You gotta tell this guy your Journey story," she keeps insisting. "Tell him the Journey story." Eventually, Dominick does so.

This is the Journey story:

"I'd seen Journey in 1980 or '81, opening for the Rolling Stones at JFK Stadium in Philadelphia," Mr. Graziano begins. "Journey comes out onstage, and Steve Perry takes the mic and says to the audience: 'You know what you guys did? You just made Journey the number-one band in America.' But the crowd was like, 'Fuck you, we want the Stones.' They threw bottles at him. So then we're in the Grand Wailea Hotel in Maui on our honeymoon—this is four years ago— and we run into Neal Schon and his wife at the hotel bar. We introduce ourselves, and I tell him I remember seeing him in Philadelphia twenty years ago, and he goes, 'Oh man, I remember that show, Perry opened up his fucking mouth.' And I was like, 'Yeah, man, they were throwing bottles at you guys,' and he was like, 'Yeah, they fucking were.'"

That's the whole story.

At first, I am substantially underwhelmed by this anecdote, mostly because it has a beginning and a middle but no discernible conclusion. However, I am wrong about this, because a few minutes later, just before I'm about to leave these people alone, the Grazianos casually mention that they've kept in touch with the Schon family ever since. Every time Journey plays in the New York area, Schon's wife makes sure the Grazianos have front-row seats and backstage passes. Georgia even made a yellow baby blanket for Schon's daughter, Amber. In other words, the leader of this mammoth rock band—the "number-one band in America"—is now (kind of) a family friend. The Grazianos will probably have a nice chat with the Schons on this crazy boat. They will ask how Amber is doing, and Georgia will always know that she helped their baby fall asleep.

Don't stop believing. I mean it. Don't.

"DEEP SABBATH"

SPIN's decision to hire me in 2002 was a direct result of the publication of *Fargo Rock City,* which (at the time) made me nervous; I had this fear that the only thing anyone would ever want me to write about was heavy metal. This was exacerbated by the fact that—a few weeks after my arrival—*SPIN* decided to theme an entire issue around metal, and I ended up writing 75 percent of it. If I took a job at *The Economist* and started covering trade policy, this perception would never change. "Did you happen to see that story about granting China most favored trade status?" people would say. "I think that Metal Dude wrote it."

These are two stories from that *SPIN* metal issue (September 2002). The first is a misguided attempt to prove how all forms of heavy metal actually derive from Led Zeppelin's fourth album, a theory I never completely believed. The second piece, however, was legitimately entertaining (at least to me). I did this brief (maybe twenty minute) Q&A with Robert Plant over the telephone, and he was tremendous. If given the choice between talking with a hip, relevant artist or talking with an older, salty rock monster from a bygone era, I'll take the latter every single time. Young musicians are always obsessed with creating a persona and saying the things they think they're supposed to say; older guys truly don't care. When I think back at the rock stars I've interviewed, the most unpredictable conversations were almost always with people over forty: Plant, Donald Fagen of Steely Dan (who acted like a college professor trying to get fired), Barry Manilow (who criticized Nine Inch Nails for lacking soul), Bono (who seemed to actively want me to analyze his livelihood), and Ozzy Osbourne (who talked about Nazis and riding elephants). The only contemporary artist I'd put in this class is Marilyn Manson; I've interviewed him four times, and he was articulate and engaging every time. Manson isn't necessarily smart, but he's a goddamn genius.

What's so great about this Plant conversation is that the only thing we really talked about was how much he hates heavy metal, which was the antithesis of why we wanted him in the magazine. He also completely disproves my "*Zoso* hypothesis," but that hardly seems surprising. I just wish he would have explained what the fuck a hedgerow is.

IN THE BEGINNING,
THERE WAS *ZOSO*

Led Zeppelin's fourth studio album—1971's unnamed *Zoso* (so called for the enigmatic symbols on its cover)—is the most famous hard-rock album ever recorded, not to mention a watershed moment for every grizzled old man who's ever carried a bundle of sticks on his back. *Zoso* is not Zeppelin's best album (that would be *Houses of the Holy*) or their heaviest (*Physical Graffiti*) or even their "most metal" (*Led Zeppelin II*). However, it's the defining endeavor for the band, and for the genre it accidentally created. Epic, ethereal, and eerily sexual, *Zoso* is the origin of everything that sounds, feels, or even tastes vaguely metallic, except maybe Metallica and that sludge from Scandinavia (both of which come from Black Sabbath's *Sabbath Bloody Sabbath*).

Need proof? Here, track by track, is everything ever blasted across your high-school parking lot, as told through the sonic vision of *Zoso*, via guitarist Jimmy Page and his dragon pants . . .

"Black Dog" = rap metal = Korn's "A.D.I.D.A.S." Identifying the dawn of the rap-rock idiom is not easy. Some suggest

Rage Against the Machine's self-titled debut (1992); others point to the Public Enemy–Anthrax collaboration "Bring tha Noize" (1991), Faith No More's *The Real Thing* (1989), or Run-D.M.C.'s "Rock Box" (1983). Paul Stanley apologists will claim it's "All Hell's Breaking Loose" (from KISS's 1983 album *Lick It Up*). However, it was truly spawned during the first fifteen seconds of *Zoso*—Robert Plant informs a young lass that he intends to make her sweat and groove (not necessarily in that order), and his wise words require no riffing. Kid Rock—ten months old at the time—definitely saw a marketing opportunity.

"Rock and Roll" = hair metal = Cinderella's "Gypsy Road." Initially conceived by Page as a boogie-bang tribute to the "roots" of rock, it's the only track on *Zoso* that sounds like prototypical blues-based pop metal, which is to say that it sounds like Aerosmith (or all the '80s gutter-glam bands who later aspired to be Aerosmith). Perhaps you recall "Rock and Roll" being eloquently covered by Vince Neil and Sebastian Bach at the 1989 Moscow Music Peace Festival (or perhaps not).

"The Battle of Evermore" = prog metal = Yngwie Malmsteen's "Riot in the Dungeons." Now, granted—"The Battle of Evermore" doesn't sound like Fates Warning or Celtic Frost or Steel Prophet. But it operates like progressive metal: it fades in like falling snow, describes Dark Lords and ringwraiths, and it certainly never explains what this battle is supposed to be about (though some speculate it's a retelling of the Battle of the Pelennor Fields from *The Return of the King*, so maybe it's about Peter Jackson). The details don't matter as much as the deeper motive, which built the "prog" template. In rock, "progressive" doesn't mean writing about the future; it means writing about a past that never happened.

"Stairway to Heaven" = metal power ballad = Warrant's "Heaven." Depending on your perspective, "Stairway to

Heaven" is either (a) the most popular song of the rock era, or (b) the most overplayed song in FM history, thereby making it either (c) the greatest track of the past fifty years, or (d) the only song worse than "Hotel California." Yet the significance of this never-released single will haunt proms for all eternity. It allowed—nay, demanded—that every metal band make at least one song that your mom might like.

"Misty Mountain Hop" = L.A. "reality" metal = Guns n' Roses' "Welcome to the Jungle." When intertwined, the lyrics from these two songs become a conversation between Robert Plant and Axl Rose, discussing what it's really like to move to California and meet the weird kids: A naïve teenager goes to the West Coast for the first time, sees crowds of people sitting on the grass with flowers in their hair, and hears them say, "Hey, boy, do you wanna score?" These are the people who can find whatever you may need, and if you got the money, honey, they got your disease. But our protagonist soon learns that if you go down in the streets today, baby, you better (you better!) open your eyes, whoa yeah, 'cause you're in the jungle, baby, and you're gonna die.

"Four Sticks" = stripper metal = Monster Magnet's "Powertrip." As long as naked women are swinging on poles in public and providing $10 lap dances to truckers and unemployed stockbrokers, there shall be a demand for this type of fast-and-heavy, darkly sleazy rock 'n' roll. All praise to Allah.

"Going to California" = unplugged metal = everything on *Five Man Acoustical Jam.* And she's buyyyyyyyyyyyying a staaaairway . . . to . . . Tesla.

"When the Levee Breaks" = stoner metal = Fu Manchu's "Boogie Van." Drums from God, lyrics from the Depression, guitars that go everywhere, guitars that go nowhere, and the sonic weight of a thousand woolly rhinos falling from

Skylab. There is no light black enough for listening to John Bonham. *Zoso* did not make people take drugs; *Zoso* made drugs, and Kyuss, and every other trance-inducing metal machine, completely necessary.

NOT A WHOLE LOTTA LOVE

Few would argue with the theory that Led Zeppelin invented heavy metal. One who will, however, is Robert Plant, the golden god who became the archetype for every metal throat who followed. And it's not just that Plant dismisses the entire genre because it rips him off; he thinks metal bands suck because they don't rip him off *enough*. It's been more than twenty years since John Bonham's death ended Zeppelin's epic reign, but Plant's unrepentance has not waned.

The fifty-three-year-old Brit is touring and has released a solo album (*Dreamland*) juxtaposing vintage blues and folk with modern trippiness. He remains willing to criticize just about every hard-rock band that's ever existed, and he even took a shot at the very idea of *SPIN* celebrating a musical idiom he clearly hates.

"After you finish this issue about the fucking absurdity of boys trying to be more than what they should be—Conan the Warrior goes on tour, or whatever—come see my new show," he said at the conclusion of our interview. "Just come along, because it's such a trip. And when you decide to do an issue about psychedelia, I'll sit in my rocking chair and tell you some stories about Janis Joplin and Jim Morrison."

CK: Even though most people consider Led Zeppelin to be the creators of heavy metal, you've always insisted that Zeppelin wasn't a metal band. So in your mind, what is "heavy metal," and why doesn't it include Led Zeppelin?

Robert Plant: You've made a mistake there; you cannot classify anything, anywhere. Classification is a killer. Otherwise, we're all stuck. It means Mother Love Bone or Linkin Park or Creed will never do anything except what they've already done. Led Zeppelin did lots of different things—working in North Africa, writing songs like "Friends" and "Four Sticks" and "Kashmir." I can't imagine "Kashmir" being considered a heavy-metal piece. I don't think "Stairway to Heaven" was very heavy metal. But we were bombastic. We took no prisoners. We took great delight in playing with bands who had the attitude and ego that was so prevalent in America at the time. Everyone was a self-proclaimed star, which was dumbfounding to me. So to turn up the intensity and be truly bombastic— that's when we just out-heavied everybody.

CK: But why is it, despite Led Zeppelin being so musically diverse, that most of the bands Zeppelin influenced only picked up on one thing that the band did, which was to play loud and heavy? I mean, did you like any of the bands that did that?

Robert Plant: Well, I think some of the Seattle bands gloried in a kind of music John Bonham always called "Deep Sabbath," which was a conglomerate of English, sketchy, blues-based thud. It was inane and had no mystery to it at all. I know from my escapades with guys from Seattle, and from working with Steve Albini, that this Sabbath style of music—that almost clumsy, plodding, slog metal— just never really sprang out of the speakers or moved into any acoustic area. It was just an aping of the Led Zep thing.

CK: Well, then, you must find it ironic that most people who love your band today also tend to love Black Sabbath.

Robert Plant: No, no. I don't agree. I've been playing in festivals in Europe for the past year, and I find those audiences want the sensitivity, too. But maybe it's because I've been playing to a lot of Latin people. I played the Isle of Wight Festival last week, and one of the songs I did was "Going to California," because it's my kind of bag. Now, whether you would call "Going to California" heavy metal, I don't know; it might be a bit embarrassing at times lyrically, but it did sum up a period of my life when I was twenty-two. And the audience was going absolutely apeshit, and these were punk guys with Mohican haircuts. So I think you're wrong.

CK: Maybe so. But it seems that whenever people talk about the dawn of heavy metal, the logic usually goes like this: Black Sabbath created a certain kind of sound that was replicated by British acts and later nü metal bands, and Led Zeppelin sort of invented the sound and image for groups like Guns n' Roses and Aerosmith. Do you disagree with that?

Robert Plant: Well, I think the guitarist in Aerosmith makes no attempt to hide his admiration for Jimmy Page, and that's inherent in a lot of their tracks. Aerosmith are basically a pop group. They write pop songs, and they're aiming for the charts and Top 40 television. And when you think of the treachery of hard rock—when you think of bands like Bon Jovi, and when you think of . . . um . . . what were some of the other hair bands from that era?

CK: Mötley Crüe? Ratt?

Robert Plant: Yeah, yeah. Those bands were hanging on to some real big pop melodies and dressing them up as something aggressive and boyish and

95

testosterone-ridden, but it was still "Livin' on a Prayer," you know? And that's not a great place to be coming from.

CK: It isn't? Why not?

Robert Plant: Well, it is if it's a career move and you want to do "Bridge Over Troubled Water" when you're sixty.

CK: Do you think a lot of those bands were ultimately influenced more by Zep's debauched depiction in the book *Hammer of the Gods: The Led Zeppelin Saga* than by what's actually on your records? It seems like they copied your espoused lifestyle more than your actual songs.

Robert Plant: Who knows? I mean, is it all a career move? Getting fucked up is quite easy if you have more than thirty dollars. It was interesting to watch all that, because I never read that book. But I don't think anyone could have lived through the stuff that [former Zeppelin tour manager] Richard Cole blubbered out to the guy who wrote it [author Stephen Davis].

CK: I really have a hard time believing that you've never read *Hammer of the Gods*. Weren't you curious?

Robert Plant: The guy who wrote that book knew nothing about the band. I think he'd only hung around us once. He got all his information from a guy who had a heroin problem who happened to be associated with us. The only thing I read was the "After Zeppelin" part, because I was so eager to get on with music and stop living in a dream state.

CK: Does it bother you that, in the eyes of a lot of people, the only reason John Paul Jones was not asked to participate in your 1994 reunion with Jimmy Page was financial? And that you and Page simply didn't want to split the revenue three ways?

Robert Plant: [*chuckles*] It's like this: Led Zeppelin

was a very strange, four-quadrant marriage. And when the marriage dissolved, when John passed away, I really didn't think I'd work with any of those guys again. When we were kids, Bonham and I were the toughest guys around. Nobody wanted to be around us, because we believed in ourselves so much and we were really unbearable. So when he passed, I really didn't want to stay with the southern guys—the two guys from London. I thought enough was enough, and I'd lost the one guy I'd been close with since I was fifteen. But when MTV asked me to do the *Unplugged* show, I thought, *I can't take all the credit for this. I can't do the Zeppelin stuff and sit there with a broad grin on my face.* So I asked Jimmy if it was possible for us to start writing again, without it becoming some sad Zeppelin reunion. And there was really no room for anybody else. There was no physical room or emotional room or creative room.

CK: But couldn't you have toured with Page, Jones, and Bonham's son Jason on drums?

Robert Plant: But what the fuck for? John Bonham's kid isn't as good as John Bonham. Look, I know you're a journalist, so I'll go along with this question. I don't make my living by making my living. My time is so important that I can't compromise my taste—or my idea of what's right—simply to match someone else's view of what's a good, calculated move. And can you imagine what a lumbering monster that tour would've been? It would have been quite sluttish to come back firing like a bunch of hard rockers. The important thing was that Page and I decided to write again.

CK: How often do you talk to Jimmy Page for nonbusiness purposes?

Robert Plant: We're going to a tennis match on Tuesday.

CK: Really? Who's playing?

Robert Plant: Fuck if I know! I just made that up [*laughs*].

CK: I realize this probably seems ridiculous to you, but there is a whole class of people who listen to classic-rock radio and wonder if you guys are actually friends.

Robert Plant: There's definitely a warmth between us, and a patience. We're like Walter Matthau and Jack Lemmon. The reality is that Page is a very clever, talented guy who has a particular slant on music, and I was always his sidekick who had a different slant on music.

CK: Earlier in this interview, you said a Led Zeppelin reunion tour would have been a "lumbering monster." But what about bands who are even older than you? Do you think the Rolling Stones are still able to maintain a sense of conviction at this point in their career?

Robert Plant: No. But I think they've gone somewhere else, and I really can't be critical. Because if they have a good time and they play well, it's a communion. And it's somewhere for people to go who remember when that stuff was shit-hot. This kind of thing happens every year. And guess what? You [as a journalist] get a salary, and I get a lot of dough if I sell a lot of records. It's called entertainment.

CK: As the man who heard them all, what is the coolest, heaviest, most "metal" Jimmy Page guitar riff?

Robert Plant: Hmm. [*pauses*] That's a very good question. I guess it's gotta be "Whole Lotta Love," doesn't it? And there's another song that isn't heavy but that I love because the guitar is fucking amazing—"For Your Life" off *Presence*. And then there's the beginning of "The Wanton Song" and "Immigrant Song." I suppose "Immigrant Song" might have it over "Whole Lotta Love," but the thing about "Whole Lotta Love" is that it's quite a sexy track.

CK: Actually, that reminds me of something: on "Whole Lotta Love" you say you're going to give some girl "every inch" of your love. But you're British. Why don't you use the metric system?

Robert Plant: That would change the whole tone of the thing! I suppose today it would have to be, "I'll give you several centimeters of bliss." But people of my generation know nothing about the metric system. I'm fortunate to say I still use inches—or at least that's what my girlfriend says, and she's twenty-nine.

DISPOSABLE HEROES

For most of my youth, Metallica fans made me nervous. By the time *Master of Puppets* was released in 1986, the kids who were already into Metallica seemed kind of nuts. These were usually weight lifters who had previously liked Mötley Crüe and Van Halen before suddenly deciding that anything overtly commercial was absolutely fake, and that singing about girls and partying was pathetic, and that real rock bands were supposed to wear blue jeans and hate their parents. Being a fan of Metallica in the '80s was not supposed to be fun. Loving Metallica was like being Catholic: if you truly believed, it was supposed to inform every aspect of your life. I could not relate to this. I preferred songs about having sex with underage girls in elevators, but Metallica always seemed to be singing about being burned alive (or something along those lines).

By 1992, everything about loving Metallica had evolved, even though the music was only slightly different (the songs were shorter and less complex, but it was still the same premise). I remember the first time I went to a party and watched two sorority girls sing along with "Enter Sandman"—it blew my mind. It was like watching Nancy Reagan smoke pot. In the early '80s, Metallica had refused to make videos; now they seemed to make a new video every six weeks. Over time, it was this "mainstreaming of Metallica" that started to fascinate me, and I went back and seriously reexamined a lot of their older material. I like their music more now than I did back when I was in high school, particularly *Kill 'Em All* and *Garage Days Re-Revisited.*

When *The New York Times Magazine* asked me to do a profile on Metallica before the release of the documentary *Some Kind of Monster,* it felt like the film was going to be a really big deal: every possible media outlet appeared to be covering it. However, *Some Kind of Monster* underperformed at the box office (at least compared to its prerelease expectations). In a weird way, all the media coverage may have actually hurt the film's commercial viability; you could almost experience the entire movie by reading about it. I still think *Some Kind of Monster* is a wonderful documentary, but everything you need to know about it can be illustrated within the span of three thousand words. Sometimes I suspect audiences assumed they already knew exactly what this movie was about, so they saw no reason to pay $10 to see it. A year after its release, I happened to interview Lars Ulrich again, and I casually asked if he was surprised *Some Kind of Monster* didn't make $20 million at the box office. He was not.

"I'm fucking amazed it even made two million dollars in America," he said. "I can't fucking believe it even got released. Do you think people in Nebraska give a fuck if A. O. Scott says some documentary is good? Do you think anyone cares what Owen Gleiberman thinks about Metallica? I never got caught up in that hype. We didn't make fucking *E.T.*"

There is a line in this story where I refer to *Some Kind of Monster* director Joe Berlinger as an "egomaniac," a classification Berlinger adamantly denies. I have casually run into Berlinger on three occasions since the publication of this article, and he always brings up the issue of his alleged egomania immediately, regardless of where we are or what we happen to be talking about.

BAND ON THE COUCH

(JUNE 2004)

There is a scene midway through the documentary *Some Kind of Monster* that defines the film's vision; it's arguably the movie's most emotional moment and certainly its most archetypical. We see the rock group Metallica—the most commercially successful heavy-metal band in rock history— sitting around a table with their therapist, trying to establish how they will finish recording their next album. The recording process has already been complicated by the departure of their bassist and the drinking problem of singer James Hetfield; Hetfield has just returned to the band after a lengthy stint in rehab. Fifteen years ago, Metallica drank so much they were referred to by their fans as "Alcoholica," and the band members all thought that was hilarious. But now, things are different; now, Hetfield can only work four hours a day, because the other twenty hours are devoted to mending a marriage that was shattered by alcohol (and the rock 'n' roll lifestyle that came with it).

Metallica's drummer, a kinetic forty-one-year-old Dane named Lars Ulrich, is having a difficult time dealing with these new parameters. He paces the room, finally telling Hetfield that the singer is "self-absorbed" and "latently controlling." Everyone slowly grows uncomfortable. "I realize now that I barely knew you before," Ulrich says, despite the fact that he's known Hetfield since 1981. The language he uses sounds like outtakes from an *Oprah* episode on self-help books—except Ulrich punctuates every sentence with a very specific (and completely unprintable) expletive.[1] The scene closes with Ulrich's mouth six inches from Hetfield's ever-stoic skull, screaming that singular expletive into the singer's face. It's the most intimate, most honest, most emotionally authentic exchange these two men have ever experienced.

This is also the scene where—if you are in the audience—you will probably laugh.

I've seen this film twice in screening rooms, and it happened both times. Virtually everyone in the theater snickered like condescending hyenas, just as they did during every other visceral, meaningful moment in this documentary. And so did I.

Now, perhaps that's cruel, and perhaps that's predictable. But it's mostly because *Some Kind of Monster* presents an uncomfortable kind of realism: it's the most in-depth, long-

---

1. The expletive being "fuck."

form psychological profile of any rock band that's ever existed; it's also the closest anyone has ever come to making a real-life *This Is Spinal Tap*. One could even argue that *Some Kind of Monster* is a rock 'n' roll film that has nothing to do with music, and that it's actually a two-hour, twenty-minute meditation on therapy, celebrity, and the possibility that just about everyone is a little damaged. That's because the men who made *Some Kind of Monster* (directors Joe Berlinger and Bruce Sinofsky) and its on-screen psychologist (a sweater-clad sixty-five-year-old named Phil Towle) seemed to need therapy as much as Metallica.

"If you strip down all human beings to their core, you'll find the same stuff," claims Towle, the "performance enhancement coach" who served as Metallica's therapist over the two years in which *Some Kind of Monster* was filmed. "You will find fear of rejection, fear of abandonment, fear of being controlled, fear of being unloved, and the desire to love and be loved. That becomes more complicated with hard-rock bands, because—when you exist in a mode of instant gratification—you're never hungry for depth of intimacy. Sex, drugs, and booze are glorified in rock 'n' roll, but those are really just symptoms of the desire for relief."

This is all probably true. In fact, part of what makes *Some Kind of Monster* so compelling is that Towle—the hyper-nurturing Midwesterner now recognized for saving Metallica—seems to possess as many insecurities as the band he was paid $40,000 a month to help. There is not one person involved in *Some Kind of Monster* who could safely be described as "okay."

And it's entirely possible that this is the point.

In order to understand how *Some Kind of Monster* came into existence, you need to know two stories. The first is the history of Metallica, a two-decade narrative that explains (a) why this movie makes people laugh, and (b) why this movie is so unprecedented. Twenty years ago, there was no band on earth who seemed less likely to release a documentary about dealing with interpersonal issues; in a way, it still doesn't seem possible.

Formed in 1981, Metallica became the first important speed-metal band; they played faster and harder than just about every group who had ever come before them. While other '80s metal bands wore spandex and sang about girls, Metallica wore jeans and sang about Armageddon; their first album was called *Kill 'Em All,* a title that was actually less aggressive than the phrase they wanted to use. Hetfield was the frontman, a scowling gun enthusiast who was raised as a Christian Scientist and now hated the world. Drummer Ulrich was a former tennis prodigy in Denmark who moved to California with his affluent family as a teenager, bonding with the antisocial Hetfield over unpopular British metal bands like Diamond Head and Angel Witch. Metallica's lead guitarist is Kirk Hammett, a dark, androgynous personality spawned from a broken home; he spent his sixteenth birthday trying to stop his father from pummeling his mother. Hammett is the personality buffer between Hetfield and Ulrich (if Metallica truly *was* Spinal Tap, he would be the Harry Shearer character). The group's original bassist was a swivel-necked San Franciscan named Cliff Burton, but he died in 1986; while touring through Europe, Metallica had a cataclysmic (and bizarre) highway accident outside of Copenhagen. Their tour bus actually fell on Burton. He was immediately replaced by Jason Newsted, a longtime Metallica superfan who had always dreamed of performing alongside his heroes; after being asked to join the band, the other three members mercilessly hazed Newsted for well over a year (for example, they would constantly—and erroneously—tell strangers that he was gay). These are hard people.

Originally a cult band for burnouts and speed freaks, Metallica went on to become the Led Zeppelin of their generation. They've sold over 90 million albums worldwide; while other metal acts were buried by the early-'90s grunge movement, Metallica only became stronger. And the driving force behind their invincibility seemed to be the fact that they did not care about anything. They fueled their tours on Jägermeister (Hetfield used to drink a bottle every night). They "betrayed" their fan base in 1996 by cutting off their hair, the speed-metal equivalent of Dylan going electric. When kids started illegally downloading their songs off Napster, Metallica had the audacity to sue their own fan base. Metallica actually did what other rock bands only aspire to do: by ignoring trends, they became immune to cultural change. They were, it seemed, unbreakable.

Until (of course) they started to break. A 2001 *Playboy* interview illustrated (and—according to the band—perpetuated) a growing sense of discontent within Metallica, eventually resulting in Newsted's decision to quit after fourteen years of service. Sensing the possibility of losing an extremely lucrative artistic entity, Metallica's management team (an organization called Q-Prime) put Metallica in touch with Towle, a man who'd previously worked with the St. Louis Rams during their 2000 Super Bowl run and had unsuccessfully tried to save another of Q-Prime's clients (the political rap-metal group Rage Against the Machine). Formerly a gang counselor in Chicago, Towle now specializes in psychotherapeutic scenarios involving big money and massive egos. The hope was that he would stop Metallica from imploding; coincidentally, those therapy sessions initiated just before Berlinger and Sinofsky started filming the band's attempt to record their next album.

They ended up filming for 715 days.

It seems Berlinger and Sinofsky had sustained a relationship with Metallica ever since the 1996 HBO documentary *Paradise Lost*, the chronicle of three teenage Metallica fans accused of ritualistically murdering children in West Memphis, Arkansas. Metallica had allowed the two directors to use the band's music in *Paradise Lost* for free, and the two parties had kept in touch, casually discussing the possibility of one day working together on a larger project.

However, in the period following *Paradise Lost*, Berlinger

and Sinofsky's professional relationship began to fray. This is the second story.

Berlinger (who looks like he could be George Lucas's kid brother) is a workaholic with a paradoxical personality: he's an egomaniac, but he's also obsessed with getting other people's approval. Though he had collaborated with Sinofsky for years (most notably on the critically adored documentary *Brother's Keeper*), he began to question the value of their partnership. Essentially, he wanted to go solo. In 2000, Berlinger broke away from Sinofsky to direct *Book of Shadows: Blair Witch 2*, the big-budget sequel to *The Blair Witch Project*.

That decision more or less destroyed Berlinger's life.

"I presided over one of the biggest flops in cinema history," says Berlinger. That's something of an exaggeration, but it's not far off—critics hated *Blair Witch 2*, and it made very little money. Berlinger blames this on Artisan Entertainment for completely reediting *Blair Witch 2*, and his complaint doesn't sound wholly irrational; some of the enforced changes were drastic. For example, Berlinger had originally wanted to use the Frank Sinatra tune "Witchcraft" as the score for the opening credits; Artisan changed it to "Disposable Teens" by Marilyn Manson.

Berlinger was devastated by the response to *Blair Witch 2*. He became a recluse and melodramatically considered quitting film altogether. Meanwhile, Sinofsky feared his collaborative relationship with Berlinger was finished. "We had serious problems that we never addressed," says Sinofsky. "We remained friends, but—when he went off to do *Blair Witch*—I was envious. And I was fearful that he wouldn't come back." However, he did come back. A depressed Berlinger longingly watched *Paradise Lost* in his living room one night, and—upon hearing the ominous strains of the Metallica song "Sanitarium"—he suddenly remembered the forgotten idea of making a rock movie. He contacted Sinofsky, and they contacted Metallica. Now, the original plan for this project was strange: they were going to film the band in the studio and make a series of infomercials (yes, *infomercials*). These infomercials would be broadcast in thirty-minute increments on late-night television, and the idea was that people would see these infomercials and order Metallica's next album. It was going to be this innovative, crazy way to sell records.

But then things got crazier.

When production on this unnamed "Metallica infomercial project" began in 2001, the group was already mired in turmoil: Newsted had officially quit the band after only one session with Towle. Newsted still considers the idea of rock band therapy to be a little ridiculous. "Something that's really important to note—and this isn't pointed at anyone—is something I knew long before I met James Hetfield or anyone else," Newsted said in an interview from his ranch in western Montana. "Certain people are made to be opened up and exposed. Certain people are not meant to be opened up and exposed. I'll leave it at that."

For the first thirty minutes of *Some Kind of Monster* (roughly three months in real time), you see a band that doesn't necessarily like each other, struggling with a record no one seems enthused about creating; it's sort of the metal version of the Beatles' *Let It Be*. But then—suddenly and without much explanation—Hetfield disappears into rehab. Ulrich and Hammett have nothing to do in the interim, except talk to their therapist. This is the point where *Some Kind of Monster* starts to change; what it becomes is not a glorification of rock 'n' roll, but an illustration of how rock 'n' roll manufactures a reality that's almost guaranteed to make people incomplete. Metallica's massive success—and the means through which they achieved it—meant they never had to intellectually mature past the age of nineteen.

"I think most people in rock bands have arrested development," Hammett says now. "Society doesn't demand people in rock bands to do certain things. You're able to start drinking whenever you want, and you can play shows drunk, and you can get offstage and continue to be drunk, and people love it. They toast their glasses to an artist who's drunk and breaking things and screaming and wrestling in the middle of a restaurant. Things like that happened to us, and people cheered. I remember reading [the Led Zeppelin biography] *Hammer of the Gods*, and I thought, *I wanna be like that all the time*. What I didn't realize is that the stories in that book took place over an entire career.[2] We were trying to act like that every single night."

To some, that might sound like a cliché sentiment for a millionaire musician to express; it almost blames society for making guitar heroes wasted and lawless. But this kind of self-discovery is part of what makes *Some Kind of Monster* a strikingly modern film: by fusing the accelerated culture of therapy with the accelerated culture of celebrity, it illustrates why the people inside those two realms can't keep up.

"Metallica's evolution as people was aborted by their surreal existence," says Towle. "Kirk Hammett once told me that coming off tour was like experiencing post-traumatic stress syndrome; he said it was like leaving a war and reentering real life. When I asked him why he felt that way, he said, 'Because now I have to empty the trash.' The profundity in that statement is in its simplicity: rock stars are infantilized by people who do everything for them. We insulate them from a reality that would actually be good for them."

This unreality does not only apply to drinking and garbage removal, either. That becomes especially clear when Hetfield returns to the band from rehab as a completely changed man (he even begins wearing eyeglasses, for some reason). Slowly, the deeper issue of *Some Kind of Monster* emerges: Hetfield and Ulrich have spent their entire adulthood intertwined, but they've never been close. For the past twenty years, they've never needed to have a real relationship with each other, even though Hetfield was the best man in Ulrich's wed-

---

2. And—quite possibly—never happened at all (see page 96).

ding. And that is what you mostly see over the last hour of this film: two middle-aged men fighting through their neuroses and confusion, earnestly talking about *intimacy* and *emotional betrayal* and *how they feel about each other.*

It is important to remember that these are the same two men who cowrote a song called "Seek and Destroy."

Why Metallica allowed Berlinger and Sinofsky to film this process remains baffling. "Lars felt the therapy sessions were actually enabled by the presence of the cameras," says Berlinger. "He felt the cameras forced them to be honest." There's certainly no question about how much the band believes in this film: when Elektra Records grew concerned over the project's escalating cost, the label considered turning it into a reality TV show (this was back in 2002, when MTV's *The Osbournes* was the hottest commodity on television). By that point, both the filmmakers and the group saw this solely as a theatrical release. They wanted complete control, so they bought the rights. Which means Metallica wrote Elektra a check . . . for $4.3 million.

That, obviously, is a lot of money. But Metallica has more money than God. That's another strangely personal insight in *Some Kind of Monster*—you get to see just how mind-blowingly rich these guys actually are. And particularly for Metallica, wealth is not something they necessarily want to brag about; remember, this is a band who *sued its own fans* just two years ago. The core Metallica disciples tend to be alienated, working-class males; one wonders how these people will react to an extended sequence in *Some Kind of Monster* where Ulrich—the most self-consciously urbane member of the group—sips champagne and sells his collection of Jean-Michel Basquiat's artwork at a Christie's auction for $12 million. Hetfield and Hammett would have both preferred to see the auction scene removed from the film (Hetfield described the footage as "downright embarrassing"), but Ulrich wanted it in the movie. He feels it is an essential aspect of his personality. And as he explains his position, you can hear two years of therapy dripping off his voice. He has no problem talking about *anything*, even if it's "downright embarrassing." I suddenly find myself wishing that every rock star I interviewed had spent twenty-four months in psychotherapy.

"Art is my passion," says Ulrich. "It just so happens that art operates in those kind of high financial neighborhoods. If people find that distasteful or obnoxious, I can't control that. It's part of who I am. If you're going to paint a portrait of the people in Metallica, that has to play a role, because that is who I am. And if people want to focus on the financial elements of art instead of the creative elements of art, I can't control that, either."

"I hate to think about this film as just being pro-therapy or anti-therapy," Berlinger says when asked about the philosophical message of *Some Kind of Monster*. "To me, it's more about how it's okay to admit you have issues."

Well, maybe so. But it's impossible to watch this documentary without drawing certain conclusions about the process it explores. On one hand, everyone I interviewed for this story concedes that Metallica would have likely broken up without Towle's assistance. But is this "enlightened" Metallica much better off? If a band's entire aesthetic is based on the musical expression of inexplicable rage, what's left when that rage is vanquished? One could suggest that Towle has exorcised the singular demon that made Metallica relevant. Moreover, the depiction of Towle's behavior during the final third of the film validates every criticism ever directed toward therapists: over time, Towle slowly seems to believe that he is a *member* of Metallica; he even tries to contribute lyrics for the album. And when a (completely reasonable) Hetfield tries to end the group's therapy, Towle attempts to convince him that this is a mistake, and that Hetfield is simply struggling with his inability to "trust," and that the band still needs his $40,000-a-month assistance. Even the filmmakers found this strange.

"When he started using the word *we* instead of the word *I*, Joe and I kept asking ourselves, 'Is this something a therapist would say [to a client]?' I always thought it was a little weird," Sinofsky says.

Not surprisingly, Towle denies any confusion over his role with the band.

"A documentary is subjective, and it's affected by what footage is selected by the documentarians," he says. "The way that it's portrayed implies that I was pushed out the door, and that's not what happened. I don't want to sound defensive about this, but the film makes it seem like I just wanted to extend my gravy train, and anyone who knows me would know that nothing could be further from the truth."

Regardless of how one views Towle's motivations, it's hard to attack his results: the guys in Metallica are, without question, much happier humans. I interviewed James Hetfield in 1996, and it was one of the worst conversations of my professional life—he was surly, impenetrable, and unable (or maybe just unwilling) to think in the abstract. When I interviewed him for this story, he was a completely evolved person: affable, nonconfrontational, and willing (almost wanting) to chat about his feelings. In fact, when I asked him about Towle's attempt to keep Metallica in therapy they no longer needed, Hetfield gave the most reasonable answer imaginable.

"Phil has issues, too," Hetfield said. "Every therapist has issues. We're all just people. We've all got some brokenness inside us. Phil's abandonment issues came up, and he tried to mask them by saying, 'You're mistrusting me.' And it's like, wow—that's a really important point in the movie."

And a really funny point, kind of. But sometimes the difference between self-actualization and self-amusement is less than you think.

UNBUTTONING THE HARDEST
BUTTON TO BUTTON

The following White Stripes story probably bothered me more than any piece I've ever written. This seems curious in retrospect, because it now reads like a workmanlike profile containing no controversy whatsoever.

This was the first official cover story I wrote for *SPIN,* and (I think) the first significant cover story on the White Stripes for any national publication in America. Putting the Stripes on the cover seemed a little crazy at the time, because their fourth album (*Elephant*) had not yet been released and it was still unclear whether this band was famous enough to be on the cover of a major magazine. This is always a tricky issue at a place like *SPIN*; at the time, the publication's circulation was something like 525,000 and there was always this unwritten theory that suggested it was unwise to put any artist on the cover who couldn't sell at least 525,000 copies of their own record (in other words, it didn't make sense to try to promote a rock magazine with a rock band who was less popular than the magazine itself). When I started the reporting for this article, their previous album (*White Blood Cells*) still hadn't gone gold. As a consequence, I think I unconsciously felt a pressure to "sell" the band to readers, which is why I included a sentence where I refer to the music of the Stripes as "so fucking good." I regret doing this. I mean, the White Stripes *are* fucking good, but that sentence sounds completely idiotic.

The whole process was difficult. Jack White's main motivation for doing the interview appeared to be his desire to explain why he hated interviews (this happens a lot with modern artists; Julian Casablancas is the same way). As a result, the piece is too self-conscious. However, the larger problem came when I turned the story in to *SPIN* and one of my editors had a problem with Jack's quotes. The editor questioned the relevance of White's race-related quotes; I felt they were the only legitimately new elements of the story. We locked horns on this point, and—as I am wont to do—I totally overreacted. I threatened to take my byline off the story, which would have been stupid. I briefly considered quitting *SPIN,* which would have been even stupider.

Late in the editing process, I talked to the *SPIN* copy chief about the situation, and he (mildly) agreed with my argument. By chance, this particular copy editor was quitting the magazine in two weeks and moving to Virginia, so he just added the quotes back into the story and pushed it through to the production staff (without really telling anyone else). However, this copy editor also gave me some wise advice before capitulating to my request: "You know," he said, "a magazine only exists in the world for one month, and people don't remember anything. They usually can't remember what they read two days ago. Six months from now, you will feel ridiculous for having been so overwrought about a few quotes from Jack White."

And I suppose I kind of did. But I also kind of didn't.

GARAGE DAYS UNVISITED
(OCTOBER 2002)

Jack White flicks his cigarette ash into a glass of water. He and Meg White are sitting on a couch in an unnecessarily swanky hotel room in downtown Chicago, trying to explain how it feels to be a punkish underground band—with modest sales and an antimedia posture—that has somehow become America's most frothed-over creative venture.

"We're in a weird spot right now," Jack says. "To be honest, I have a hard time finding a reason to be on the cover of *SPIN.* It was like being on the MTV Movie Awards [where they performed their recent single "Fell in Love with a Girl"]. You start asking yourself, 'What are we getting from this? What are we destroying by doing this? Does it mean anything?' So you try it. You wonder if you'll end up being any different than everyone else, and usually, the answer is no."

Actually, the answer is maybe. If you ignored the White Stripes' songs, you'd assume they were a novelty act: they wear only matching red, white, and black clothing, they have no bassist, and they've built their public persona around a fabricated relationship (they claim to be siblings, but they're actually an ex-couple whose divorce was finalized in 2000). However, this joke has no punch line. The White Stripes represent a sound (postmodern garage rock) from a specific place (downtown Detroit), and it's packaged within a conscious mix of sonic realness and media boondoggle. They have done what all great rock bands are eventually supposed to do—they've reinvented blues music.

As we talk, guitarist Jack speaks in full, articulate paragraphs. Drummer Meg mostly hugs a pillow and curls her legs underneath her body, hiding feet covered by rainbow-colored socks that resemble Fruit Stripe gum's zebra mascot. The night before, the duo played the Metro club near Wrigley Field, and it was an acceptable ninety-minute show. Tonight they'll play a blistering set at the Metro that won't start until 12:55 A.M., and it will annihilate the molecules of Illinois's air: They will do an extended version of a new song ("Ball and Biscuit") that makes references to being a seventh son and includes a grinding guitar solo, shredded over the beat from Queen's "We Will Rock You." They'll cover the Animals' "House of the Rising Sun." Everything will be raw and unrehearsed and imperfect.

And that's why it's so fucking good.

"We have to go back," Jack insists. "The last twenty years have been filled with digital, technological crap that's taken the soul out of music. The technological metronome of the United States is obsessed with progress, so now you have all these gearheads who want to lay down three thousand tracks in their living room. That wasn't the point."

"The point," says Meg, "is being a live band."

Perhaps Meg is right. However, classifying the White Stripes as two kids in a stellar live band scarcely describes their curious career arc and often contradictory aesthetic. Supposedly formed on Bastille Day in 1997, they got mild attention for being bassless and dressing like pieces of candy. After they'd released two albums (1999's eponymous debut and 2000's *De Stijl*, named after a Dutch art movement that emphasized primal abstraction) and toured with Pavement and Sleater-Kinney, there was a growing suspicion that Jack and Meg were succeeding where Jon Spencer and his moronic Blues Explosion had failed—there is little irony in what the Stripes create. "We wanted things to be as childish as possible, but with no sense of humor," Jack explains, "because that's how children think." Of course, children also lie; children will conflate truth and fiction for no reason at all.

Like Pavement in '92, the Stripes brought romance and mystery to an underground devoid of rock 'n' roll fantasy. By the release of *White Blood Cells* in the summer of 2001, they'd evolved into a cultural phenomenon. Eventually, they signed a lucrative deal with V2 (which has since rereleased their earlier albums), had their own Lego-centric MTV hit, and were embraced by modern-rock radio programmers suffering from a post-Bizkit hangover.

V2 president Andy Gershon, who reportedly signed the band for $1.5 million, was initially reluctant. "Your conventional wisdom is that they're a two-piece, they need a bass player, they've got this red-and-white gimmick, and the songs are fantastic, but they're recorded very raw . . . how is this going to be on radio?" he says. "But for me, it was like, the record's amazing."[1]

Along with the Strokes and the Hives, the White Stripes are part of a back-to-basics real-rock revival awkwardly termed "neo-garage." With roots in the '60s stomp of teenage bands

---

1. I have no fucking idea why rock magazines insist on interviewing "industry insiders" for these kinds of profiles. Are we really supposed to be surprised that the guy who runs the White Stripes' record label thinks the White Stripes are awesome? The inclusion of this quote was not my idea.

responding to the British Invasion, garage rock is about simple, direct catharsis. For years, this music was the province of aging coolsters, but neo-garage infuses that old sound with glam electricity. The duo hails from southwest Detroit, more specifically from a lower-middle-class Hispanic section uncomfortably referred to as Mexicantown. They claim to be the youngest offspring in a family of ten children. They claim to have formed one day when Meg wandered into their parents' attic and began playing Jack's drum kit. This is not true. But this much is true: Mexicantown is where Jack White grew up and operated an upholstery shop, and Meg is from the same zip code; she once worked as a bartender at a blues bar in the trendy northern Detroit suburb of Royal Oak. Jack is twenty-six. Meg is twenty-seven. The White Stripes are "Detroit People," and they are the most visible band in the Detroit garage-rock scene, a conglomeration of pals extending far beyond the Stripes themselves.

Detroit is full of underproduced, consciously primitive rock bands, all playing the same bar circuit; you could waste a weekend trying to name every band in the 313 area code (a lot of them can be found on the *Sympathetic Sounds of Detroit* compilation, which Jack White recorded in his living room). There are the Von Bondies, a sloppy, MC5-ish rave-up quartet, and the Clone Defects, an arty, quasi-metal band. Slumber Party are borderline shoegazers; the Come Ons play traditional '60s-ish pop. The Dirtbombs bridge the gaps between glam, Detroit's Motown past, and the blues-rock future. The Piranhas are destructo-punk and already legendary for their "Rat Show" at a now-defunct club called the Gold Dollar in 1999 (their singer performed with a bloody, freshly executed rat duct-taped to his naked torso). The Detroit Cobras are probably the hottest band of the moment (and supposedly ignoring an avalanche of major labels trying to sign them). Yet the White Stripes remain the most conflicted of media darlings: unlike most of their blue-collar peers, they have a well-cultivated look, an artistic sensibility, and a mythology that makes the Stripes a *concept* as much as a band (almost like a garage-rock KISS). But the real reason they're the biggest little rock group since Sonic Youth is more difficult to quantify: audiences hear something in their music that's so fundamental it almost feels alien.

According to Jack, what they're hearing is truth (or at least his version of it).

"We grew up in the late '80s and '90s, and what was good in rock 'n' roll for those twenty years? Nothing, really. I guess I liked Nirvana," White says. "And sometimes when you grow up around all these people who only listen to hip-hop, something inside of you just doesn't connect with that. Some people will just kind of fall into that culture—you know, white people pretending to be black people or whatever[2]—because they're involved in an environment where they want to fit in and they want to have friends, so they decide to like what everyone else likes and to dress how everyone else dresses. Meg and I never went along with it."[3]

I try to get Meg to comment; she defers to Jack, smiles, and looks away. Meg seems really, really nice and really, really bored. She and Jack laugh at each other's jokes, but they mostly behave like coworkers. I ask her how she feels about the way people have portrayed her—like when reporters infer

---

2. In retrospect, I truly cannot fathom why this sentiment seemed so controversial at the time.

3. There's one other detail about Jack White that undoubtedly affected this piece: He doesn't trust the media, so his impulse is to contradict anyone he suspects is attempting to manipulate his image. This quality is rare. Most celebrities want to be lead, so they'll agree with any question that intimates an obvious answer; if you ask the average movie actor if his latest performance was more physically demanding than his previous roles, he'll almost always agree that it was (even if it wasn't). Most celebrities want the journalist to like them. White does not; his natural reaction is to disagree with whatever the question seems to suggest. For example, if a reporter says to him, "The guitar playing on this record reminds me of Led Zeppelin," White will immediately claim that he doesn't like Led Zeppelin and that the analogy is weak. However, if that same reporter had said, "Everyone thinks this album sounds like Led Zep, but I think it sounds more like the Stooges," White would say, "Oh really? I'm very influenced by Jimmy Page. This is our Zeppelin record." Within the context of any profile that's supposed to illustrate who he is as a person, there's nothing Jack White won't disagree with.

profound metaphorical insight from her unwillingness to chat.

"Some people," Meg says, "put more thought into shyness than necessary."

Wendy Case is considerably less shy than Meg White.

In fact, Wendy Case is considerably less shy than David Lee Roth. She is the thirty-eight-year-old lead singer/guitarist for the Paybacks, a band Case describes as "hard pop." Her hair is blond on top and brown underneath, she laughs like a '73 Plymouth Scamp that refuses to turn over, and she can probably outdrink 90 percent of the men in Michigan. We are riding in her black Cherokee down Detroit's Cass Corridor.

"If you're gonna look for one unifying force [in the Detroit scene], the thing is that we all still drink," Case says. "You get together and you drink beer, and you listen to music. That's pretty much the nucleus of every social situation."

The Cass Corridor is a strip of urban wretchedness jammed between the north shadow of Detroit's skyline and Wayne State University. It's basically a slum, filled with dive bars and homeless people who spend afternoons having animated conversations with the sky. This is where Detroit's garage rock has flourished, so it's no surprise that most of this town's bands are no-nonsense buzzsaws. That said, the depth and intensity of their musical knowledge is surprising. The recent Dirtbombs album, *Ultraglide in Black*, is mostly covers (Stevie Wonder, Phil Lynott), and the Detroit Cobras' *Life, Love and Leaving* is all covers.

"We'll all sit around and listen to an old Supremes record or a Martha Reeves and the Vandellas record and marvel at the production level, especially considering how cheaply it was done," says Eddie Harsch, a guy who used to play keyboards with the Black Crowes and currently plays bass for the Cobras. "People in Detroit know their records."

This is certainly true for the Stripes, who pepper shows with Dolly Parton's "Jolene," Meg's rendition of Loretta Lynn's "Rated X," and the menacing, tommy-gun riff of Link Wray's "Jack the Ripper."

Jack explains it this way: "We've never covered a song simply because it would be cool or because we'd seem really obscure for doing so. Certain circles of musicians will all get involved with the same record at the same time, and suddenly it will be cool to like the Kinks' *Village Green Preservation Society* for a month. But why didn't people feel that way three years ago? I've always hated the whole idea of record collectors who are obsessed with how obscure something is. Usually when somebody brings up something obscure, I assume it's not very good, because—if it was—I would have heard it already. Record collectors are collecting. They're not really listening to music."

We talk a little longer. But then Jack does something odd: he reaches behind his waist and rips the tag off his black pants. It's the type of weird moment that makes the Stripes so baffling and compelling. In and of itself, it's not exactly mind-blowing that a guy ripped the tag off his pants. But this small, theatrical gesture punctuates Jack's quote better than words ever could. It looks rehearsed, even though that's impossible (it's hard to imagine Jack buys a new pair of trousers for every interview). Yet everything the White Stripes do raises a question. How can two media-savvy kids (posing as brother and sister and wearing Dr. Seuss clothes) represent blood-and-bones Detroit, a city whose greatest resource is asphalt?

"One time I was joking around with Jack," recalls Detroit Cobras guitarist Maribel Restrepo, who lives ten minutes from where Jack resides in southwest Detroit. "And I said, 'If you tell little white lies, they'll only lead to more lies.' And he goes, 'You can't even do that, because the minute you say anything, that's all people will talk about. It gets to where you don't want to say anything.'"

It's not that less is more; it's that less is everything. When Meg White hugs her pillow and tells me that people put more thought into shyness than necessary, I want to play along with her—even though she's lying. It's almost as if we don't want to know the truth about the White Stripes. The lies are much better.

THE ICE PLANET GOTH

This article is a combination of two forms of quasi-journalism: it's 50 percent a "Look at All These Misplaced Weirdos" story, and it's 50 percent an "Enjoy My Self-Reflexively Peculiar Personal Experience" story.

In many ways, this was among the easiest pieces I ever wrote; all I had to do was show up. One day every year, a whole bunch of goth kids go to Disneyland (partially because they like the iconography, but mostly because it seems like a crazy thing for goth kids to do). As such, these kids really want attention; they were not difficult to find, and it was not difficult to convince them to talk about themselves. I simply spent the day walking up to pasty strangers in black capes and asking them why the fuck they thought Space Mountain was "fabulous."

This was actually the second story I wrote about goths; the first was in Akron, the day after the Columbine school shootings. That, obviously, was a somewhat more serious article, my core thesis being that the overwhelming majority of existing goth kids did not aspire to wear trench coats to biology class before shooting every cheerleader in the face. To me, that was the most insane thing about Columbine: prior to April 20, 1999, it wasn't just that goth kids weren't considered violent; prior to that tragedy, goth kids weren't even considered *scary*. They were just the kids who listened during English class.

SOMETHING WICKED THIS WAY COMES
(DECEMBER 2002)

If you can't find a reason to hate Disneyland, you're just not trying. Like the insincere smile of an aging bank teller, Disneyland represents a contradiction with no discernible upside: it's hokey and archaic, yet gaudy and corporate. It's all kitsch sunshine and crass consumerism, and any self-respecting cynic would despise its existence.

Unless, of course, said cynic enjoys Bauhaus.

Don't let anyone tell you the Age of Irony is over. It's alive and well in California, and here's proof: goth kids love Disneyland. On the final Sunday of every August, droves of goth-tacular witches and warlocks drive to Anaheim and enter the foreboding inner sanctum of Mickey's Toontown. Welcome to Bats Day in the Fun Park, the annual SoCal collision of goth culture[1] and family fun.

---

1. Few subcultures are as visually distinct—or as publicly misrepresented—as the goth movement. Part fashion and part philosophy, "gothness" is preoccupied with all things lugubrious. Goth icons can be traced through the centuries (Edgar Allan Poe, Hammer Film Productions, Black Sabbath), but the scene fomented around punks like Siouxsie and the Banshees and "Bela Lugosi's Dead," the 1979 debut single by English glam ghouls Bauhaus. Best known for vocalist Peter Murphy's craven caterwaul, Bauhaus inspired a generation of bands like the Sisters of Mercy and Mission U.K. (and legendary London club the Batcave). The fans were easily identifiable—pale, stoic, and dressed completely in black. Goth became commercially viable during the mid-'80s with the success of the Cure. Its popularity exploded in the '90s, when it merged with metal and industrial dance music, spawning Nine Inch Nails and Marilyn Manson. These "angry" goths typified modern dark-side culture and were branded enemies of society—when Eric Harris and Dylan Klebold shot their classmates at Columbine High School, they were characterized as "goth" only because they wore the uniform.

"L.A. goth is very different from goth everywhere else in America," explains Bats Day coordinator and Disney super-fan Noah Korda, the diminutive thirty-one-year-old who spearheads the pilgrimage. "I mean, it's cold everywhere else. In places like Chicago, it's gloomy. But goths in California are mostly happy people. I was just the kind of person who was always interested in creepy crap. For me, this has never been about being sad or alienated."

Bats Day began in 1998. At the time, it was just an excuse to be weird. A few regulars from Hollywood goth clubs like Helter Skelter and Perversion decided to drop acid and walk around Disneyland on a summer afternoon. The following year it was officially dubbed Bats Day, and it has grown ever since. When the sun was at its zenith on August 25 of this year, more than five hundred black-cloaked iconoclasts were tromping around Mickey's playland. It is not, however, a Disney-sanctioned event. "We don't contact the park," says Korda. "And they probably wouldn't care, but just in case, I don't want to give them a chance to come up with a reason to shut it down. But it's got to be pretty obvious that this is going on."

At times during Bats Day, it was impossible to swing a dead cat in Disneyland without hitting a goth (of course, if you had swung a dead cat around Disneyland, a few of these kids probably would have found that awesome). Here's a Dionysian diary from the Day of the Disney Dead.

10:10 A.M.: The sun is already pouring through holes in the powder-blue California sky as I meander through the gates of Disneyland, assaulted on all sides by small children shrieking for merchandise and ice cream. At the point of entry, I see a sign that reads "Here you leave today and enter the world of yesterday, tomorrow, and fantasy." I take ten steps into this world and immediately see a man selling overpriced Kodak disposable cameras. Yesterday and tomorrow aren't quite as charming or futuristic as one might anticipate. My suspicion was that 10:00 A.M. would be too early for goth hunting, but there are already dozens of specimens congregating near some

123

poor sap in a Goofy suit, and a few of them are pushing baby carriages and donning mouse ears. I begin chatting with a forty-year-old goth legal secretary named Crickett Hoffman. I ask her to explain the paradox of supposedly gloomy humans frolicking in the happiest place on earth.

"Goths tend to be kids at heart," says Hoffman. "When you're young, you think the goth movement is about depression and alienation. But if goths were really that depressed, there would be no goth movement. They'd all kill themselves."

10:54 A.M.: Several goths are gawking at a woman portraying Ariel, the chesty little mermaid from that movie about the little mermaid, which I think was called *The Little Mermaid*. Although there are no goths at a nearby headgear outlet called Hatmosphere, I spot several of them wearing newly purchased Captain Hook pirate hats. This prompts me to consider starting work on a nonfiction book titled *Sir Francis Drake: The First Goth?*

11:07 A.M.: My first error: I see a goateed guy wearing a skull T-shirt, accompanied by a black-haired girlfriend with more tattoos than Tupac and a complexion the color of cocaine. I ask him how many years he has participated in Bats Day in the Fun Park, but it turns out he has no idea what I'm talking about. "We just came here for the hell of it," says twenty-seven-year-old Brandon Stratton. "I had no idea any of this was going on." Stratton and I then have a brief conversation about Tim Burton movies while his girlfriend stares at me silently, probably fantasizing about how I would look swinging from a gallows.

Noon: The entire goth army convenes at Sleeping Beauty Castle for the first of three group photos, all taken by Noah Korda. While we wait for Korda to organize the sinister posse, I strike up a conversation with Scott McElhaney, a six-foot-two forty-year-old who vaguely resembles Marilyn Manson and has an interesting backstory: After spending twenty-one years in the navy, he has taken a job with a defense contractor, building and testing military infrared sensors. This is an admittedly ungothlike move, but McElhaney says goth-dom was never his bag to begin with. "I don't think I'm really goth," he says. "I'm more of a hearse person. But hearse people are certainly sympathetic to the goth sensibilities." It seems that McElhaney is a member of Phantom Coaches, a subsection of humanity united in their love of cars that tote corpses (McElhaney drives a 1970 hearse with a Cadillac chassis but concedes that the ultimate ride is the '59 Superior driven by Bud Cort in *Harold and Maude*). However, there is more to Phantom Coaches than just cars: the group also enjoys celebrating Halloween, hanging out in cemeteries, and listening to "gothabilly" music, which is sort of a synthesis of the Stray Cats with Siouxsie and the Banshees. The highlight of our mass photograph in front of the castle is the appearance of Snow White's nemesis, the Evil Queen, an *über*-wicked woman roundly cheered by hundreds of goth minions who evidently see her as some kind of role model. These guys certainly dig the black-hearted bitches. Moments later, an actress portraying the virginal Snow White tries to get into the picture, and everyone boos her into submission.

12:36 P.M.: "Disney came up with a wonderful idea, and a bunch of other people came in and perverted it," Krystle Becknauld tells me, finally expressing the kind of goth sentiment I had expected to hear. She is particularly venomous toward Disney's California Adventure, the modernized, upscale park that lies just south of the original Disneyland. "That other park destroyed this area. Now they have Ferris wheels and cotton candy. Walt Disney never wanted that shit." Becknauld is a snarked-up, blond eighteen-year-old poised to enter her freshman year at Cal State Long Beach. She walks the park with three males wearing floor-length black leather trench coats. I tell them they are insane, as it is at least 80 degrees and I am sweating through my T-shirt.

"Well, of course you are," one responds. "The sun is beating down on your raw, exposed flesh."

1:01 P.M.: One of the misconceptions about this culture is that goths are lonely. At Disneyland, the opposite seems to be true: many of these demi-spooks appear to be in successful, mutually necromantic relationships. I ask a group of three happy goth couples to describe the perfect mate, and they all say it's the person that they're currently with. I then ask them to pick the celebrity they'd most like to have sex with. The guys choose Rose McGowan. The girls select Peter Murphy.

1:43 P.M.: What do you feed a hungry goth? Apparently, Monte Cristo sandwiches from a restaurant called the Blue Bayou in New Orleans Square. A party of five goths waits for a table in the Blue Bayou's lobby, and I mention that Disney's mainstream parkgoers appear oddly unalarmed by the number of people bumping around in capes and hooded death robes. However, these goths feel differently about the level of tolerance. "I was just in one of the stores," says twenty-eight-year-old chemist Jennifer Nogle, "and all the normals were asking the staff questions like 'What's with these people? Are they part of some weird religion?' Get real."

Nogle's reference to "normals"—goth slang for nongoths—raises an interesting point: people are constantly asking goth kids what makes someone goth. However, an equally valid question is: What makes someone a normal?

"They are not us," Nogle says with focused conviction. "They wear polo shirts."

2:50 P.M.: As a single rider on the Indiana Jones Adventure, I am seated next to . . . a cute goth teenager! I strike up some winning banter while we wait for the train car to commence rolling.

"So," I begin, "are you enjoying your day at Disneyland?"

Silence.

I try again, this time from a different angle. "So, do you

think Marilyn Manson will survive the departure of Twiggy Ramirez? Because I thought that 'Disposable Teens' song was tremendous."

More silence. I am running out of material.

"So," I ask, "do you think Harrison Ford is goth?"

"Why do you keep talking to me?" she finally says, and suddenly the ride begins. Now it's too loud to talk. Animated rats are falling from the ceiling of a cave, and I remember that *The Last Crusade* was totally ridiculous.

3:46 P.M.: Things to do in Disneyland if you're goth:

1. carry a Cure lunchbox as a purse,
2. make devil horns whenever photographed,
3. insist you're "not really goth."

4:00 P.M.: The second mass photograph of the day. This one is taken at Tomorrowland, which is how people at Disney during the 1950s saw the future, which means the future now resembles the early 1970s, which means their future is our past, which means Tomorrowland is kind of like *Star Wars*. While Noah Korda snaps a photo of the growing mass of black storm troopers, I ask a pentagram-tattooed woman named Linda Knowles whether she felt ostracized by the 1999 Columbine school shootings, an event wrongly blamed on the goth subculture. To my surprise, she felt even more ostracized after September 11. "I was in a grocery store in Laguna [California] right after September 11, and I was wearing a T-shirt from Salem, Massachusetts, because my husband and I had just been there for vacation," Knowles says. "And this woman points to me and says, 'You're one of those witches! Osama bin Laden was a fall guy. It was the witches who blew up the Twin Towers!' So, obviously, there is still some prejudice against the goth lifestyle."

5:32 P.M.: Five goths convince me to go on Splash Mountain with them. This is one of those rides where you sit in a log and get completely soaked, which I normally disdain. But I've never seen wet goths before, so I go along for the trip.

I find myself inside a log on an underground river. Everything smells like chlorine and Hot Topic. The girls in front of me are giggling at the animatronic rabbits surrounding us, and I find myself thinking, *How did America become terrified of these people?* Two trench coat–cloaked kids in Colorado may have become twisted killing machines and ruined it for everybody else, but these goths are the kind of folk who laugh at fur-covered robots. The ride concludes when the log plummets fifty feet into a mini tsunami. I bid my soaked newfound acquaintances good-bye as they reapply their makeup.

7:20 P.M.: I hate to keep beating a dead jackal, but the logic behind goth summer fashion is profoundly fucked up. Why would anybody wear a black sweatshirt in August? Why would people who live in Southern California drape themselves in black velvet, unless they were appearing in an Alannah Myles video? The goth movement would be better off had it flourished in Iceland. If Björk had made a record about vampires instead of polar bears, the world would certainly be less sweaty.

7:45 P.M.:

Q: How do you make fifty goth kids sprint across Disneyland?

A: Put up a sign that says "Smoking Section."

There are only three smoking sections here at Disney, and they all look like backstage at a Sisters of Mercy concert. Apparently, the Marlboro Man is pretty goddamn goth.

8:00 P.M.: As night falls on the Disneyland Park, the entire Bats Day flock of five hundred descends like locusts on the Haunted Mansion for a final snapshot. It's impossible to ignore how happy they all seem—smiling, talking on cell phones, and joking about watching *The Crow* and drinking hemlock. And something becomes completely clear: for the first time in a long time, a lot of these goths feel comfortable and accepted. Today, they are the insiders. They are the people who can sarcastically point at others with impunity; they are the freaks who took over; they are, quite suddenly, the normals. When the tapestry of alienation becomes the status quo, disaffection merely becomes fashion. It's a goth world after all.

FITTER, HAPPIER

Radiohead was the smartest collection of musicians I've ever interviewed, and I have no idea what band would rank second. I do know it wouldn't be that close. All they wanted to talk about were books. The dumbest guy in Radiohead is still smarter (by himself) than all three members of the Beastie Boys and two-fifths of the Strokes.

When I was flying to Oxford, England, for this story, I read Naomi Klein's five-hundred-page manifesto *No Logo.* I was a little afraid that Thom Yorke might want to talk about Canadian anticorporate ideology for the totality of our interview. As it turns out, he never mentioned it once. However, I must have discussed this subject with Colin Greenwood, even though I don't remember doing so. The reason I assume we must have talked about Naomi Klein is because I opened up *No Logo* when I was putting this anthology together, and there was a rudimentary map inside: during dinner, Colin had sketched me a map of downtown Oxford so that I could find a farmers' market that sold lychee tea.

Finding this map makes me optimistic. I have interviewed so many rock stars who turned out to be pricks and/or morons; it was refreshing to meet a band who actually turned out to be cooler than I anticipated. There have been countless occasions when I've listened to a song and imagined what its words and sounds were supposed to represent, and I inevitably perceive each element to be complex and subtle and conscious. However, when the songwriter eventually explains his thought process during the music's creation, I often realize that (a) the musician barely cares what the song is supposed to mean, and that (b) I've actually invested more intellectual energy into the song than the goddamn artist. Which is fine, I suppose; I mean, my favorite band is KISS, so there are certainly some self-created holes within my argument. But it was still satisfying to discover that Radiohead's music seems smart *on purpose.*

NO MORE KNIVES
(JULY 2003)

Meeting Thom is easy.

Everyone will tell you it's not, and they're all wrong. There are people who will insist Thom Yorke is a misanthropic sociopath, and that he ends interviews for no good reason. They will suggest that the likelihood of him speaking candidly is roughly the same as the chance of him unscrewing two bolts from his neck and removing his cybernetic faceplate, suddenly revealing a titanium endoskeleton that was built by futuristic space druids.

But this is not true.

Thom Yorke is weird, sort of. But you've met weirder. He's mostly just an intense, five-foot-five-inch thirty-four-year-old who wears hooded sweatshirts with sleeves too long for his limbs, and this makes him look like a nervous kindergartener. He doesn't appear to have combed his hair since *The Bends* came out in 1995, and his beard looks "undecided," if that's possible. But here's the bottom line: he's pleasant. Not exactly gregarious, but polite. He is neither mechanical nor messianic. And this is what everyone seems to miss about him, and about Radiohead as a whole: they may make transcendent, fragile, pre-apocalyptic math rock for a generation of forward-thinking fans, but they're still just a bunch of dudes.

I'm sitting with Yorke in the restaurant of an Oxford, England, hotel called the Old Parsonage. He was twenty minutes late for our interview, explaining that he had to run home and do some yoga because he was "feeling a bit weird." He's studying the restaurant menu and complaining that he's running out of things he can eat—not only is he a vegetarian, but he's stopped eating anything made with wheat (for the past six months, he's had a skin rash, and he thinks wheat is the culprit). Eventually he settles on roasted tomatoes and butter beans, a meal he calls "expensive" (it costs about seventeen dollars). We're talking about politics (kind of) and his two-year-old son Noah (sort of), and I ask him how those two subjects dovetail—in other words, how becoming a father has changed his political beliefs and how that has affected the songwriting on *Hail to the Thief*, the sixth studio album from earth's most relevant rock band.

His answer starts predictably. But it ends quickly.

"Having a son has made me very concerned about the future and about how things in the world are being steered, supposedly in my name," he says between sips of mineral water. "I wonder if our children will even have a future. But the trouble with your question—and we both know this—is that if I discuss the details of what I'm referring to in *SPIN* magazine, I will get death threats. And I'm frankly not willing to get death threats, because I value my life and my family's safety. And that sort of sucks, I realize, but I know what is going on out there."

Yorke's reluctance is not a surprise. Since April, Radiohead have stressed that *Hail to the Thief* is not a political record and that the album's title is not a reference to George W. Bush's controversial victory over Al Gore in the 2000 presidential election (in fact, Yorke claims he heard the phrase during a radio program analyzing the election of 1888). This is a bit paradoxical, because that argument seems both valid and impossible: there are no overtly political lyrics on the record, but it *feels* political. And Yorke is not exactly nonpartisan: at a recent antiwar rally in Gloucestershire, England, he publicly declared that "the U.S. is being run by religious maniac bigots that stole the election."

So what are we to make of this?

"If the motivation for naming our album had been based solely on the U.S. election, I'd find that to be pretty shallow," he says. "To me, it's about forces that aren't necessarily human, forces that are creating this climate of fear. While making this record, I became obsessed with how certain people are able to inflict incredible pain on others while believing they're doing the right thing. They're taking people's souls from them before they're even dead. My girlfriend—she's a Dante expert—told me that was Dante's theory about authority. I was just overcome with all this fear and darkness. And that fear is the 'thief.'"

Well, okay, maybe labeling Yorke a "normal dude" might be something of an exaggeration. Perhaps he is a tad paranoid. But he's no paranoid android; he's just a paranoid humanoid, and he certainly has a sense of humor about it. After he casually mentions his girlfriend, I ask him if he'll ever get married.

"That's a totally personal question—next," he says gruffly, and for a moment it feels like I'm watching an outtake from Radiohead's 1999 documentary, the mediaphobic *Meeting People Is Easy*. But then I laugh. And he laughs. And suddenly he's just a bearded humanoid who's eating tomatoes, completely aware of how ridiculous our conversation is. "What is this?" he asks. "Do you work for *Us Weekly* now?"

Most of what you believe about Radiohead is wrong.

"The first time I ever saw Thom, he was jumping over a car." This is not something I expected Radiohead guitarist Ed O'Brien to say, but he appears quite serious. "Thom was an amazing gymnast in high school," he continues. "Nobody knows that about him, but you can get a sense of it just by watching him move around. He's really strong. He did this handspring right over a car. It's like how Morrissey was a great long-distance runner in high school—nobody knows that, either."

O'Brien is the fifth member of the band I have spoken with over the past eight hours, each in a different room of the

Old Parsonage. I've been rushing from room to room for answers, not unlike the final ten minutes in a game of Clue. O'Brien is the last person I'm speaking with today, and he's different from the other four guys in the band: he's significantly taller (six feet five), he's the only one who doesn't reside in Radiohead's native city of Oxford (he lives an hour away in London), and he talks like an intelligent hippie (if such a creature exists). He's also rumored to be the most "rock-oriented" member of Radiohead, preferring the conventional structures of older songs, like "Ripcord" and "Just."

Here, again, my assumption is wrong.

"Do people really think I like straight-ahead rock?" he asks when I bring this up. "There is an irony in that, because I've always been more interested in making sounds, which is why I tend to gravitate toward *Kid A* material. If I ever made a solo record—and I have no plans to do that, but if I did—it would be all ethereal music. I like to smoke. I like a toke or two. So I like music in that vein."

Part of the reason O'Brien is perceived as Radiohead's designated rocker is that he's the most interested in classic rock; he especially enjoys discussing U2, who appear to be Radiohead's third-biggest musical influence (the first two being the Smiths, whom all five members love unequivocally, and the Pixies, from whose records Jonny Greenwood learned how to play guitar). For the most part, the other four members don't talk about mainstream rock.

"I'm interested in bands as beasts," O'Brien says. "I'm interested in U2 and the Rolling Stones and Neil Young and Crazy Horse. I love the dynamic of musicians working together and all the voodoo shit that comes with it. It's a complicated thing to do over the expanse of time, which is why I respect U2 so much. Don't get me wrong—I adore the Stones, but they haven't made a good record since 1972. *Exile on Main Street* was the last great Stones album.[1] But U2 have been at it for

---

1. O'Brien apparently doesn't like 1978's *Some Girls*, which is crazy.

twenty years, and that song 'Stuck in a Moment You Can't Get Out Of' was amazing. And that's after twenty years. That's when the Stones were making *Still Life*."

It's intriguing to hear O'Brien discuss band dynamics, because Radiohead rarely discuss the internal mechanics of their organization; their dynamic is relatively unknown. The band members tend to describe the creative process as their "methodology," and here's how it works: Yorke writes the material alone (usually on piano) and gives demo CDs to the other four. They all listen for a few weeks and deduce what they can contribute; they then meet, rehearse, and arrange the songs as a unit (according to Jonny, arrangement is their favorite step). They perform the songs live (in order to see what works and what doesn't), and then they go into the studio to record them.

With *Hail to the Thief*, the recording process was intentionally short. Most of the record was cut in two and a half weeks in Los Angeles with longtime producer Nigel Godrich, often one song per day (supposedly, the very first sound you hear on the album is Jonny plugging in his guitar on the initial morning they arrived at the studio). What's surprising is how conciliatory the other four band members are to Yorke. They're all accomplished musicians, but he directs the vision of the band. And this seems to cause no problem whatsoever.

"In a band like the Smashing Pumpkins, that kind of songwriting situation caused problems, because one gets the impression certain members of that band felt replaceable," O'Brien says. "But if you feel good about yourself, you will be honest and generous toward other people. I hope Thom makes a solo album in the future; there's no doubt he will.[2] And it will be fucking amazing. But as a band, we are all individually essential. In Radiohead, no one is replaceable."

Obviously, this is the kind of hyper-democratic statement

---

2. This would be 2006's *Eraser*. It's interesting to note that even though the other members of Radiohead don't necessarily understand Yorke, they're remarkably good at speculating about his behavior.

all bands make, but it seems slightly more genuine with Radiohead. Due to the layered complexity of their soundscapes—almost nothing is verse-chorus-verse, guitar riff–bass line–drum beat—collaboration and cross-pollination are unavoidable. It appears that Jonny's musical contribution continues to expand; for example, he wrote all of the song "A Wolf at the Door" (Yorke just added the words). At thirty-one, he's the youngest member of Radiohead, and he also may be the most cognitively musical. He likes to talk about details.

"For every song like 'I Will,' which arrived fully formed and was immediately perfect, there are songs like 'Sail to the Moon,' which weren't great," Jonny says. "I'm not being rude, but 'Sail to the Moon' wasn't very well written, and it had different chords and only half an idea. It only came together after the whole band worked on it and figured out how the structures should be, and [drummer] Phil [Selway] had some insight on how the song could be arranged. And then it became just about the best song on the record."

In a way, it all sounds remarkably simple, but things weren't always this easy. O'Brien says *Hail to the Thief* represents "the end of an era" and that they've taken "this kind of music" (however you want to define it) as far as it can go. But that statement seems more reflective of their new outlook on life, which is that being in this band is an exceptional—and relatively painless—experience. They like being Radiohead.

Six years ago, they did not.

"The worst point [in our career] was playing shows in the U.K. right after *OK Computer* came out," says bassist Colin Greenwood, Jonny's older brother. "There is nothing worse than having to play in front of twenty thousand people when someone—when Thom—absolutely does not want to be there, and you can see that hundred-yard stare in his eyes. You hate having to put your friend through that experience. You find yourself wondering how you got there."

Colin is saying this as he eats in the hotel's parlor room. It's the second of four meals he will consume today (he claims nervousness over *Hail to the Thief* has raised his metabolism). Colin is both the band's friendliest and goofiest member and just about the most enthusiastic person I have ever met. Sometimes he closes his eyes for twenty seconds at a time, almost as if the world is too brilliant to look at; there appears to be no subject he is not obsessed with. He tells me I must visit the Oxford University Museum of Natural History to see the stuffed dodo birds (which I do) and insists I check out a cartography exhibit at the Bodleian Library (which I do not). He gleefully mentions having seen a baby deer while driving to the *SPIN* photo shoot, as if it had been some rare sighting of the Loch Ness monster. He mentions about fifteen different books during our interview and even gives me one as a present (Brian Thompson's *Imperial Vanities*). Everyone in this band probably reads more than you do; hanging out with Radiohead is kind of like getting high with a bunch of librarians. At one point, I ask Colin (who is married to American writer and literary critic Molly McGrann) a theoretical question: If the music of Radiohead were a work of literature, would it be fiction or nonfiction?

"I think it would be nonfiction," he says. "Thom's lyrics are sort of like a running commentary on what's happening in the world, almost like you're looking out of the window of a Japanese bullet train and things are sort of flying by. It's like a shutter snapping in succession."

That's an apt description of the lyrics on *Hail to the Thief*, particularly on less abstract tracks like "A Punch-up at a Wedding" (a narrative about the clichéd reactions to a social faux pas), "We Suck Young Blood" (which examines the vapidity of celebrity), and "Myxomatosis," perhaps the most interesting entry on *Hail to the Thief*. Myxomatosis is a virus that inadvertently devastated the British rabbit population after it was introduced in the 1950s, covering the countryside with bunny carcasses. The disease is not what the song is literally about,[3] but hearing Yorke's explanation illustrates why

---

3. Unfortunately.

trying to dissect the metaphors in Radiohead's music is virtually impossible. The dots do not connect.

"I remember my parents pointing out all these dead rabbits on the road when I was a kid," Yorke says. "I didn't know that much about the virus, or even how to spell it. But I loved the word. I loved the way it sounded. The song is actually about mind control. I'm sure you've experienced situations where you've had your ideas edited or rewritten when they didn't conveniently fit into somebody else's agenda. And then—when someone asks you about those ideas later—you can't even argue with them, because now your idea exists in that edited form.

"It's hard to remember how things actually happen anymore, because there's so much mind control and so many media agendas," he continues. "There's a line in that song that goes, 'My thoughts are misguided and a little naïve.' That's the snarly look you get from an expert when they accuse you of being a conspiracy theorist. In America, they still use the 'conspiracy theorist' accusation as the ultimate condemnation. I've been reading this Gore Vidal book [*Dreaming War*], and I know Vidal is always accused of being a conspiracy theorist. But the evidence he uses is very similar to the evidence used by a lot of well-respected British historians. Yet they still call him crazy. To me, that's part of what 'Myxomatosis' is about—it's about wishing that all the people who tell you that you're crazy were actually right. That would make life so much easier."

This self-analysis is noteworthy, because it speaks to where Yorke is coming from intellectually. However, it avoids one trenchant question: What does mind control have to do with a virus that kills rabbits?

The answer is "nothing."

Yorke named the track "Myxomatosis" for the same reason he repeats the phrase "the rain drops" forty-six times during the song "Sit Down. Stand Up." He simply liked the way it sounded on tape. The syllables fall like dominoes, and the consonance collapses like a house of cards. Sometimes you can't find the meaning behind a metaphor because *there is no metaphor.*

Yorke's preoccupation with picking words for how they sound (as opposed to what they mean) is part of why Radiohead's cultic following cuts such a wide swath (every album except 2001's *Amnesiac* has gone platinum): if phrases have no clarity and no hard reality, people can turn them into whatever they need. If you need the words on *Hail to the Thief* to be political, they certainly have that potential; if you need *Hail to the Thief* to explain why your girlfriend doesn't love you, it can do that, too. It's a songwriting style Yorke borrowed from Michael Stipe; not coincidentally, Stipe's R.E.M. were the last rock intellectuals taken as seriously as Radiohead are taken today.

"What I love about them," says Stipe, calling from a recording studio in Vancouver, "is that Radiohead's music allows me to craft my own film inside my head. That's what I like about all music."

Stipe[4] and Yorke's relationship is hard to quantify, as it's always difficult for *über*-famous rock musicians on different continents to have any kind of conventional friendship (since traveling together on R.E.M.'s 1995 *Monster* tour, they've maintained a sporadic phone and e-mail dialogue). However, this much is clear: the guidance Stipe provided Yorke at the height of Radiohead's fame almost certainly kept the band from breaking up. To hear Stipe explain it, their interaction was almost academic—he talks about the complexity of "dealing with words" and how all performers "are missing some-

---

4. Here's a detail about Michael Stipe I couldn't jam into the article, mostly because I thought the sentiment would be distracting: when we spoke on the phone, my first question was directly about Yorke's cultural position, and Stipe said, "Well, Thom has entered that rarefied class of songwriter—these are people like Bob Dylan, Joni Mitchell, and myself. The things he says now take on a different kind of significance." This, I suppose, is completely true—but what a fucked-up thing to say about oneself! Were those the only three people he could think of?

thing in their DNA" and that it's almost impossible for artists to balance their inherent insecurity with the ego required to display oneself in public.

Yorke's description is considerably simpler.

"The nicest thing Michael did for me was pull me out of a hole I would have never escaped from otherwise," Yorke says. "This was right after *OK Computer* came out. All he really did was listen to me talk about the experience I was going through, but there's not a whole lot of people who can relate to that kind of situation, you know? That was very nice of him. I would like to pull a few other people out of holes at some point."

I tell Yorke he should consider contacting White Stripes frontman Jack White about this, but he says, "I don't think he needs my help." This is another of Yorke's quirks: he tends to assume that everybody on earth has their life more together than he does. Sometimes he puts his hands on the sides of his skull and inadvertently replicates the figure in Edvard Munch's painting *The Scream*. Conversationally, he seems completely rational and calm, but he's convinced he's losing his mind, and that this is probably Bill O'Reilly's fault.

"I absolutely feel crazy at times," he says. "Anybody who turns on the TV and actually thinks about what they're watching has to believe they're going insane or that they're missing something everyone else is seeing. When I watch the Fox News channel, I can't believe how much nerve those people have and how they assume that people are just going to swallow that shit. And I find myself thinking that *I must be missing something*."

This is who *Hail to the Thief* is ultimately for, I think—people who look for order in the world and simply don't see it. Colin thinks much of the album is about the destruction of human space by corporate forces (he draws thematic comparisons between *Hail to the Thief* and Jonathan Franzen's essay collection *How to Be Alone*); Jonny thinks it might be about accepting the condition of the world and concentrating on one's own family; Selway talks of "dark forces" that drove the record's creation; O'Brien casually wonders if "it might be too late for this planet." (Part of Radiohead's enduring mystery might be that even the other guys in the band don't fully understand what Yorke's lyrics are trying to convey.) Yet the songs are all about the same thing, really: learning how to understand a new kind of world. And while this isn't always simple, it's not necessarily depressing. In fact, it might be why Yorke still claims that *Hail to the Thief* is a record "for shagging," which is what he told the press months before the record was released. Apparently, we're all supposed to listen to "Myxomatosis" and get laid.

"I think this is a sexy record," Yorke says, and there is at least a 50 percent chance that he's serious. "The rhythms are very sexy. It's where the beats fall. It has its own sexy pulse."

Hoping for clarification, I ask him to name the sexiest record he owns.

"That's a good question," he says. "Public Enemy was pretty sexy. '911 Is a Joke' was a sexy song."

And I find myself thinking, *I must be missing something*.

THE AMERICAN RADIOHEAD

This story created an interesting problem, and I don't think I ever truly resolved it. I interviewed Wilco's Jeff Tweedy on a Friday afternoon, and it went extraordinarily well. I went back to New York the following week and wrote the piece for *SPIN*. And then—a few days after I gave the story to my editor—we found out that Tweedy had entered rehab the day after I spoke with him. Obviously, that complicated things, because I wasn't sure how much this revelation impacted the story. You could argue that it changed absolutely everything, or you could argue that it changed nothing. I ultimately reinterviewed Tweedy over the phone and added about four hundred words for contextual purposes, but I still wonder if I should have traveled back to Chicago and rereported the entire thing.

There were two things that didn't make the story (and which I later wrote about in an essay for *Minneapolis City Pages*). At one point, Tweedy and I were standing in the pantry of his home in northwest Chicago (he was looking for his stocking cap), and he started talking about how his eight-year-old son was the drummer in a grade-school rock band that played Jet songs. Now, nearly everybody I know thinks Jet is ridiculous; they've become the band hipsters are legally required to hate. So I made some joke (and I have no idea why) about how Jet was terrible and that it was somehow predictable that the only people who would want to cover Jet songs would be second graders. Tweedy didn't understand why I would say something like that. He looked at me like I had just made fun of a quadriplegic and asked, "Well, don't you like rock music?" And then I felt stupid, because I realized that (a) Jet plays rock music, and that (b) I like rock music, and that (c) *I actually liked Jet,* both tangibly and intangibly. So that was something I realized about Jeff Tweedy: musically, he remembers what is obvious.

After about five minutes, Jeff Tweedy found his stocking cap. We got into his car and started driving to the studio where Wilco makes music (we were listening to demos of the song "Hummingbird," as I recall, and the demos were—oddly—on cassette). We were waiting at a red light, and I asked him if there would ever be an Uncle Tupelo reunion with Jay Farrar. Surprisingly (and without much hesitation), he said, "Maybe." This shocked me, because Tweedy hasn't really spoken with Farrar in roughly ten years. I asked him what would be the biggest hurdle in making this reunion a reality. He said something I could never have anticipated: "I don't know if I could play those songs anymore," Tweedy said. "The bass parts on some of those songs are really fast. I don't think I can play bass that fast anymore." This, obviously, is crazy; this is like saying you're considering reuniting with your estranged wife after a ten-year separation, and you're mostly nervous that she might have rearranged the living room furniture. Yet—somehow—this sentiment struck me as remarkably insightful; it was the kind of highly important detail that normal people never consider when they expect artists to unconditionally satisfy their dreams. So this was the other thing I realized about Jeff Tweedy: musically, he notices what is not so obvious.

GHOST STORY

(JULY 2004)

Jeff Tweedy didn't vomit today. He vomited yesterday, but not today.

We are on the second floor of Tweedy's home in northwest Chicago, a pale green residence that could just as easily be owned by an employee for the Illinois Highway Department. There is a sign in the bathroom that reminds me to brush my teeth. Tweedy is lying on a bed designed for a child, thinking about smoking an American Spirit cigarette and quite possibly having a panic attack. His four-year-old son Sam is running around the house completely naked, incessantly repeating the phrase "Thank you!" while he sprints from room to room. Tweedy's eight-year-old son Seth is playing drums in the basement, and he's remarkably advanced; he's already in a band called the Blisters, fronted by a fifth-grade vocalist (they cover Jet songs). Tweedy's wife Sue keeps apologizing because the house is overrun with teacups and plastic soldiers; Tweedy can't remember if his wife's name is spelled "Suzy" or "Susie," so he begs me to refer to her simply as "Sue" if I mention her in this article (apparently, he's gotten in trouble for this before). At the moment, I can't tell if Jeff Tweedy is completely relaxed or desperately nervous, because he always seems to act exactly the same; it's just that he tends to puke more than most frontmen.

"Here's the scoop—I'm nuts," Tweedy says. He smiles, but he does not laugh. "I need to get on the first floor, I think, or maybe we should go outside. Have you ever swam out into the ocean and suddenly realized you've gone too far out? Sometimes being outside feels like the shore to me. It's hard to explain. It's sort of like getting so high that you're afraid you'll never be able to get back inside your body and you'll never be normal again, except I'm obviously not high right now."

Retrospectively, Tweedy's last statement might raise a few eyebrows. This conversation is happening on Friday afternoon, March 26. Tomorrow night, Jeff Tweedy will have a major panic attack that will necessitate a trip to the emergency room, and then he'll have another major attack on Sunday. He will subsequently check into a dual-diagnosis rehabilitation clinic that will simultaneously treat him for an addiction to painkillers and a mental illness that causes monolithic migraine headaches and uncontrollable nervousness. It's all a bit confusing, because Tweedy isn't lying when he says he's not high; in fact, he hasn't taken any painkillers in the five weeks prior to this interview, even though he's still addicted to Vicodin. That's part of the reason he'll end up in the hospital tomorrow night.

But these are all things I won't learn for a month.

Amidst the chill of early spring, things still seem normal. Tweedy is wearing an unwashed Godzilla T-shirt and sarcastically compares himself to Dave Pirner. We go into his backyard, and it's a Tonka Toy graveyard. Our ostensible intention is to discuss the new Wilco album *A Ghost Is Born*, which we did do . . . but only for twenty minutes. The other two hours of the conversation mostly dwell on "the nature of art," which undoubtedly sounds like pretentious bullshit. And I'm sure it would have been were it not for the fact that Tweedy is probably the least pretentious semi-genius I've ever interviewed.

"It's just that I'm uncool," Tweedy says when asked about the overt normalcy of his middle-class life. "I have a great life, but it's an uncool life. It was a wonderful revelation to move to Chicago and make music and just be normal. So many artists reach a certain level of success, and then they cross over; they surrender everything to the service of their persona. Take somebody like Madonna, for example: you could never get to be that huge unless you surrendered every other impulse in your body to the service of your persona. Even with Bob Dylan, there was clearly a point early in his career where he was completely able to immerse himself inside that persona. And I think it's disastrous that so many people destroy themselves because they can't do it. They don't have the intestinal fortitude. I mean, how many fucking people has Keith Richards killed? How many countless people has Sid Vicious killed? How many young girls has Madonna made insane?"

This probably sounds like the kind of sentiment you'd hear from a graying thirty-six-year-old father who hasn't had a drink in thirteen years, drives a minivan, and exists in a state of omnipresent nervousness. And it should, because that's who Tweedy is.

The story of Wilco—and the arc of Tweedy's career—is ultimately a story of sonic expansion, a fact that's too often lost on people; almost every Wilco album arrives with a minicontroversy that overshadows everything else (and obviously, that's going to happen with this album, too). It began with the breakup of Uncle Tupelo, the St. Louis band Tweedy formed with lifelong friend Jay Farrar in 1987. Though Tupelo did not invent alternative country, they legitimized it as a culturally consequential genre. When Uncle Tupelo ended acrimoniously in '93, Farrar formed Son Volt while Tweedy absorbed the other members of Tupelo and started Wilco, a band whose first record (*A.M.*) sounded similar to their previous work. In 1996, Wilco released *Being There*, a double album that opened the band's sonic parameters; 1999's *Summerteeth* was essentially a pop album that had almost no connection to alt country whatsoever.

It was 2002's *Yankee Hotel Foxtrot*, however, that radically changed the public perception of Wilco and turned them into the Midwestern equivalent of Radiohead. The story of *Yankee Hotel Foxtrot* has been told so many times (and in so many publications) that it hardly seems worth covering again, but here's the short version: upon their delivery of *YHF*, Wilco was dropped from Reprise Records (an imprint owned by Warner Bros.) for making an album that was too "inaccessible," only to resell the same material to Nonesuch Records (an imprint *also* owned by Warner Bros.). The record eventually sold 400,000 copies and turned Wilco into critically adored iconoclasts with enough integrity to flatten a Clydesdale. This paradox was illustrated in the documentary film *I Am Trying to Break Your Heart*. However, that movie also unveiled the rift that prompted guitarist Jay Bennett to exit Wilco upon *YHF*'s completion, and certain scenes implied that his departure was due to a power struggle with Tweedy. This is a perception Tweedy still finds irritating, since it seems to keep happening to him: in Uncle Tupelo, everyone thought Farrar was the dour John Lennon character and Tweedy was the less substantial Paul McCartney; in Wilco, Tweedy was cast into the exact opposite relationship with Bennett.

"That is not something I haven't noticed," Tweedy says. "Every time I make a record that goes in a different direction, people seem to assume that whatever was good about the previous record must have been the work of The Other Guy. This happens on every record I make, and it's not something that's directed at Wilco as a band—it seems specific to me. In Uncle Tupelo, I was supposedly the pop lightweight. But then in Wilco, everyone seemed to think that somebody else must have brought the pop sensibility in."

According to every member of the band, *A Ghost Is Born* was a collaborative effort that reflects a growing interest in explorative music, heavily influenced by the kraut rock sensibilities of drummer Glenn Kotche and new keyboardist/technophile Mikael Jorgensen. "Less Than You Think" is a fifteen-minute track with twelve minutes of nonmelodic drone. The guitar sound on "At Least That's What You Said" is strikingly similar to Neil Young and Crazy Horse. There's also a ten-minute song called "Spiders (Kidsmoke)" that sounds like the fusion of two songs, and it's preceded by a track called "Hell Is Chrome" that appears to address the existential issue of being trapped by perfection.

Then again, I might be totally wrong about this.

CK: This might seem like a weird question, but do you like Bob Seger?

Jeff Tweedy: What?

CK: I think "Spiders (Kidsmoke)" sounds like a Kraftwerk song that evolves into a Bob Seger song.[1]

---

1. This was not actually my thought; my editor at *SPIN*, Jon Dolan, mentioned this connection to me the very first time we heard *A Ghost Is Born*. I thought, *You know, that's completely accurate.* Two weeks later, I brought it up during my interview with Tweedy, but I didn't explain that it wasn't my original idea (it didn't seem worth the trouble, particularly since I didn't think Tweedy would give a fuck who came up with a theory he doesn't even agree with). When I eventually turned this story in, Dolan was mildly nonplussed that I had hijacked his insights, which I can wholly understand (particularly since I prefaced the sentiment by saying, "*I think . . .*"). As such, I cut it out of the original story. This sort of thing happens sometimes. For example, in 1997 my friend (and then coworker) Ross

Jeff Tweedy: Well, I'm not a big Bob Seger fan. I don't hate him. He's written some amazing songs, and he's written some amazingly terrible songs. I mean, who would admit they like Bob Seger now that "Like a Rock" is in your face every fucking second of the day? But stuff like "Turn the Page" and "Mainstreet" were great. And you know, now that I think about it, the guitar sound on "Mainstreet" is actually pretty close to the guitar sound on "Hell Is Chrome." So maybe you've uncovered something. Maybe I actually love Bob Seger.

CK: Is "Hell Is Chrome" about the value of disorder?

Jeff Tweedy: I think so.

CK: Are you just trying to be agreeable right now?

Jeff Tweedy: I don't know. Maybe "Hell Is Chrome" is about wanting the inverse. It's hellish for me to so badly want order in a world where you can't have it. My impulse when I write is an almost obsessive-compulsive desire for order. It almost hurts.

Here again, Tweedy describes himself with words that don't fit his behavior; he portrays himself as a man who is losing his mind, but he seems completely calm and rational as he does so. Apparently, this comes from years of practice.

"I really don't know how bad his panic attacks are," says bassist John Stirratt, one of the original members of Uncle Tupelo and the only current member of Wilco who knew Tweedy before he quit drinking at the age of twenty-three. "It's varied over the years that I've known him, but the

---

Raihala was interviewing Art Linkletter, and Linkletter became upset when Ross used the terms *hobo* and *bum* interchangeably (apparently, Linkletter had worked as a hobo in his twenties and found the word *bum* to be mildly offensive). Whenever I tell this anecdote to strangers (which happens quite often, for some reason), I sometimes imply that Linkletter told this to me directly, simply because it's too complicated to explain who Ross is and how I know the details of this dialogue. I concede this is lying, but it's lying for the sake of simplicity.

migraines have definitely gotten worse in the latter years. I mean, he was always wound up in a way, but I can't say I really understand it."

It's possible that Stirratt doesn't understand it because Tweedy is reticent to explain anything that suggests he is struggling. It seems like he *wants* to talk about these things, but he usually stops himself; he's afraid it will make him seem like a clichéd rock narcissist.

"I have always been rigid in my hatred of the stereotype of the debauched, tortured artist," Tweedy says. "In fact, I might have actively tried to subvert that idea [in the past], because it turned me off so many times when I was young. And it's not like I'm saying everyone should live a clean life, because I've done drugs and all that. I have no problem with those things. It's just that I felt—like most teenagers—that I had real pain in my life, and I kept reading interviews from artists I loved who proceeded to say things that simultaneously diminished what they did and how I felt. I hate the idea that artists suffer more than anyone else. They're just in a different position."

People who like Wilco tend to be interested in musical details, and these are the key details for *A Ghost Is Born*: it was produced by the mercurial Jim O'Rourke, who also contributed some instrumental parts. When Wilco plays live, many of those guitar parts will be played by jazz-o-centric Nels Cline (best known for his work with the group Quartet Music), who will tour as a fifth member of Wilco. Several songs on *A Ghost Is Born* were created through a process the band called "fundamentals," where Tweedy autonomously played an acoustic guitar and sang random lyrics while the other members listened to him in a different room; the other band members would then perform along with Tweedy for thirty straight minutes (in other words, the band could hear Tweedy, but Tweedy couldn't hear them). These half-hour sessions were all burned onto CDs, and Tweedy would listen to the discs at home and mine individual songs from the jam session.

The rest of my April interview with Tweedy was, for lack of a better term, affable. He doesn't *seem* addicted to anything except nicotine. His day-to-day life sounds ideal: he wakes up late, reads for a few hours, picks up his kids from school and plays with them for a few hours, takes a late nap, and then drives to the Wilco band loft and works on music deep into the night. There is always a sense of longing in Wilco's music, and that same feeling resonates in Tweedy's dialogue; he will admit that it makes him sad that Farrar claims to not even listen to the music he makes. "I found an interview with Jay where he said he's never heard any Wilco, and I was really disappointed. I always check out his stuff. There might have even been a time after Uncle Tupelo broke up—when I was making *Being There*, definitely—when I was still thinking about [Farrar] in the process of making the album. I mean, when I was in Uncle Tupelo, I wanted to write songs that knocked Jay out. And I wanted him to think Wilco was fucking rocking, you know?"

We talk about God for a bit, partially because there's a track on the new record called "Theologians" that outlines Tweedy's disdain for dogmatic religion. We also talk about politics, mostly because Tweedy has never felt more political than he does right now ("I'm almost scared to say this," he says at one point, "but I'm really starting to believe George W. Bush wants to experience the Rapture in his lifetime.") However, the most telling thing Tweedy says probably comes when I ask him a few minor details about the lyrics to "Heavy Metal Drummer," the second-best song off *Yankee Hotel Foxtrot*. What he tells me illustrates more about his personality than anything someone else could deduce from his songs.

"People always get confused about 'Heavy Metal Drummer,' because they think I was the drummer in a band that covered KISS songs. That's not what it's about. I can tell you what it's about. Hopefully, it won't ruin it for you." For the first time, Tweedy becomes almost goofy, gesturing with a cigarette lodged in his right paw; this is clearly a story he enjoys telling. "That song is really just another reminder about not being judgmental and reductive. There were many,

many nights in St. Louis where me and my friends would go see some punk band at the cool punk club, and then we'd all go to the landing on the Mississippi River, because the bars on the landing had a four A.M. liquor license. And all us punk guys would sit there and scoff and feel superior to all the heavy-metal bar bands with the big hair and the spandex, most of whom were having the fucking time of their fucking life. So who was losing? Me. I was. Those guys were getting laid, they were deluding themselves into thinking they were gonna be huge stars, and they were living. And I was dead. I was staring into my drink."

He laughs.

"I don't think we'll play that song anymore."

A few hours later, we said good-bye, and I went home.

Exactly one month later, Tweedy calls me on the telephone. He has just spent two twelve-day stints in an unnamed Chicago clinic (after the first twelve days he still felt twinges of panic, so he readmitted himself for another twelve). I ask him how he is doing, and I mention that many of the things he said to me thirty-one days ago have now taken on a different context. He is not surprised.

"I'm doing better," he says. "Considering the whole rock-star cliché of going into rehab, I can see how my actions might seem contradictory to how I presented myself when we last spoke. But the fact of the matter is that I really didn't represent myself in any way that wasn't true."

In short, this is what happened: Tweedy was prescribed Vicodin for his migraines. The pills helped; in fact, they helped too much. Sometimes he would swallow ten in one day. In February, he decided to stop taking them, because he felt they were becoming a problem. But he also decided to stop taking *all* his medication, including the pills that are supposed to control his panic episodes. This is a drug called benzodiazepine.[2] After a few weeks, he went back on the ben-

---

2. Benzodiazepine is the generic of Valium.

zodiazepine, but now it was too late; it no longer stopped him from having attacks. This is when everything escalated.

"I stopped taking everything else when I stopped taking the painkiller," he says. "I just became phobic about all medicine. But when I went back on the panic medication, it was too late. I was actually detoxing off the panic medication in rehab, because it's really dangerous to detox off benzodiazepine too quickly; you can have seizures. When I went into the emergency room on that Saturday, I thought I was dying. But I needed to go to rehab for the Vicodin, too. I needed to understand how addiction and mental illness were interrelated, because I had never really put those two things together."

That might be the strangest aspect of Tweedy's time in rehab: at least from his own description of the events, it sounds like he was dealing with mental illness more than he was dealing with a drug problem. He now calls rehab "the greatest experience of [his] life" and wishes he had heard about dual-diagnosis facilities years ago.

"I always thought I was different," Tweedy says, which is the kind of thing people who get out of rehab always seem to say. "I could always quit other things I had experimented with, and I wasn't pursuing oblivion. I never wanted to get fucked up, and I don't like being fucked up. It wasn't like I was taking Vicodin to party."

That's the kind of rock star Tweedy is, I guess: he takes drugs, but not to party; he vomits, but not from drinking; he goes to rehab, but he ends up liking it. If every band was like Wilco, rock music would be a whole lot stranger.

BOWLING FOR THE FUTURE
(AND POSSIBLY HORSE CARCASSES)

When I was hired by the *Akron Beacon Journal* in May of 1998, I was initially classified as their "pop culture reporter," a title that seemed very novel and forward thinking at the time. However, this created a problem: the newspaper already had a mildly territorial movie critic, a moderately territorial music writer, and an insanely territorial TV writer (who also seemed to openly despise me). The publication also had a reporter who specifically covered religion, another who covered the advertising industry, and about three or four people who wrote about the collision of people with politics. As such, I was supposed to cover popular culture without infringing on the idioms of film, rock 'n' roll, television, religion, media business, or politics. This did not allow for a lot of obvious story angles; I recall writing copious articles about (a) skateboarders and (b) the impending dangers of Y2K.

One autumn afternoon, I was aimlessly driving around Akron (probably listening to *The Jim Rome Show* and looking for fucking skateboarders), and I started to notice all these signs for psychics; it seemed to be the only industry in Akron that was thriving. And because (at the time) Akron was home to the Professional Bowlers Association Hall of Fame, I concocted this lame conceit that revolved around me talking to psychics about my future as a professional bowler. This is the only time in my career where I tape-recorded people without their knowledge, which technically makes this story "investigative journalism," although I doubt if debunking the supernatural insights of elderly women in Ohio is a particularly gonzo act. If you ask crazy people crazy questions, they will say crazy things. This wasn't even like shooting fish in a barrel; this was like shooting fish in a barrel of Vaseline.

Because this appeared in a daily newspaper, the writing is pretty stiff and straightforward. In retrospect, it seems silly that we felt an obligation to include the specific addresses of everyone involved; I realize newspapers are supposed to serve as the public record, but is this information anyone will ever need to use? And did I really need to interview the city assessor? This piece should probably be funnier than it is, and I wish the main idea wasn't so predictable. Which, I suppose, are the two primary criticisms of most of my writing: that it's not especially funny, and that it's not particularly insightful.

Still, it was nice to get a joke about dead horses into the *Beacon Journal* lifestyle section.

LOCAL CLAIRVOYANTS
SPLIT OVER FUTURE
(DECEMBER 1998)

Is life akin to bowling, or is bowling akin to life? The best answer to both of these questions is probably "shut up." However, there *is* a relationship between these entities, albeit a tendril one: In bowling, your score is not only dependent on what you've done, but also on what you *will do*. Your current state of affairs is contingent on what will happen next. It's the same in life. The larger significance of a (symbolic) strike thrown today is meaningless until you've experienced another (metaphorical) frame tomorrow. It's impossible to understand the present if you cannot see the future.

With this analogy in mind, I made a psychic journey.

In an attempt to know the unknowable, I sought answers from astrologers, tarot card readers, and other psychic friends who (supposedly) peer into the abyss of the unknown. Their supernatural succor came at a price; in the Akron area most fortune-tellers charge in the neighborhood of $30 for forty-five minutes of clichés.

Akron even has a local "phrenology ordinance" that's supposed to regulate this craft. It was instituted in the 1950s to control racketeering by gypsies; today, fortune-tellers are not supposed to operate without a $25 license. However, this ordinance is almost never enforced. "I'm kicking around the idea of repealing that ordinance altogether," said Akron city assessor Jim Young. "I think it's kind of worthless." That sentiment seems to be shared by most Northeast Ohio law enforcers; in nearby cities like Kent and Tallmadge, administrators didn't know of any such law. If you're willing to pay for fake conversation, no one's going to stop you.

To discover my own future, I went to five local readers. As a unifying inquiry, I posed the same question to all five: "Do I have a legitimate shot at making the Professional Bowlers tour?" I felt this was the kind of an aggressively straightforward inquiry any valid psychic should be able to answer. In fact, I would think *anybody* could answer this question, because I almost never go bowling.

However, I never lied about my ability. If a psychic asked how long I've been bowling, I said, "For over ten years." (Which is true; I have bowled at least once a year since 1987.) If the psychic asked me how good I was, I simply replied, "I probably need to become more dedicated if I hope to make the tour." (For example, I would almost certainly have to consider bowling without being drunk.) I was not hoping any of these people would tell me something I didn't know; I merely wanted to see if even one of these psychics could tell me something that was already obvious.

EXPERIENCE ONE

The reader: "Sheryl" (or perhaps "Cheryl"), who practices at 4663 State Route 43, just outside of Kent. She usually charges $35, but she only asked me for $20 because my aura was so dark she could not properly read my character (apparently, I'm an opaque purple).

Ambience: Sheryl does her tarot readings in the pantry of her home. The mystical environment was somewhat hampered by her eleven-month-old child, who screamed during much of the reading.

Insight: Due to the alleged darkness of my aura, the reading was kind of depressing. Sheryl insists my chakras are out of alignment. It seems we all possess seven chakras, and they are the energy forces that give us life. They are supposed to be equidistantly spaced throughout my body, and mine are not. Sheryl told me she could fix my chakra problem for $290. When I asked why this would cost *exactly* $290, she said, "That's what I feel. It's not me setting a price. It's because I look at the cards and see a certain price." Perhaps these cards were designed by Alan Greenspan.

On the PBA: "I see that as something that's going to be good for you. It's going to happen by the middle of next year." Rock.

EXPERIENCE TWO

The reader: Gladice Smalley, sixty-six, who works and lives at 741 September Drive in Green, Ohio. She charges $30.

Ambience: Smalley has a quaint office; the walls are decorated with the signs of the zodiac and a Mickey Mouse calendar.

Insight: Gladice has a stream-of-consciousness delivery and very big hair. She works with a deck of cards she calls "Witch and Gypsy cards," although she swears she is neither. Gladice also has a bitter distaste for suicide: she claims it's a waste of effort, because anyone who kills himself will be reincarnated in twenty-four to forty-eight hours. (I was impressed by the strict parameters of the reincarnation process; human souls must be couriered by FedEx.) The greatest revelation about me regarded my past life: it turns out I was once a well-educated woman who died in 1919. Upon hearing this, I did some research in the library. In January of '19, there was an explosion in a Boston molasses factory; a surge of molasses killed twenty-one people and several horses. I can only assume I was part of this disaster; I've always mysteriously feared molasses (and, to a lesser extent, dead horses).

On the PBA: "Absolutely," Gladice replied when asked if I'd make the tour. She said it will take me twenty-nine months, and I will be dominating the tour in just seven years. And how does she know this? Because my astrological chart has a "grand square." Apparently, Oprah Winfrey's chart has the same square. Perhaps the former me who died at that molasses factory was a big egocentric black woman. Somehow, this makes me feel sad.

EXPERIENCE THREE

The reader: Rosemarie of Rosemarie's Astrology and Tarot Card Reading, at 2045 Romig Road in Akron. She charges $25 or $35, depending on the degree of detail you desire.

Ambience: There were many pictures of Marilyn Monroe on the walls, and—during my reading—*The Howie Mandel Show* was on TV in the living room.

Insight: Rosemarie was the only reader who seemed skeptical of my motives. At one point, she asked, "Are you here to find out things about yourself, or are you here to give me a hard time?" This woman might not have ESP, but that doesn't mean she's not perceptive. Nonetheless, she gave me a sincere reading. Her opening statement was highly complimentary: "You are a good, honest person, and you like to do things for other people. You are an intelligent person, but people don't give you credit for how intelligent you truly are." (Unfortunately, I can think of about five things wrong with that statement.) Rosemarie predicted that I would soon have an important relationship with a woman whose name prominently featured the letters C and L. (Cyndi Lauper? Cloris Leachman?) She also said I will be taking a trip in "early 1999" with "three or four friends" to a "hot climate." This is marginally prophetic, because I am indeed taking a trip in January. However, I will be traveling alone, and my destination is Fargo, North Dakota.

On the PBA: "I see it possibly happening in about six months, because you can achieve anything you want in life," she said. "But bowling is not your ultimate destiny."

The reader: Phyllis, a "licensed reader" at 40 Southwest Avenue in nearby Tallmadge. She has three rates: $15 for one question, $25 for a partial reading and four questions, or $35 for a full reading with unlimited questions. I like this system!

Ambience: A radio supplied background music throughout our session; it was tuned to WQMX, a country station. I often felt the psychic energy of Shania Twain's abs.

Insight: Phyllis used no cards or crystals; she just looked into my eyes. "I can read your face the way you read a book," she said. This must be ideal for killing time in airports. Phyllis asked me lots of questions and always acted like she already knew the answers; she seemed a tad smug. Her queries ranged from "Why do you feel that something is missing in your life?" (answer: "I do not know how to accept unconditional love") to "Why do you fear the darkness of the night?" (answer: "Wolf attack"). At one point, she asked me if I was stalking my ex-girlfriend. And much to my utter confusion, Phyllis inexplicably advised me to become a commercial jingle writer, which (I suppose) does sound like a nice way to make a living.

On the PBA: "That [bowling] is something you should do as a hobby," Phyllis said. "Bowling is not what you're on earth to do. I see more of a future with your jingle writing. I'm not saying that bowling is impossible, but you must become focused."

The reader: Jo Anne Stover, a professional astrologer and certified hypnotherapist, who works above a New Age store called The Acorn Grows at 841 North Main Street in Akron. Her price is $30.

Ambience: The Acorn Grows seemed like the kind of place where Bilbo Baggins would shop: lots of incense and an inordinate amount of unicorn paraphernalia.

Insight: Jo Anne openly admitted that she is not psychic. She took data (like my birth date) and punched it into the computer on her desk. She also read tarot cards, but she did it academically. Although this mathematical assessment was no more accurate than any of the other readings, I suppose it did seem more "professional," somehow. Jo Anne told me I'm very fertile and it would somehow be beneficial for me to walk barefoot in fresh soil. (I was vaguely disturbed by both of these statements.) She did give some specific information about my future: according to the tarot cards, my 1987 Chrysler LeBaron will soon have transmission problems.

On the PBA: According to Jo Anne, three celestial bodies control bowling. Mars, Uranus, and Neptune are the "bowling planets," and (astrologically) their placement in the sky—at the time of my birth—was perfect for success on the waxed lanes of Middle America. Moreover, one of the tarot cards I drew from her deck featured a blond boy laughing manically. "That's you," she said. "That's you, laughing at all the people who said you'd never succeed as a professional bowler."

Take that, nonbelievers! I shall laugh in your face when I win my first PBA title by throwing a 286 against some bozo I've never heard of. Supernatural forces are on my side, you pathetic, naysaying trolls. Once I get my auto mechanic to check the chakras in my transmission fluid, I shall be unstoppable.

BUT I STILL THINK
"ALL FOR LEYNA" IS AWESOME

When I was writing *Sex, Drugs, and Cocoa Puffs* in the spring of 2002, I would occasionally forward the rough essays to my editor at *The New York Times Magazine,* mostly because I had this fear that they all fucking sucked (and that he would tell me if they did). One of those essays was about Billy Joel. My editor found it slightly bizarre that I liked Billy Joel, since he was living under the impression that I sat in a bomb shelter listening to Warrant and snorting cocaine off a Ouija board. He asked if I wanted to write a profile on Joel for the *Times* magazine, and I said, "Of course." This has retrospectively confused some[1] people, as they assume the story I did for the *Times* also appears in *S,D&CP.* This is not true; I think there are only two or three sentences that appear in both versions. But here's why I mention this: *The reason I was asked to do a story on Billy Joel was because I liked Billy Joel.* And this proved ironic, because now Billy Joel hates me.

When I delivered the story to the *Times* magazine, my biggest fear was that it was boring (and maybe even a tad fawning). Joel just seemed sad and alone, and we talked about how he missed being in a relationship. It seems like we talked about girls and love all afternoon, and the conversation was excellent—there was very little small talk. It was almost all "big talk." Still, nothing we discussed seemed remotely controversial; Billy just seemed like a rich dude who eventually came to realize that money and success can't kill loneliness. That isn't groundbreaking material.

Yet—somehow—this story got more media attention than anything I've ever written. It seems like half the people who read it thought it was some kind of a hatchet job, and the other half thought

---

1. And by "some," I mean "six or seven, maybe."

it was a three-thousand-word personal ad for Billy Joel (for months afterward, women across the country would e-mail me pictures of themselves, requesting that I put them in touch with Billy, as if I were his butler or something). In the wake of this piece, there were suddenly all these tabloid reports that Joel fell off the wagon and started drinking again; he also crashed his Mercedes in the Hamptons, which suddenly seemed suspicious. Billy even went to the *New York Post* and claimed that I had (somehow) fucked him over with this story, although he didn't dispute any of the quotes.

Part of me feels bad about all this, but I honestly have no idea what I could have done differently. I mean, profile writing is a rather rudimentary process: you ask people questions, and then you write about the most interesting things they say. There's really no other way to do it.

THE STRANGER
(SEPTEMBER 2002)

Billy Joel has led the kind of life only a fool would hope for. No realist would ever dream of attaining the level of success he has achieved. He has sold more than 100 million records, which is more than any solo artist except Garth Brooks and Elvis Presley. He has dated supermodels, and he married one of them. Drunk people will sing "Piano Man" for as long as there are karaoke bars, so he shall live forever. This fall he will embark on a stadium tour with Elton John, and they will sell out Madison Square Garden on the strength of songs that are two decades old; next month, Twyla Tharp will take a play to Broadway titled *Movin' Out*, which will interpret twenty-four of Joel's songs through the idiom of modern dance.

And yet as Joel and I drive around the Hamptons in his

surprisingly nondescript car, none of these facts hold his attention for long. We talk about his sixteen platinum records, and his memories of making *An Innocent Man*, and his love of Italian motorcycles, and the obsessiveness of his dental habits. But whatever subject we touch on, the conversation inevitably spirals back to the same thing.

Women.

Since he sold his East Hampton mansion to Jerry Seinfeld, Joel has been living in a modest rented house nearby. But he tells me that he is trying to rent an apartment in Manhattan for the sole purpose of meeting women. "I'm not going to meet anyone out here," he says. "The happiest times in my life were when my relationships were going well—when I was in love with someone, and someone was loving me. But in my whole life, I haven't met the person I can sustain a relationship with yet. So I'm discontented about that. I'm angry with myself. I have regrets."

Our conversation continues in this vein for most of the afternoon, and after a while I find myself in the peculiar position of trying to make Billy Joel feel better. I point out that many things in his life have gone amazingly well; I remind him that he's in the Rock and Roll Hall of Fame. "That's a cold comfort at the end of the day," he tells me. "You can't go home with the Rock and Roll Hall of Fame. You don't sleep with the Rock and Roll Hall of Fame. You don't get hugged by the Rock and Roll Hall of Fame, and you don't have children with the Rock and Roll Hall of Fame. I want what everybody else wants: to love and to be loved, and to have a family. Being in love has always been the most important thing in my life."

This sentiment is so universal that it's cliché. But that's not a criticism. In fact, it's probably why Joel is able to connect with people in a way that even he doesn't completely realize: he musically amplifies mainstream depression. He never tried to invent a new way to be sad.

Joel's sardonic gloom has been at the vortex of almost all his most visceral work. "Honesty" (on *52nd Street*) implies that the only way you can tell that someone really cares about you is if they tell you you're bad. "All for Leyna" (on *Glass Houses*) is about an emotionally capricious lover who leaves the song's protagonist shattered and alone. "And So It Goes" (a ballad released in 1990) has Joel insisting that every woman he loves will eventually abandon him. Even "Scenes from an Italian Restaurant" (on *The Stranger*) is about how relationships that seem perfect are always doomed.

"Billy does take things harder than most people," says Jon Small, a Long Islander who met Joel in 1965, played drums in Joel's first two bands, and was briefly married to the woman who would become Joel's first wife. "Emotionally, he takes things harder than I ever did. But all us guys in his inner circle always knew that Billy writes his best when he's having problems. He works best in drastic situations, and those are always due to his relationships."

That, of course, is the paradox: Joel's art is defined by his life, and his best work is his most morose. He can achieve greatness only through despair. But for Joel, at fifty-three, that artistic transference seems to be failing. There was a time when sadness spawned genius; now it just reminds him that he's alone. "I'm kind of in a dark place," Joel says. "And I know some people are actually excited about that, because they think I'll write an album about being sad. But that's not what my music is about. There have been times when I've done that, but I'm not going to do it again."

Joel hasn't made a pop album in almost ten years, even though his last one (*River of Dreams* in 1993) moved five million units. There's always a chance he might someday decide to make another, he says, but he currently has no plans to try; he describes himself as unmotivated, uninspired, alienated from the concept of commercial songwriting, and uninterested in composing lyrics. He still plays around with what he calls "thematic fragments" of instrumental music, but he has no concrete aspirations for any of it.

"I don't have a new project," he says. "I'm not doing anything but personal life stuff." He talks like a guy who has conquered every goal he dreamed about as a teenager, only to discover that those victories have absolutely nothing to do with satisfaction.

Cold Spring Harbor, his first album, came out in 1971. Joel hated it; a mistake during the production sped up the album's master tape, making his vocals sound shrill and chipmunkesque. (He recalls smashing the LP against a wall the first time he played it for friends.) His second solo release, *Piano Man* (in 1973), was an artistic advancement and his first defining moment as a musician—and probably the moment that marginalized him forever.

"In the big picture of pop music, I don't know if what I've created is seen as being that important or that necessary, at least not if you ask the experts," he says. "I was tagged right after *Piano Man*: I was a balladeer, I didn't write substantive music, my records were overproduced, I played too many ballads. Oh, and of course my favorite: 'He studied piano.' I had never realized that one of the prerequisites for being critically acclaimed was not knowing how to play your instrument. That stuff bothered me for a long time."

Joel's musical output from 1976 to 1982 (*Turnstiles* through *The Nylon Curtain*) was one of the most successful runs in rock history. But the records he made during that period are consistently maligned by virtually every school of rock scholarship. "*Rolling Stone* magazine would not say anything positive about me, and they were the tastemakers at the time," Joel explains. "There were people from the old guard who insisted I wasn't a real rock 'n' roller. Well, okay, fine— I'm not a real rock 'n' roller. You got me."

The reasons for that critical disdain are hard to pin down. There are no lyrics from "The Stranger" as ridiculously melodramatic as the worst lines from "Born to Run" ("Just wrap your legs 'round these velvet rims / And strap your hands across my engines"), nor was Joel's public posture any less organic or more calculated than that of the Sex Pistols. But guys like Bruce Springsteen and Johnny Rotten have a default credibility that Joel will never be granted, and it's not just because he took piano lessons. The problem is that Joel never seemed cool, even among the people who like him. He's not cool in the conventional sense (like James Dean) or in the self-destructive sense (like Keith Richards), nor is he cool in the kitschy, campy, "he's so uncool he's cool" way (like Neil Diamond). He has no intrinsic coolness, and he has no extrinsic coolness. If cool were a color, it would be black—and Joel would be kind of a burnt orange. The bottom line is that it's never cool to look like you're trying . . . and Joel tries really, really hard.

"He just doesn't get it," Robert Christgau tells me over the telephone. "The person I compare Billy Joel to is Irving Berlin; that's the positive side of what he does. But Billy Joel also has a grandiosity that Irving Berlin never got near. That's what's wrong with him. If he wanted to be a humble tunesmith—a 'piano man,' if you will—he would be a lot better off. But he's not content with that. He wants something grander. And that pretentious side infects not only his bad and mediocre work, but also his best work."

Christgau has covered music for *The Village Voice* since 1969 and is sometimes considered the "dean of rock critics." When I told him that Joel suspects critics will never include him among rock music's pantheon of greats, it took him about fifteen milliseconds to agree.

"Well, he's right," Christgau says. "He's not good enough. He and Don Henley are really notable for how resentful they are about their lack of respect. You don't catch Celine Dion complaining about a lack of critical respect, and she's a lot worse than Billy Joel. But she doesn't care. Billy Joel cares deeply about that respect, and he wants it bad."

Perhaps as a response to three decades of slights, Joel made a classical album in 2001 called *Fantasies and Delusions: Music for Solo Piano*. Influenced by Chopin and credited as the work of "William Joel," *Fantasies and Delusions* sold remarkably well, topping the classical charts for months—though arguably, Joel could smash a piano with a ball-peen hammer for seventy-five minutes and release it as a live album, and it would still sell remarkably well. But that record—and the college lecture tour he undertook to accompany it—didn't reinvent Joel at all. It just convinced the Robert Christgaus of the world that they were right all along.

In 1970, Joel tried to commit suicide by chugging half a bottle of furniture polish. The conventional wisdom has always been that this attempt stemmed from the fact that his career was floundering. (His attempt at a psychedelic heavy-metal band—an ill-fated two-piece called Attila—had just imploded.) In truth, Joel says, it was over problems in his relationship with Elizabeth Weber, the woman who would become his first wife. "I was absolutely devastated," he recalls. "I couldn't bring anything to the relationship. That was the driving force behind my suicide attempt."

Weber is the subject of one of Joel's most famous songs, "Just the Way You Are." It's a love letter that says everything anyone ever wanted to hear: you're not flawless, but you're still what I want. He tells Weber not to try "some new fashion" or dye her hair blond or work on being witty. It's a criticism of perfection, but in the best possible way; it's like Joel is saying that he loves Weber because she's not perfect, and that he could never leave her in times of trouble.

The irony, of course, is that Joel and Weber divorced five years after "Just the Way You Are" won a Grammy for Song of the Year. Some would say this contradiction cheapens the song and makes it irrelevant. I'd argue that the opposite is true; the fact that Joel got divorced from the woman he wrote this song about makes it his single greatest achievement. It's the clearest example of why Joel's love songs resonate with so many people: he expresses absolute conviction in moments of wholly misguided affection. This is further validated when he admits—just forty minutes after telling me about his suicide attempt—that he was never really in love with Weber at all, even on the night he tried to kill himself. He thought he was in love, but he wasn't.

"I shouldn't have gotten married," he says of his union

with Weber. "She said we either had to get married or our relationship was over, so I said, 'Okay.' I was twenty-four. I was too young to get married, although it ended up lasting eight years. Was I really in love? I don't think so. But when I married Christie, I really wanted to get married and I really wanted to have kids."

"Christie" is Christie Brinkley, the gangly sex kitten Joel married in 1985 and lionized in the hit single "Uptown Girl." Brinkley agreed to be interviewed for this article, only to change her mind at the last possible moment. She is the mother of Joel's sixteen-year-old daughter, Alexa, and is generally perceived to be the love of his life—although he insists that his six-year relationship with Carolyn Beegan in the 1990s and his more recent courtship of Trish Bergin, a TV news anchor, were almost as deep. In fact, tabloid speculation was that Joel's breakup with Bergin was the reason he spent ten days in alcohol rehab this summer, a rumor Joel confirms, saying that Bergin was the reason he "started drinking all that wine."

But as the hours pass and we keep talking, he slowly widens the scope of his melancholy. "The more I think about it, the more I think it was all four of those relationships," he says. "I never really stop thinking about any of them."

So how much wine do you have to drink before you need to check yourself into rehab?

"A lot," says Joel. "A lot." Joel says he was on a "well-documented bender" for three months before checking himself into Silver Hill Hospital in Connecticut in mid-June. This would date the bender's origin to right around the time of his March 15 concert with Elton John at Madison Square Garden, an evening in which Joel was widely described as disoriented, exhausted, and erratic. (Throughout the performance, he shouted out the locations of famous World War Two battle sites like "Midway!" and "Guadalcanal!") In early June, he drove off the road in East Hampton and wrecked his Mercedes; a week later, the *New York Post* was reporting, "BILLY JOEL IN REHAB AFTER GALPAL DUMPS HIM."

"I was amazed by the way all of that played out in the media," he says now. "To me, a musician going to rehab is like a normal person going to get his teeth cleaned. Don't these people ever watch *Behind the Music*? It's a cliché. If I had known that the story was going to be reported in the way that it was, I would have considered not going at all."

Part of what perplexes Joel is that he feels as if he is no longer the kind of celebrity who warrants tabloid coverage; when I argue that the news media are always going to be interested in anyone who has sold twenty-one million copies of his greatest-hits collection, he reminds me that he hasn't made pop music in almost ten years.

"I don't think what has happened to me is that different from what happens to most people," he says. "The only difference is the scale. People seem to think my problems are larger than life, but they're not larger than my life. Yes, I was married to Christie Brinkley, but it didn't work, just like a lot of marriages don't work out. I don't sit around thinking: *Oh, my God! I'm this famous guy who lost his famous wife!*"

It's a contradiction: Billy Joel is keenly aware that he is "Billy Joel," but he doesn't seem to fully understand how that designation is the cause of virtually everything good and bad about his life.

"On the one hand, it probably is easier for me to meet women than it is for most people, because I have a certain degree of fame," he says. "But on the other hand, I have certain problems in relationships that other people don't. I was recently on a date with a woman, and she told me: 'You're one of those guys who comes with all this *stuff*. You're always being written about and photographed and all that star stuff.' And it dawned on me that she was probably right."

Movin' Out, Twyla Tharp's $8 million show based on Joel's songs, will have its official Broadway debut on October 24. But it has already absorbed some of the baggage that Joel has carried for years. When the unorthodox musical opened in

Chicago in late July, theater critics described it as "inane" and "cliché-ridden," prompting major changes to the first act. And though those barbs were mostly directed at Tharp, it's easy to see how they could strike Joel as well, even though he played virtually no role in the production. The characters in *Movin' Out* include Brenda and Eddie (the couple from "Scenes from an Italian Restaurant") and Tony (from the song "Movin' Out"), all of whom have their lives thrown into chaos by the Vietnam War (illustrated by tracks like "Goodnight Saigon"). Tharp describes it as the story of the entire baby boom generation, a demographic for which Joel has often been tagged as an apologist. "He chronicled the time in which I lived," the sixty-one-year-old Tharp says. But there are elements of Joel's work that Tharp considers timeless. "There is a large component of the loner in all of Billy's music," she says. "It's something, for better or worse, that has been part and parcel of the idea of the artist in the twentieth century and nineteenth century. In our culture, the perception of the artist is that of a loner."

Oddly, one of the loneliest songs in Joel's entire lonely oeuvre didn't make it into "Movin' Out." It's called "Where's the Orchestra?" and it seems particularly apropos, since it uses the theater as a metaphor for loneliness. The lyrics are one long allusion to watching an alienating, dissatisfying play ("I like the scenery / Even though I have absolutely no / Idea at all / What is being said / Despite the dialogue"), and it doesn't take a rock critic to see it as a metaphor for the emptiness Joel himself feels. It's also the Billy Joel song that I have always related to the most on a personal level; in fact, I sometimes tell people that they would understand me better if they listened to "Where's the Orchestra?"

I tell this to Joel, thinking it might make him feel better. But I think it makes him feel worse.

"That song still applies to me," he says in a weirdly stoic tone. "I heard it the other day, and it still moved me, because I feel like that today. I've only felt content a few times in my life, and it never lasted. I'm very discontented right now.

There are situations in my life that didn't pan out. I'm like most other human beings. I try and I fail. The whole metaphor of that song is that life is a theatrical play, and it's all a tragedy, and—even though you can enjoy the comedic, ironic elements of what you're experiencing—life will always come up and whap you on the head."

To punctuate this statement, he whaps himself on the side of his skull with an open hand. It's the kind of thing that should be funny, but somehow it isn't. Probably because when Billy Joel hits himself, he isn't smiling.

SOMEONE LIKE YOU

I've probably written more about tribute bands than any sensible man should. I really like them, though. Tribute bands often reflect what I like about rock 'n' roll more than the authentic bands they replicate.

DUDE ROCKS LIKE A LADY
(JUNE 2005)

"In the days of my youth, I was told what it means to be a man," yowls a waifish rock chick named Brooke Gengras, and three hundred lesbians know exactly what she means (even if I do not). While thundersticks detonate behind her, Brooke goes on to relate how she's had her share of good times and her share of bad times, but she can't seem to manufacture any concern about the woman who left her for a brown-eyed man; here again, the lesbians seem to agree completely. On the other side of the stage, a woman named Steph Payne is wearing dragon pants and carrying a Les Paul guitar and walking backward like Jimmy Page in *The Song Remains the Same*, although I don't recall being able to see Jimmy's black bra every time he reared his head back. Fifteen minutes from now, a woman in the audience will invade the stage and attempt to kiss Payne, but Payne will keep playing (in fact, she will play heavier).

You get the impression this has probably happened before.

We are inside the Supper Club in Times Square; there is a

blizzard on the streets of Manhattan, but the amplifiers are melting inside. The Supper Club is hosting a semi-private party for Showtime's lesbian soap opera *The L Word,* and we are experiencing the headline entertainment: Lez Zeppelin, an all-girl tribute to the greatest rock band ever to sing about *The Hobbit.* Tonight, Lez Zeppelin will play just four songs— "Good Times, Bad Times," "Black Dog," "Whole Lotta Love" (including the theremin solo), and "Rock and Roll." Their replication of these songs is 80 percent flawless and 99 percent awesome. They sound like what would have happened if Heart had somehow written four songs that were all better than "Barracuda." And there are a few jarring moments when it will feel like the most powerful all-female band in rock history is not the Runaways or L7 or Sleater-Kinney; it will feel like the most powerful all-female band in rock history is four women playing cock rock to a room full of hard-drinking, cable-subscribing lesbians. That might sound sexist (and perhaps it is), but it also might be true.

The rise of bands like Lez Zeppelin is the kind of multilayered cultural phenomenon that would make Camille Paglia so ecstatic that her brain would implode. The fact that women can play music originally written and performed by men—and that they can play this music so fluently—should not surprise anyone. What makes this noteworthy is their *choice* to play this music, especially since the majority of successful female tribute bands gravitate toward the most masculine, misogynistic music in pop history. It all feels "political," somehow. Mötley Crüe glorified "Girls, Girls, Girls," and so does the all-girl Crüe tribute Live Wire. Iron Maiden told mothers to bring their daughters to the slaughter, and L.A.'s Iron Maidens make the identical request. There is an all-girl Italian band called KISSexy that even includes a fifth member (she portrays replacement guitarist Vinnie Vincent), apparently so that they can play the KISS songs released after Ace Frehley quit in 1982, most notably "Lick It Up" (which is about licking) and "Fits Like a Glove" (which is not about gloves). And the question that might be even more compelling is why so many guys want to watch girls appropriating dude metal, particularly since the feminine reinvention of a song like "Custard Pie" significantly alters how intimately male audiences can relate to its message.

Steph Payne thinks she has the answer.

"I have this theory," she tells me a few weeks after the *L Word* gig. "A contractor was going to do some work in my apartment, and I told him about our band. Well, he flipped out; he told me that he saw Zeppelin at Madison Square Garden in 1973. And this big contractor dude—this heavy-duty, heterosexual bricklayer—told me that Robert Plant was the only man he ever wanted to sleep with. My theory is that there were a lot of guys like this contractor: guys who were sexually turned on by Led Zeppelin, because Page and Plant were fucking beautiful. They were thin, they had long, flowing hair— they looked like girls. My theory is that a lot of male Zeppelin fans really *did* want to sleep with Led Zeppelin. So those kinds of guys love the fact that we're girls, because they can watch us play those songs and still feel normal. They can actually go there in their mind without freaking themselves out."

So perhaps this phenomenon is a little less political than it seems.

"We've had to kick guys out of our shows for jacking off," Nici "Riff" Williams tells me, and I am not surprised. Williams plays bass in AC/DShe. "He wasn't just kicked out, but physically dragged out—in a daze—by guys who were a little bit more testosterone-driven than he was. We were playing in a place in Folsom, California, north of Sacramento. The venue has a balcony, and I guess this guy was sitting right above the stage, jacking off. One of the security guards saw him and started to kick his ass. He ended up getting dragged out of the place with his pants down."

I am speaking with both Williams and Amy "Bonny Scott" Ward, the founding members of San Francisco's best-known, all-female tribute to pre-1980 AC/DC. Unlike many of their tribute peers, AC/DShe is not a collection of career musicians who decided to scrap their original bands in the hope of making more money as begrudging copycats; AC/DShe is the *only* band Williams and Ward have ever played in. Williams, in fact, had never even picked up a bass until she thought up the name AC/DShe and decided such a group needed to exist. It is not that these women merely love AC/DC—they actually feel a responsibility to make AC/DC more popular. This is their religion.

"Our ultimate goal is to spread the gospel of AC/DC," explains Ward. "We are trying to turn people on to AC/DC. A lot of young kids come to our shows. They've never seen AC/DC, but they've grown up on AC/DC because of their parents. There's nothing cooler than playing to a shitload of kids in the front row—kids who are nine or ten, wearing AC/DC shirts, singing all the words. I know that sounds fucking corny, but it's cool. The second goal is to eventually meet AC/DC. I mean, if we could meet AC/DC, then we've achieved everything. And being in this band gives them a reason to *want* to meet us. Otherwise, we're just a couple of bimbos going to an AC/DC show, trying to make it backstage. This is the proper way to meet your heroes."

AC/DShe's motivations are both modest (i.e., meeting a popular rock band) and abstract (making one of the world's most popular bands more popular). This curious brand of pragmatism is probably central to their success—and within the limited confines of the tribute idiom, AC/DShe is just about as successful as possible. They have played to five thousand people in Chicago and more than ten thousand miscreants at biker rallies; they've been flown to Wales to perform at AC/DC's Big Ball, an international festival celebrating the music of Australia's most precious metal. Curiously, they are not the only all-female AC/DC tribute in America; there are at least four others, and Seattle's Hell's Belles are (arguably) just as famous as AC/DShe. Yet Hell's Belles are not AC/DShe's main musical rivals, even though they should be. AC/DShe's main musical rival is Zepparella.

As you may have guessed, Zepparella is another all-female

Zeppelin tribute. Two of the women in Zepparella—their lead guitarist and drummer—joined after leaving AC/DShe. It is a complicated situation. These former members of AC/DShe ("Phyllis Rudd" and "Agnes Young") also play in an original band called Bottom, which has opened shows for Zepparella. They wanted to do this while remaining in AC/DShe, which Williams and Ward saw as unacceptable. Both women were reticent to discuss this (inarguably unique) rivalry, but it's clear that some feelings remain bruised.

"The one thing that I will say," Ward adds cautiously, "is that we've always been on the up and up with those girls. We had been playing with them for three years, and it was great. Zepparella is a completely different thing, and a completely different audience. But I do think it's really fucking hard when your Angus Young is also Jimmy Page. I think that the image we portray—you know, the idea that we're doing this simply because we're huge AC/DC fans—would have been tarnished a little bit."

Ward's argument is that someone wanting to simultaneously play in an AC/DC tribute *and* a Led Zeppelin tribute is precisely what she hates about other cover bands: that they are not serious about the music they lionize, and that it's simply a financial decision. They are only in it for the money. Ward and Williams (along with AC/DShe rhythm guitarist "Sarracuda" Young) remain focused on what they feel is most important, namely (a) delivering dirty deeds at cut-rate prices; and (b) consistently re-creating Bon Scott's last night on earth. AC/DShe may be better at *drinking* like AC/DC than they are at *sounding* like AC/DC. Their rider requests almost nothing beyond Budweiser and Maker's Mark, which they guzzle throughout their performances. Williams notes that there is no bass line during the first and second verse of "Highway to Hell," thereby allowing her to shotgun two beers during one song ("That's kind of my bass solo," she says). These are, in many ways, the kind of women that male AC/DC fans dream about meeting. And though that is not AC/DShe's singular aspiration, it's not something they're ashamed of.

"Some other tribute acts do take this all-girl thing to a totally different level," Ward says. "We were never trying to be political. We would never say, 'We're chicks and we can rock, too!' I mean, *of course* chicks can rock. But there are other all-girl bands where that is absolutely their agenda, and they're feminists and they make feminist statements. We've been asked to play at political events and to do fund-raisers, but we always say no. Our agenda is to have no agenda. Rock 'n' roll has nothing to do with politics. Even if we *agree* with the politics, we still refuse to do those events, because AC/DC would never do anything like that."

Seven years before he sired the fourth-most-famous Stroke, Albert Hammond wrote a song about how it never rains in Southern California; according to Hammond's paradoxical lyrics, it actually pours. And it is pouring tonight in Los Angeles as I walk toward Club Vodka to see Cheap Chick, SoCal's finest (and presumably only) all-female Cheap Trick tribute. I am not sure what they will look like, but they are easy to spot: I see four women freaking out over a Nissan mini-van, and one of them is wearing a New York Yankees baseball cap and checkerboard sneakers. I walk over to say hello and anticipate meeting four twenty-five-year-old ironists, but these are not the people I encounter. The reason they are freaking out over this minivan is because someone just gave it to them. It was a gift from Nissan, and it's precisely the kind of gift they need.

You see, Cheap Chick are soccer moms.

Well, not all of them, I suppose; only two of them have kids. However, everybody in Cheap Chick is a little older—and a little more sensible—than I expect. "I'm Kristi and I'm forty-one, and I'm proud of being forty-fucking-one," says Kristi Callan, lead singer and mother of two. "I play Robin Zander, and I also edit books for money. I do whatever I can to make money."

It seems that someone from Nissan is a fan of Cheap Chick, so he decided to give them a Nissan Quest as an innovative form of viral marketing: he apparently hopes to rebrand the concept of *soccer moms* into the hipper category of *rocker moms*. The members of Cheap Chick seemed like ideal candidates for such an evolution. "Nissan's target market is active moms," says bassist Pamita Neptuna, who also has two children. "They want to appeal to the kind of woman who would be in a rock band. We're not unusual for a band, but we're unusual for moms." As such, the members of Cheap Chick now share a complimentary $30,000 vehicle that would be perfect for touring, if they did, in fact, tour. Which (of course) is something they can't really do, because somebody has to drag the kids to soccer practice twice a week. It's a vicious circle.

Neptuna is the reason Cheap Chick became a reality; the band was her idea, and she handles all the publicity and booking. "My talent does not lie with being a phenomenal bass player," she says. "My true talent is talking people into doing stupid things."

All four members of Cheap Chick had previous careers in music, but all four now hold day jobs. During the 1980s, Callan was in a Bangles-esque group called Wednesday Week who were briefly label mates with the likes of Poison on Enigma Records. In the '90s, drummer Judy Cocuzza played with the cartoonish, all-girl punk-metal outfit Betty Blowtorch (in Cheap Chick, she calls herself Bunni Carlos—a play on Cheap Trick's Bun E. Carlos that can only be appreciated on paper). Guitarist Robin Beacham is both the quietest and sexiest member of the band, and inadvertently the most confusing: because her real first name is Robin, people always assume she portrays singer Robin Zander, even though she actually portrays Rick Nielsen. This is the kind of dilemma nontribute acts never have to worry about. Beacham joined Cheap Chick after declining an opportunity to personify Tony Iommi in the all-female Black Sabbath tribute Mistresses of Reality.

Perhaps because of their ages—or maybe just because of their collective worldview—Cheap Chick seem detached from all the gender-based questions that typically hound any group of women who play music created by men. Though they concede that part of their audience simply wants to watch hot women playing rock music, they find that neither interesting nor insulting. "Growing up, I never thought that I was a girl playing the drums and that there were also guys who played the drums," claims Cocuzza. "I always just thought, *I play the drums*. It took me a long time to realize that everybody else thinks I'm a girl. I mean, I'm *aware* that I'm a girl, but it never made a difference to me."

That's a good attitude, especially since Club Vodka is (more or less) a strip club. The bar features two stages: one for Cheap Chick and one for cheap chicks. I assume the strippers will take a break during Cheap Chick's set, but they do not; they inexplicably perform throughout the entire concert. It's a confounding dissonance: while one woman rips through the solo to "Southern Girls" and flicks guitar picks into a mixed audience of 150, another woman (who's literally a Southern girl from Alabama) uses those same riffs to slither like a python against a cold metallic pole. During "He's a Whore," a brunette stripper jumps on the main stage and tries to molest a visibly uncomfortable Beacham, forcing the guitarist to constantly flee the dancer's ridiculously fake breasts. The rest of the band finds this hilarious. It's almost like a bachelorette party, except the soundtrack is power pop.

Cheap Chick close the night with "Surrender" and "Dream Police." Outside on Melrose Avenue, it's still pouring. It's a good thing that this Nissan has antilock brakes.

The first night I watch Lez Zeppelin perform, I presume they are all lesbians. This seems like a valid assumption, inasmuch as (a) they were performing at a party for *The L Word*, and (b) they are in a band called Lez Zeppelin. After I interview the band in a Manhattan rehearsal space, I decide that my initial math was wrong; I decide that two of them are lesbians and two of them are not. When I see them a third time, I realize that three of them are totally straight (and at least two are totally married). In fact, they might *all* be straight, for all

I know. This is their "mystery," much like the way the real Led Zeppelin refused to admit whether or not they had sold their souls to the devil in order to receive supernatural rocking power and/or a higher royalty rate from Atlantic Records.

"Definitely maybe not," says drummer Wendy Kershen when I first ask if Lez Zeppelin are predominantly (or partially) homosexual. "But maybe. Maybe, or maybe not. Actually, I had to have a sex change to join this band."

As it turns out, the name Lez Zeppelin is a marketing tool. According to the band, it was simply the cleverest linguistic manipulation they could think of. However, it's clear that Payne—a former rock writer for *NME* and *Rolling Stone*— understands exactly what she is doing. "Our gender is definitely an important part of what we do, but it doesn't necessarily have anything to do with us being lesbians," she says. "There is certainly some unusual power in the idea of girls playing this particular music, and that doesn't have anything to do with whether or not those girls are gay or straight. It's just the profound intensity of females playing cock rock."

Because Lez Zeppelin live in New York City, they exist in something of a bubble; they don't face much artistic opposition. On the West Coast, Cheap Chick and AC/DShe are surrounded by the hordes of tribute acts (both male and female) who now dominate the Sunset Strip (on the same night I saw Cheap Chick, the opening band was Nirvana tribute Penny Royal—and both were competing against nearby shows by the Skid Row tribute Monkey Business, the Black Sabbath tribute Wicked World, the ELP tribute Knife Edge, and the Rolling Stones tribute Sticky Fingers). This is not the case in New York, where the scene is less visible. Payne found Kershen by placing an advertisement in *Drummer Girl* magazine; in a bizarre (and possibly unbelievable) case of serendipity, Kershen had just given up on forming an original band and locked herself inside a studio, hoping to learn John Bonham's drum fills. Payne (who once toured as a backing musician for erstwhile girl grouper Ronnie Spector) had already hooked up with Lisa Brigantino, who—weirdly—played bass, organ, and mandolin, which happen to be all the same instruments John Paul Jones played in Zeppelin. What's even more coincidental is that Brigantino delivers the kind of droll commentary you'd expect to hear from John Paul Jones, assuming J.P.J. wasn't British and possessed ovaries: she is entirely professional and relentlessly understated.

"When Steph told me about her idea to play this music—which I was familiar with, but not to the extent of the other three—it intrigued me, and it seemed like a challenge," Brigantino says, slightly bored by the question. "It seemed like a way to increase my musicianship, and it created an opportunity to play several instruments every night. Historically, women in rock are rarely seen as instrumentalists, and that is what we're trying to achieve. These songs are intricate and heavy and wonderful to play. As someone who grew up playing a lot of different instruments, I caught a lot of flak from guys and always felt this pressure to prove myself, simply because I was a woman and no one expected me to be any good."

As Brigantino explains her motives for reinventing "Trampled Underfoot" for audiences who reflexively adore the original, the meaning of Lez Zeppelin (once again) starts to seem philosophical; she is trying to prove a point, and that point is tangibly tied to her femininity. So maybe this trend does mean something; maybe all-female tribute bands really *are* political. But then I start chatting with Lez singer Brooke Gengras, and I realize I may be overthinking all of this. There is a point to Lez Zeppelin, but it has nothing to do with the *Lez* and everything to do with the *Zeppelin*.

"This band is just so fun, and it's because I fucking love Led Zeppelin, man." Gengras calls herself "Roberta Plant" and wears '86 Air Jordans. If asked to describe her enthusiasm, the key modifier would be *unbridled*. "I mean, I fucking love John Bonham, but I'm never gonna get to play with him, and my other band isn't going to sit around and play fucking Zeppelin covers all night, so fuck it."

Roberta Plant looks a little like Parker Posey; her other band is called Easy, but this band is easier. All she has to do is sing the songs that changed her life. And if men (or women) want to watch her do that simply because she's a woman, that's fine; being a woman doesn't have any impact on why she loves *Physical Graffiti* and *In Through the Out Door*.

"Actually, the hardest thing is just memorizing the lyrics," she says. "When I was learning 'Stairway to Heaven,' I had to close my eyes and create this entire movie in my head—I had to come up with this entire visual fucking thing, just so I could fucking remember all six verses of this weird-ass shit. I had to look up *hedgerow* in the dictionary."

Well, so did the rest of us.[1]

---

1. See page 90.

TAKING THE STREETS
TO THE MUSIC

I blew this one. *The New York Times Magazine* sent me to London to do a profile on Mike Skinner, a young, white semi-rapper who performs under the name The Streets. He had just put out an album I loved, so I was pretty jacked about doing this. I'd also never been to London, so that seemed intriguing. Unfortunately, I choked during the interview.

Many reporters try to "save" questions for the end of interviews, because they don't want to make the subject upset. I rarely do this; I occasionally ask the toughest, most uncomfortable questions at the front end of an interview. The best interviews always involve a certain degree of creative tension. However, I should not have tried this with Skinner. Because his lyrics were so smart and sophisticated, I overlooked the fact that he was still a young guy who wasn't political or aggressive or interested in verbal sparring; he just wanted to hang out, talk about bullshit, and get this interview out of the way.

Still, I wrote the story and turned it in to the magazine. This initiated a new problem, because my editor and I suddenly recognized something about Mike Skinner that we both should have recognized before I ever left the U.S.: The Streets isn't famous here. For most people who read *The New York Times,* this would be the first time they'd ever heard of him. As such, it wasn't clear why we were even doing the story; it wasn't like American culture was on the precipice of being overrun by boyish British rappers. I rewrote the story completely, this time basing the narrative around a Streets show in a Brooklyn club that happened a few months after I had gone to England. This gave the article more context, but not much. The new draft was also more confusing, because almost everyone at the show in Brooklyn was white; it suddenly seemed like this story was about race (although in no specific way). A few months passed; I assumed my editor would just kill the story entirely. But then—almost a full year after the original interview—Skinner released a few random songs over the Internet, so the *Times* mag cut down the second draft of the story from 3,000 words to 1,200 words and ran it as a two-page "Perspectives" piece.[1]

But ANYWAY, what follows is the original draft of the story that never ran, an artifact that has probably grown more dated and pedantic within the time it took you to read this introduction.

UNTITLED GEEZER PROFILE
(SPRING 2003-ish)

It has been brought to my attention that geezers need excitement.

Supposedly, this reality is self-evident. And it seems that if these geezers do not find that excitement within the context of their own lives, they have a propensity to incite violence. This revelation is, apparently, common sense. Simple common sense. And I have no idea what any of this is supposed to mean, and I am waiting for Mike Skinner to explain it to me.

Providing that explanation is what he does for a living.

Walking among the unwashed, unhip masses of the world at large, Skinner is merely another kid from Britain, a twenty-four-year-old who looks like he just turned fifteen. Do not feel depressed if you've never heard of him, as he is not famous. Except that he is, if you happen to be the kind of person who actively searches for pop geniuses. In certain circles, in certain clubs, and pretty much anywhere in London, Skinner is one of those "voice of a generation" types: as the writer-rapper-producer for a one-man hip-hop entity known as The

---

1. And I'm sure the details of this editing process are absolutely fascinating to you, aren't they?

188

Streets, Skinner has experienced the kind of meteoric ascension (at least among critics) that changes a messenger into his own self-styled medium. His debut record, *Original Pirate Material*, has been dubbed the first transcendent hip-hop album to emerge from England . . . which is kind of like being dubbed the sexiest female at a gnome convention. But Skinner's title might eventually mean more. At least for the moment, Skinner incarnates a British youth movement everyone else has ignored. His lyrics are defined by their lack of action: The Streets speaks of "The Geezer Lifestyle"—the mundane, day-to-day pursuits of antitrendy, blue-collar white males in England's lower-middle class. It's a lifestyle that Skinner depicts in almost all his songs (most notably on a track called "Geezers Need Excitement," the philosophy of which I paraphrased in the opening paragraph of this story).

However, the more I ask Skinner who and what a geezer truly is, the more I suspect that the motivation behind my question is more complex than the reality of his answer. In fact, that's the point, and that's what I don't understand.

"I guess *geezer* is just like if you were to say *man* or *dude* or something like that," he says with his left hand shoved halfway into his pants and his British accent leaning to the right like verbalized italics. "Like, I could have just as easily said '*Dudes need excitement*,' and it would mean pretty much the same thing."

Really? That's all there is to this? *Geezer* is just a word?

"Well, no. I guess not," he responds. "I guess maybe there is a roughneck quality to *geezer*. But it mostly just means a guy I would consider cool. D'know what I mean?"

Well, no. Not quite. But maybe.

The narratives on *Original Pirate Material* are almost like little episodes of *EastEnders*, filtered through the slang and sensibilities of *Trainspotting*. Skinner and his geezer posse drink beer and brandy and eat fish and chips, and they discuss bong technology and Carl Jung and a future that seems vaguely dystrophic. They appear to play a lot of video games.

189

Unlike American rappers, Skinner does not talk of *bitches* and *hos*; he chases *birds*. He tells his listeners that they should be happy if they don't relate to his message, because that means they've never really been depressed. Yet the tangible content of *Original Pirate Material* is not nearly as compelling as the way it's delivered; Skinner might be the most aggressively British Brit in pop history. Like Thatcher-era dub poet Linton Kwesi Johnson, Skinner's vocal style is closer to conversation than rapping; his accent isn't harsh, but it's *vast*. It's relentless. And it's so staunchly Anglo that even the people who love him seem unwilling to classify his work as rap music. *Entertainment Weekly* proclaimed *Original Pirate Material* as the single finest album of 2002, but they call it "punk." *The Village Voice* described it as "England's first great hip-hop record, mostly because it's not a hip-hop record." *SPIN* argued that Skinner "doesn't really rap," while *Rolling Stone* enthusiastically insisted his record was all a "great rap goof." The reasons behind these contradictory accounts are myriad, but the core explanation is that Skinner shares none of the clichés of conventional American hip-hop; he's propulsive, but never bombastic. It's more intellectual than urgent, and it represents a different kind of urbanism: even when Skinner speaks rapidly, he sounds completely and utterly bored.

"My life isn't that interesting, really. I get up at nine, I work on music until around six or seven, maybe I watch the telly for a few hours, and then I go to bed. Sometimes I go out and get [drunk], but not all that often," Skinner says. "Everyone has me down as this crazy, drinking, drug-taking, working-class hero. And when I get drunk, I suppose I do get crazy. I suppose everybody does. But what I notice is that I can give a three-hour interview and mention doing drugs once, and that quote always shows up in the article. Sometimes I'll say something to a journalist, and I immediately know they're going to use it to create whoever they need me to be."

This is an interesting twist, because we had been discussing marijuana legalization just twenty minutes before he told me this; I'm pretty sure the memory of that exchange is why he said what he did. He knows what he's doing.

"My day is not as interesting as everyone wants to think," Skinner says again. "Okay, so I eat a bacon sandwich and push the knob on a computer for six hours, and then maybe I smoke weed or maybe I don't. That's sort of my job, if you can call it that. I am a workaholic. It's just that I really don't do anything."

At the moment, Skinner is sitting across from me in a 12 x 12 foot room that contains almost nothing: it has a table, two chairs, one pitcher of water, one drinking glass, and one tape recorder. There is an overhead light, but the bulb is dark; late-afternoon light pours through a window. This is the kind of room that would seem well suited for interrogating potential al Qaeda operatives, except that there's also a poster of the rock band Oasis against the far wall. We're in the back room of a south London management company called Coalition, and the twenty-four-year-old Skinner is looking at me like a six-month-old beagle puppy: huge brown eyes, big ears, paws that seem too big for his body, and a general sense of optimism. He's dressed like a suburban teenager who has put exhaustive effort into appearing as casual as possible—multiple layers of T-shirts and sweatshirts, a silver watch that's too big for his twig-thin wrists, low-slung pants, and a pair of cross-trainers that Nike awarded him for being cool in public. Around his neck he wears a razorblade, a potentially deadly accessory he somehow managed to buy from the Duty Free cart during an airplane flight to Japan. I gather that this is how geezers are supposed to dress, since Skinner has come to define the postmodern definition of what that's supposed to mean.

Those who keep insisting that The Streets isn't actually a rap act could use Skinner's interview posture as proof—he does not talk about the things one has come to expect from hip-hop practitioners. He hasn't been shot nine times (like 50 Cent), nor does he casually mention murdering people (like Jay-Z). He never praises God or criticizes his biological parents; when he discusses the complexities of "The Game," he's usually referring to PlayStation 2. And while most rappers use media interviews to validate their "realness" or to self-mythologize their persona, Skinner does neither; he won't even tell me in which part of London his apartment is located, beyond admitting that he arrived at our interview via the subway. He expresses a closeness to his immediate family but gives few details, only disclosing that his father used to repair and sell televisions and his mother worked at a hospital. When he tells me he has a girlfriend, he taps his temples and obliquely says, "And that's good, because that keeps you focused." His responses are closer to what you'd expect from a Ralph J. Gleason interview with Bob Dylan: Skinner says everything he creates is straightforward autobiography, and that he can't describe his lyrics any better than how they already exist on the album. There is nothing on *Original Pirate Material* that is not intentional, nor is there any better way to express them.

"Everything I rap about is really just an example of me talking about myself. I mean, I could talk about the tape recorder sitting on this table, but I'd really just be talking about *my* perception of what it is. I'd be talking about myself," he says. "I've never been interested in the idea of someone being able to get *anything* they want out of a song. My sister, she thinks that you should be able to find your own meanings of things in songs. She likes Radiohead. I'm not like that. All that, 'I'm just a fish in the sea, I'm so lonely'—that's kind of bollocks. There is nothing on my record that you can't understand literally."

Except, of course, the part about geezers needing excitement, lest they create violence. And everything else, really.

After ninety minutes in the interrogation room, I convince Skinner to go to a tavern across the street called the Barley Mow Pub. As we leave the Coalition office, we pass the desk of a publicist who has made dozens of photocopies of a *Rolling Stone* story about The Streets, headlined "England's Eminem."

192

I suspect Skinner gets that a lot. We leave the building and look for an ATM, and I ask him what he thinks of the comparison (and if he'd seen Eminem's semi-autobiographical film *8 Mile*).

"Oh, I suppose it's because we're both white and we both tell stories," he says, only mildly interested in the question. "I'm not as angry as he is, although I don't think he's as angry as he is, either. I quite liked *8 Mile*, though. It was sort of like *The Karate Kid*, you know? Have you seen *The Karate Kid*? Very similar kind of thing."

I mention that most Americans compared *8 Mile* to Prince's semi-autobiographical film *Purple Rain*.

"Oh, was that album based on a movie? I had no idea. Good songs on that one, though." He briefly impersonates Prince, somewhat less convincingly than when he sarcastically impersonated Thom Yorke while discussing his sister's love of Radiohead.

In truth, the rational connection between Eminem and The Streets is almost nonexistent; if not for a shared lack of pigment, they'd never be mentioned in the same sentence. For one thing, The Streets operate in a genre of hip-hop categorized as "garage" (pronounced to rhyme with the word *marriage*, at least in the U.K.). Though the difference is subtle, the garage designation ostensibly means that most music on a Streets record only has two beats per measure; conventional rock, rap, and techno usually have four. But there's also a philosophical difference between Marshall Mathers and Mike Skinner that makes the latter especially compelling; he's arguably the first significant hip-hop artist to completely remove the element of race from his music. Eminem addresses his race tangibly (the second track on his last LP was titled "White America"). Seminal Caucasian rappers like the Beastie Boys always seemed hyperconscious of their whiteness; when their first album came out in 1986, just about everyone assumed the Beastie Boys were mocking black culture. Their racial iconography was always an issue. So when a record like *Original Pirate Material* includes no references whatsoever to race, it's oddly jarring; it's like listening to a Christian rock album and noticing they never mention Jesus.

When I ask Skinner about this, he perceives the answer to be self-evident: he says segregation does not exist in England. He mentions how he used to love listening to records by Compton gangstas like Snoop Doggy Dogg, but that Snoop seemed to live on an altogether different planet. Quite simply, being white is something Skinner never thinks about. "When I first got into this, all anyone ever talked about was being real," he says. "I was actually terrified of making anything that wasn't real, because that seemed to be the whole thing. That's why I don't talk about race very much. It wouldn't be real for me."

Nelson George, the author of *Hip-Hop America*, is not surprised.

"It's all about context," Nelson says when I ask about the significance of Skinner's race-free worldview. "MCs in America are obsessed with race. In England, MCs are obsessed with class."

In the case of Skinner, that's true, although his obsession is built on the belief that the class system notion is ridiculously anachronistic. "The really posh people in England are the only ones who still care about class," he says. "Nobody our age thinks like that anymore. I mean, even people on the dole have TV. They still have the Internet. That's why the people who still worry about class have become less concerned with how much money someone has. Now, class is all about *breeding*, because that's all they have left to separate themselves."

Because so much of his material comes (or at least *appears* to come) from the perspective of a lower-middle-class ruffian, The Streets has been consistently portrayed as a representative of the working class. This is not really true; Skinner hates the working-class designation and insists his life has been relatively easy. He's been painted as a prototypical backstreet kid from Birmingham, the bleak industrial city that's musically best known for spawning Black Sabbath. This is also partially inaccurate; Skinner lived in Birmingham for several years, but he was born in London and returned there for good three years ago ("I never really picked up the Birmingham accent," he says). Still, his persona as a cultural intruder is not a complete fabrication. He is not working class because of poverty, but he's driven by working-class common sense.

"What I hate about London is that there are so many loafers claiming to be artists," he says at the pub. "I was raised on function. If you have a job in Birmingham, you're a waitress. You sell insurance. You build something people can use.

"A few years ago, I was working for a company here in London. I stuffed envelopes. Now, this company had been given something like fifty thousand quid during the Internet craze—but I could not figure out what they did. And I'm a pretty clever bloke. I guess they were technically selling bandwidth, but all they really did was put on nice shirts in order to convince people to repackage something that didn't exist in the first place. That—to me—sums up London."

This story is funny, but it's also important, or at least it is to me. It's important because that's pretty much how I felt when I moved to New York, and it's probably the reason certain American outsiders relate to *Original Pirate Material* with a depth that defies logic or geography. For reasons I could never fully fathom, the Geezer Culture Skinner so often describes in song always reminded me of Midwestern slacker culture from the early 1990s: it puts the same emphasis on thought over action. It feels the same resentment toward privilege. And it embraces the experience of the nonevent—Skinner is a genius at describing what it's like to do nothing. This is why he can tell personal stories that feel general, and it's why The Streets can resonate with listeners who don't even know what he's necessarily talking about. His stories don't matter; what matters is the way he tells them. The realities may be different, but all the details are the same.

"Look, you don't know my background. You've never been to where I'm from," Skinner says. "But there is something about the way I talk that makes you understand, right? So it doesn't matter what I do. If my next record is about flying in a private jet and drinking champagne[2] with my girlfriend Jennifer Lopez,[3] and then Jennifer Lopez dumps me, you'll be able to understand that as much as you can understand when I talk about seeing some brunette bird at a pub or when I talk about watching Courtney Cox on the telly or anything else. D'know what I mean?"

Sort of. However, it still seems like there's something Skinner's not telling me. Even though we're in a pub, he refuses to drink, opting instead for orange juice. He says this is because he's just coming off antibiotics, but I don't believe him. We talk a little about video games (his current favorite is *Getaway*, the U.K. version of *Vice City*), and about what he likes and dislikes about the United States (he loves the fact that Americans value and reward success, but he thinks too many Americans exist in a "culture of intellectual laziness"). Nothing he tells me is outrageously illuminating. But just before he leaves to go do "something" (he wouldn't say what), we chat about why certain things happen and why certain people end up in certain situations. And then Skinner offhandedly mentions something that might show a glimpse of the impetuous, working-class Streets that represent the generation he's supposedly voicing. It's the culture of cerebral underthinking.

"See that tap over there on the bar?" Skinner says, pointing toward the pub's business end. "Let's say someone told me to remove it right now. I'd most likely just take a screwdriver and take it apart immediately. I'd never unhook the hoses underneath or anything like that, and I'd probably piss beer all over myself. I'm a doer. I just do things."

---

2. Or becoming addicted to cocaine, at least if one were to consider the content of his third album, 2006's *The Hardest Way to Make an Easy Living*. In fact, I almost get the impression Skinner started abusing cocaine just so he would have something interesting to rap about.

3. Or some unnamed, crack-smoking teen superstar, as described in the song "When You Wasn't Famous." Skinner was a very forward-thinking geezer.

I mention that this is a strange metaphor, and he agrees. But I'm not sure what he thinks he's agreeing with. Is he agreeing that it's strange to remove a beer tap without unhooking its hoses, or is he agreeing that it's strange to remove a public beer tap simply because somebody told him to do so?

"That's a good point," he says, and I suspect he might mean it, because he genuinely seems confused. "I don't know. I'm a thinker, I guess, but sometimes things just need to be done."

So I guess it's all true: sometimes, things just need to be done. There doesn't need to be a reason. Geezers don't need a reason. Geezers need excitement. Geezers need something else.

FIVE INTERESTING CORPSES

I write about dead people. A lot. However, I always seem to end up writing about how certain individuals' deaths inadvertently reflect some abstract trend in society they never consciously embodied. Is this how dead people want to be remembered? Probably not. But I guess this is how those of us who stay alive try to make a living.

THE RATT TRAP
(DECEMBER 2002)

Dee Dee Ramone and Robbin Crosby were both shaggy-haired musicians who wrote aggressive music for teenagers. Both were unabashed heroin addicts. Neither was the star of his respective band: Dee Dee played bass for the Ramones, a seminal late-'70s punk band; Crosby played guitar for Ratt, a seminal early-'80s heavy-metal band. They died within twenty-four hours of each other last spring, and each had only himself to blame for the way he perished. In a macro sense, they were symmetrical, self-destructive clones; for anyone who isn't obsessed with rock 'n' roll, they were basically the same guy.

Yet anyone who is obsessed with rock 'n' roll would define these two humans as diametrically different. To rock aficionados, Dee Dee and the Ramones were "important" and Crosby and Ratt were not. We are all supposed to concede this. We are supposed to know that the Ramones saved rock 'n' roll by fabricating their surnames, sniffing glue, and playing consciously unpolished three-chord songs in the Bowery district of New York. We are likewise supposed to acknowledge that Ratt sullied rock 'n' roll by abusing hairspray, snorting cocaine, and playing highly produced six-chord songs on Hollywood's Sunset Strip.

There is no denying that the Ramones were a beautiful idea. It's wrong to claim that they invented punk, but they certainly came the closest to idealizing what most people agree punk is supposed to sound like. They wrote the same two-minute song over and over and over again—unabashedly, for twenty years—and the relentlessness of their riffing made certain people feel like everything about the world had changed forever. And perhaps those certain people were right. However, those certain people remain alone in their rightness, because the Ramones were never particularly popular.

The Ramones never made a platinum record over the course of their entire career. Bands like the Ramones don't make platinum records; that's what bands like Ratt do. And Ratt was quite adroit at that task, doing it four times in the 1980s. The band's first album, *Out of the Cellar,* sold more than a million copies in four months. Which is why the deaths of Dee Dee Ramone and Robbin Crosby created such a mathematical paradox: the demise of Ramone completely overshadowed the demise of Crosby, even though Crosby cowrote a song ("Round and Round") that has probably been played on FM radio and MTV more often than every track in the Ramones' entire catalogue. And what's weirder is that no one seems to think this imbalance is remotely strange.

What the parallel deaths of Ramone and Crosby prove is that it really doesn't matter what you do artistically, nor does it matter how many people like what you create; what matters is who likes what you do artistically and what liking that art is supposed to say about who you are. Ratt was profoundly uncool (read: populist) and the Ramones were profoundly significant (read: interesting to rock critics). Consequently, it has become totally acceptable to say that the Ramones' "I Wanna Be Sedated" changed your life; in fact, saying that would define you as part of a generation that became disenfranchised with the soullessness of suburbia, only to rediscover salvation through the integrity of simplicity. However, it is laughable to admit (without irony) that Ratt's "I Want a Woman" was your favorite song in 1989; that would mean you were stupid, and that your teenage experience meant nothing, and that you probably had a tragic haircut.

The reason Crosby's June 6 death was mostly ignored is that his band seemed corporate and fake and pedestrian; the reason Ramone's June 5 death will be remembered is that his band was seen as representative of a counterculture that lacked a voice. The contradiction is that countercultures get endless media attention: the only American perspectives thought to have any meaningful impact are those that come from the fringes. The voice of the counterculture is, in fact, inexplicably deafening. Meanwhile, mainstream culture (i.e., the millions and millions of people who bought Ratt albums merely because that music happened to be the soundtrack for their lives) is usually portrayed as an army of mindless automatons who provide that counterculture with something to rail against. The things that matter to normal people are not supposed to matter to smart people.

Now, I know what you're thinking; you're thinking I'm overlooking the obvious, which is that the Ramones made "good music" and Ratt made "bad music," and that's the real explanation as to why we care about Dee Dee's passing while disregarding Robbin's. And that rebuttal makes sense, I suppose, if you're the kind of person who honestly believes the concept of "good taste" is anything more than a subjective device used to create gaps in the intellectual class structure. I would argue that Crosby's death was actually a more significant metaphor than Ramone's, because Crosby was the first major hair-metal artist from the Reagan years to die from AIDS. The genre spent a decade consciously glamorizing (and aggressively experiencing) faceless sex and copious drug use;

it will be interesting to see whether the hesher casualties now start piling up. Meanwhile, I don't know if Ramone's death was a metaphor for anything; he's just a good guy who died on his couch from shooting junk. But as long as you have the right friends, your funeral will always matter a whole lot more.

HOW REAL IS REAL
(DECEMBER 2004)

If the appreciation of reality-based entertainment can be broken into two classes—and at the moment, it seems like everything in America is destined to be broken into two classes—there is no clearer schism than a movie like *Swimming to Cambodia* and a TV show like MTV's *The Real World*. On the celluloid of the former, you find a darkly insightful, tragically neurotic, blue-state intellectual trying to explain why his own life is unfathomable. On the videotape of the latter, you find drunken red-state coeds who allegedly represent the totality of their generation. They seem to derive from two totally different places; many of the people saddened by the death of Spalding Gray wouldn't even know who *Real World* cocreator Mary-Ellis Bunim was (and certainly not that she died earlier this year). Yet the philosophical dissonance between these two is less than logic might dictate; both found entertainment within the banality of everyday life, and both saw meaningful drama in the ostensibly undramatic.

Gray may not have invented the monological art, but he certainly did it better than anyone else who tried. He was just an odd man talking about his own trivialities, but it sometimes felt like a person twisting (and ripping) his subconscious mind in public. He was never enigmatic about his potential for suicide; he wrote about those increasingly dark fantasies as overtly as possible. In 1997's *It's a Slippery Slope*, Gray superficially wrote about learning to ski but mostly wrote about the affair that ended his first marriage; early in the monologue, he finds himself pacing around Washington Square Park and thinking about the woman who would eventually become his mistress. But even those thoughts inexplicably turn morbid: "Should I call her?" he wondered. "Should I 'touch base' with her? Drop in for some tea? And I'm dwelling on the fact that I'm going to turn fifty-two, and I'm thinking about Mom, and how she committed suicide at fifty-two, and did that mean I was gonna do it, too?"

As it turns out, Gray lasted ten years longer than his mother, ultimately plunging off the Staten Island Ferry in January. Retrospectively, the conditions of his suicide seem so predictable they almost feel unoriginal. Yet—somehow—it was still a shock to hear that this had happened, and that Gray had actually done what he always suggested; for days after his disappearance, people optimistically speculated that Gray was merely researching his next book and would emerge unscathed. And this is the fundamental paradox of Gray's life and death: no matter how intimately an artist expresses his own unhappiness, we always assume he's still a *character*. Spalding Gray's genius was that he could make his external monologues sound like internal dialogues; his genius derived from his authenticity, and that authenticity was the reason he could sit behind a table and talk solipsistically for ninety minutes without ever seeming dull. It was his authenticity that made him entertaining. But it still didn't make people believe what he was saying. It didn't matter how many times Gray stared into the eyes of his audience and essentially said, *"I am going to kill myself."* Somehow, that sentiment merely seemed funny.

What's retroactively noteworthy about Gray's performance technique—the process of sitting in a chair and emoting directly into a camera—is how it's become the most omnipresent expository device on television. This is how we are supposed to understand the true nature of the people on reality TV: throughout every episode of virtually every show, cast members confess their feelings to an unresponsive video lens, telling us who they love and who they hate and what makes them sad or happy or annoyed. This is how the plot moves. That narrative style was essentially introduced to mainstream television by Mary-Ellis Bunim, who coconstructed MTV's *The Real World* in 1992 and went on to make programs like *Road Rules, Making the Band,* and the wildly successful, vaguely depressing Paris Hilton vehicle *The Simple Life.* Bunim died in late January, succumbing to breast cancer at the age of fifty-seven. Her illness and her passing were weirdly private; I use the modifier "weirdly" because that level of discretion—and the very real tragedy that was cloaked behind it—was the antithesis of what made her TV work so influential and compelling.

Bunim started her career making soap operas; she was the executive producer for daytime series like *As The World Turns* and *Santa Barbara.* The plan for *The Real World* was to craft soap opera storylines with actual people; though shot in a documentary style, the motivation was different than traditional documentary filmmaking. The twentysomethings cast on *The Real World* were not complex subjects meant to be uncovered and examined; they were supposed to be archetypes of youth culture, and they were supposed to make the melodramatic choices (and exhibit the melodramatic behavior) that would drive a serial TV program. They were supposed to be hyperreal versions of who they already were. What they did, ultimately, was unknowingly embody the same aesthetic Spalding Gray invented when he first became a monologist. "I became a kind of inverted Method Actor," Gray wrote. "I was using myself to play myself. [It was] a kind of creative narcissism."

There is no better description of what it means to appear on reality TV than those two sentences.

Part of what made Bunim's *Real World* so polarizing was its name—by actively using the word *real* in the title, it immediately made critics want to question the veracity of every plot. By now, everyone knows that unseen editors have more control over the story than the on-screen participants; unlike Gray, the crux of Bunim's success was not built on authenticity. However, the question of what is (and isn't) real is still there, and it's the reason why imperfect fact will always be more interesting than flawless fiction. We are addicted to blurry lines. In his one-man film *Monster in a Box*, Spalding Gray sits next to a huge manuscript, the unabridged pages of his novel *Impossible Vacation*. The book is fiction, but—by all accounts—it's almost completely autobiographical. Throughout *Monster in a Box*, Gray points to sections of the text and describes the condition of his life during the writing of that particular passage. In other words, he talks about his real life while explaining why it was difficult to write an unreal version of his real life. It is a nonfiction movie about the writing of a fictional book that was actually true. And as a result, we kind of believe everything, and we kind of believe nothing. We believe, I suppose, whatever we want. Which is why the suicide of Spalding Gray still seemed shocking (even though it wasn't), and it's why Mary-Ellis Bunim's *Real World* never seems real (even though it is).

THE TENTH BEATLE
(DECEMBER 2005)

The Beatles are the most famous rock group who existed, or will ever exist. They are, in fact, the second-most famous four-human collective within any context whatsoever (the four Gospel writers are number one; Notre Dame's 1924 Four Horsemen backfield rank a distant third). Moreover, the Beatles are the only band whose population is central to their iconography: John, Paul, George, and Ringo shall always be the Fab Four. And because that number is so important (and so finite), pop historians have spent the last thirty-five years trying to decide who deserves classification as Beatle Number Five. Pete Best was the group's original drummer, so he usually gets to be the Fifth Beatle. Producer George Martin had almost as much sonic impact as the guys in the band, so he warrants credit as the Sixth Beatle. Stuart Sutcliffe played bass with Long John and the Silver Beatles in 1960, influenced the group's fashion aesthetic, and even had a movie made about his tragic life (1994's *Backbeat*); he's the Seventh Beatle. Journeyman musician Billy Preston is credited on some studio albums and performs live with the band in the documentary *Let It Be*, so he's (at worst) Beatle Number Eight. When Ringo Starr had tonsillitis in 1964, he was temporarily replaced by the Ninth Beatle, an easygoing fellow named Jimmy Nichol. Which brings us to Eric Griffiths, a man with the curious legacy of being "The Tenth Beatle."

In 1957, Griffiths and John Lennon were acquaintances at the state grammar school Quarry Bank; they sometimes smoked cigarettes and discussed the possibility of starting a band with anyone they could find who happened to own an instrument. The goal was to play skiffle, a rudimentary musical genre that fused folk with jazz, blues, and country. Working out of Griffiths's home, the pair organized the lineup and arranged the songs. Originally called the Blackjacks, their loose cooperative would evolve into the Quarrymen. By the fall of 1960, the Quarrymen had become the Beatles. But Griffiths was already gone, his role as collaborator usurped by the younger, cuter, more talented Paul McCartney. Ironically, Griffiths would later claim that Lennon was initially threatened by McCartney and wanted to start a different band without him, but Griffiths convinced him otherwise; if this is true, one could argue that Eric Griffiths *saved* the Beatles.

There are conflicting accounts about why Griffiths never became a full-fledged Beatle. The first theory is that he was asked to become the bassist when George Harrison joined the group, but Griffiths could not afford (or did not want) to purchase a bass and amplifier. The second story (as explained in Bob Spitz's biography *The Beatles*) is that John and Paul silently fired him; they scheduled a rehearsal at McCartney's home and simply never invited him (Griffiths deduced his expulsion when he unknowingly phoned the house in the middle of the rehearsal). Either way, Griffiths's brief tenure and ignominious departure illustrates the abject weirdness of being a human footnote: he is now best known for *not* being involved with something. His celebrity only serves to validate just how famous the Beatles were (and are): the Beatles were so famous that Griffiths is notable merely for having known them.

How much this turn of events hurt Griffiths remains open to debate. He certainly never stopped thinking about the past; after a long career in the British prison industry, he reunited several of the original Quarrymen in the late '90s and recorded a skiffle album titled *Get Back Together*. One can only assume he spent a lot of decades dreaming of an alternative reality where he cowrote "Please Please Me" and fled from hordes of screaming teenage girls in cat's-eye glasses. When Lennon was murdered in 1980 and Harrison passed in 2001, we were all reminded of how their lives changed the world; when Eric Griffiths died from pancreatic cancer last January, we were only reminded of the life he never had.

HERE'S "JOHNNY"
(APRIL 2005)

Celebrity deaths rarely affect me emotionally. However, I was pretty chagrined when Johnny Carson died in January. I don't recall liking him (or even consistently watching him) that much when he was still on TV, but I enjoy thinking about him now; he suddenly seems more compelling, somehow. This being the case, I read a lot of his obituaries (of which there were about four thousand), and I kept seeing the same message delivered over and over again: "There will never be another guy like Johnny Carson." This was expressed in different ways and through different means, but the core premise was always the same—Carson was this unique, original voice who represented a certain brand of understated comedic dignity, and no one will ever be that person again. And (maybe) this is true. But I don't think so. I think there could be another person like Johnny Carson, or at least another person who possesses his collection of qualities. What there will never again be is a *thing* that's like "Johnny Carson." And the reason I put Carson's name in quotes is because the idea of "Johnny Carson" is much different than who he actually was as a person. What this means is that another Johnny Carson could exist, but no one would care (or at least not as much). And this is not because society changed, and it's not because our values are different; this is because we all possess the ability to stop "Johnny Carson" from happening, and that is exactly what we choose to do. And this makes us consciously happier, but unconsciously sadder.

Choice makes us depressed.

We just don't realize it.

Certainly, I am not the first person who ever suggested this hypothesis. A professor of social theory at Swarthmore College, Barry Schwartz, recently wrote a book (*The Paradox of Choice*) that suggests "the culture of abundance robs us of satisfaction." Schwartz is a critic of what's referred to as "choice overload"; he thinks that walking into a store and having thirteen different options for uncooked pasta or eighty potential alternatives for a new cell phone injects an extra level of stress into an otherwise simple transaction. However, that problem is not what I'm talking about, because I don't worry about stress. What I worry about is something

The Paradox of Choice only touches on tangentially—the loss of shared experience. The reason Johnny Carson was important was not because he was funny or clever or cool, even though he was all of those things; the reason he was important was because he was the last universally shared icon of modern popular culture.

I do not know one person who grew up during the 1960s or '70s who wasn't intimately aware of who Johnny Carson was and what Johnny Carson did. In a way, he seemed more famous than everybody. It did not matter if he was entertaining or not, and it did not matter how much you liked him. Even if you were consciously watching something else at 11:00 P.M., you were ultimately just *not* watching *The Tonight Show*. I recall an episode of *Alice* where Vic Tayback (that was the bald guy who played Mel) briefly did a semifaithful impersonation of Johnny Carson, even though *Alice* was on CBS and *The Tonight Show* was on NBC. One could argue that the single most memorable line of Jack Nicholson's career was when he mocked Ed McMahon in *The Shining*. "Johnny Carson" was, almost in totality, the entire construction of watching television late at night. Everybody knew this, even if they didn't own a television. It was a specific piece of knowledge that all Americans had in common.

Obviously, that could never happen today. There will never again be "cultural knowledge" that everybody knows, mostly because there is simply too much culture to know about. A few years ago, the OutKast song "Hey Ya!" was wildly popular, and it seemed to have an uncommon social reach; white people liked it, black people liked it, advertisers liked it, communists liked it, kite enthusiasts liked it, etc. etc. etc. I recall having a conversation with a bunch of rock critics who kept referring to this as "The 'Hey Ya!' Moment," when everyone alive seemed to be simultaneously connected through a pop single. However, I can think of fifty people *I know personally* who have never heard of OutKast or listened to "Hey Ya!" nor could they recognize what this tune sounds like or have even a rudimentary conversation about its popularity. "Hey Ya!" was the most universally appreciated song of the past ten years, but it was still a niche phenomenon; in order to know about OutKast, you had to care about music. This was not the case with Carson. To care about "Johnny Carson," all you had to do was be alive. There was nothing else to know about it.

Now, don't confuse my argument with the notion of nostalgia, because nostalgia is not what I am writing about. I don't want to go back in time. I do not want fewer options. I get two hundred channels through my cable service, but I would like two hundred more. If I could magically create a situation where the Rolling Stones had recorded ten studio albums with Mick Taylor instead of five, I would create this situation immediately. In the present tense, we always want the maximum number of alternatives; in the short term, choice improves our lives, and we're completely aware of that. The problematic rub is that—over time—choice isolates us. We have fewer shared experiences, and that makes us feel alone. The proliferation of choice makes us feel vaguely alienated, and that makes us depressed. But this relationship is not something we're conscious of, because it seems crazy to attribute loneliness to freedom. We just think we're inexplicably less happy than we should be.

Yet this sadness is not so inexplicable.

In his new book *Blink,* Malcolm Gladwell adroitly writes about how our attitudes about things like race and morality operate on two levels: The conscious (i.e., "apartheid is wrong," "all people are equal"), and the unconscious (i.e., our immediate, visceral associations that occur before we can edit our internal thought process). Our emotional relationship with choice works in a similar fashion. In 2002, I interviewed Aerosmith's Steven Tyler about drugs and groupies, and he said something along the lines of, "Having sex with the same woman a thousand times is way more interesting than having a thousand one-night stands with a thousand different women, because those one-night stands are all the same." This is the kind of platitude rock stars say all the time; in fact, I am forced to paraphrase it from memory, because that sentiment was too clichéd to include in the article. Every aging rock god (except maybe Gene Simmons) eventually comes to this same conclusion; in fact, anyone (famous or not) who decides to get married is unknowingly agreeing with Steven Tyler. At some point, most people decide that sleeping with the same person improves the quality of their life, even though it eliminates romantic choice. We all unconsciously understand this. However, nobody consciously believes this is true until *after the fact*. If you ask any single man if he'd prefer to (a) have sex with a thousand different women or (b) have sex with one woman a thousand times, he will always take option "a," even though he knows this decision is virtually guaranteed to make him feel awkward and alone. In the present tense, we always want as much individual choice as possible; once that present has passed, we're happier if we've experienced the same limited options as everyone else.

If you're having drinks with a stranger in a bar and "Swallowed" comes on the jukebox, and you say, "You know, this is the one Bush song I like," and the guy you're talking to says, "Yes, this is probably as good as any Pixies song," you will immediately like this guy more. If you then stroll over to some girl and mention that you just happened to see Lars von Trier's *The Five Obstructions*, and she says, "That is my favorite self-reflexive Danish documentary of the past five years," the odds of you kissing this woman immediately increase 40 percent. If you then sit down at a table with five bozos who are intensely discussing the 1985 Atlanta Hawks— and you just happened to have had a poster of Dominique Wilkins on your wall when you were in junior high—you will immediately feel more comfortable. This is not the purpose of art and culture, but it's probably the biggest social benefit; these shared experiences are how we connect with other people, and it's how we understand our own identity. However, all the examples I mentioned are specific and personal; they are only pockets of a shared existence. They are things individual people choose to understand, and finding others who understand them equally are products of coincidence. But "Johnny Carson" was not. "Johnny Carson" was the last thing that everybody understood, even if they didn't try. Which is why we may have another Johnny Carson, but we'll never have another "Johnny Carson." When given the choice, we'd all rather be happy now . . . even if that guarantees we'll all be sad later.

FARGO ROCK CITY,
FOR REAL

I am including the following story for two reasons, neither of which is, "Because it's good." In many ways (in fact, in *most* ways), this story is horrible. It was my attempt to explain the Fargo, North Dakota, "rock scene" when I was twenty-three years old. In retrospect, it now reads like a satire of daily newspaper entertainment reporting, which was certainly not my intention at the time. But that's also what's kind of cool about it; the description of all the 1995 bands in Fargo (and its sister city, Moorhead, Minnesota) is probably pretty close to the rock scene of *every* small-market town in 1995. If you spent the middle part of the '90s in, say, Little Rock, Arkansas (or Des Moines, Iowa, or Boise, Idaho, or anywhere with a population below 200,000), you could probably delete all the artists' names and replace them with any of the going-nowhere bands who happened to be playing in your hometown. The article wouldn't make any less sense (or be any less accurate).

The other reason I like this story is because 1995 was a goofy cultural moment for pop music; by '95, alternative rock had been completely mainstreamed by every element of society (even in North Dakota). However, young musicians still looked to punk and grunge as a way to identify themselves as "underground." Which was hilarious, since trying to be underground by liking alt rock in 1995 would have been like trying to be underground in 1978 by liking Boston.

I have added copious footnotes to this story where they were necessary, which is pretty much everywhere.

TO BE SCENE, OR NOT TO BE SEEN

UNDERGROUND ROCK IS ALIVE
AND LOUD IN FARGO-MOORHEAD . . .
BUT WHO'S LISTENING?
(SEPTEMBER 1995)

Whenever you get into a discussion about the Fargo-Moorhead music climate,[1] the word you most often hear is not *alternative, hardcore, grunge,* or even *music*. The word you hear the most is *scene*. Regardless of whether the context is positive ("We've really got a nice scene developing here"), negative ("Those kids are just into the scene without caring about the music"), or merely expository ("Our band seems to get slagged on by a lot of the local scenesters"), the F-M alt-movement[2] is obsessed with the concept of establishing an underground scene—the people, the atmosphere, and the perceptions that go hand-in-hand with subterranean rock 'n' roll.[3]

It's probably the clearest local illustration of youth culture: the backbone of the establishment is created by kids under eighteen, and the major players are all in their early to midtwenties. Outsiders tend to view this faction as "the Ralph's Bar[4] punk clique," which really isn't accurate. Contemporary

---

1. Which I'm sure happens to you all the time.

2. It remains unclear what this movement was the "alternative" to . . . I suppose going to the mall, although I recall seeing a lot of these same rock kids at JCPenney.

3. In retrospect, it is hard to understand why anyone would actively try to "establish" other people's "perceptions," but it seemed like it at the time.

4. This was a bar in Moorhead where all the local punk bands performed, but it also hosted some surprising national acts, most notably a very early performance by the White Stripes. When the city decided to

punk rock is more of a philosophy than a sound,[5] and—unlike the late-'70s British scene—it doesn't have much to do with fashion.[6] Modern punk is just stripped-down, straightforward music with no frills and few compromises.[7] How accurately that label fits the F-M music fraternity is unclear; some bands are straightforward simply because they lack talent, and some are uncompromising because they're never in a position to be tempted by success. Nonetheless, the current status of the F-M music scene is thriving.[8] As the gap between mainstream and alternative culture closes, more and more young people are drawn to what grassroots, underground rock represents.

There is also a solid base of local musicians; although promoter Jade Nielson admits the scene has grown stagnant,[9] he thinks the level of virtuosity has never been higher. "There has kind of been an overkill because there have been too many shows without enough different bands," Nielson[10] said. "But, at this point in time, there's no question that there is more talent in town than ever before, simply because the musicians are a little older and more mature."

Nielson tends to get most of the credit for shaping the current musical direction of Fargo-Moorhead, and it's easy to understand why. The twenty-four-year-old promoter has

---

destroy Ralph's in 2004, someone tried to make a documentary film about the bar that would somehow save it from destruction. I was drunkenly interviewed for this documentary, and I think I may have claimed I saw this aforementioned White Stripes show. I did not.

5. Trenchant!

6. This was not the only difference.

7. Jesus Christ.

8. Sort of.

9. Despite the fact that I just called it "thriving."

10. At the time I wrote this story, Jade Nielson was perceived as the hippest person in Fargo. Considering how young he was at the time, it seemed rather amazing that he could actually convince shitty communist grindcore bands like Killdozer to play in North Dakota. The key, as it turns out, was geography. Bands would have dates in Minneapolis and Missoula, and they needed a place to perform in between. Jade was apparently the first human who ever figured this out.

turned the back room of Ralph's Bar in Moorhead into one of the Midwest's premier underground venues; in the past year, he's produced shows by Jon Spencer Blues Explosion, Southern Culture on the Skids, Mule, Railroad Jerk, and last Monday's Killdozer concert (as well as an outdoor summer rock festival headlined by the Jesus Lizard[11]). He began seriously promoting bands in 1993 at the now-defunct Elks Club in downtown Fargo.

"When I first starting doing these shows—especially the all-ages shows—it didn't matter who was playing. The audience was basically kids who wanted to hang out with their friends and be seen, along with a small core who were really into the music. We'd get a bigger crowd if I brought in somebody established, like Arcwelder,[12] but it was basically the same people going to every show," Nielson said. "Now, the crowd is definitely affected by the music itself. People are picking and choosing what they'll pay to hear. I even see that at Ralph's."

In terms of influence, however, the biggest single show was probably put on by rival promoter Bjorn Christianson and GodheadSilo[13] drummer Dan Haug. Their 1991 Fugazi concert at the Elks is consistently mentioned as the primary catalyst for the subsequent proliferation of F-M hardcore interest.

-----

11. This was Jade's biggest gambit. The event was earnestly called something along the lines of "Fargo-palooza," and it was an all-day outdoor show on the banks of the Red River. Unfortunately, the success of the event was dependent on walk-up ticket sales, and the show happened to fall on an afternoon when it was over 95 degrees. Hardly anyone showed up, and it was a financial disaster. The entire scene kind of caved in soon after (at least for a while). The Jesus Lizard were pretty awesome, though.

12. Arcwelder was never particularly beloved by anyone except bookish dudes working at college radio stations, but they were still "established," somehow. They also had cross-demographic name recognition, since most farm kids in North Dakota know how to arc weld.

13. GodheadSilo was a local drum-bass two-piece who actually moved to Seattle and were signed by Sub Pop. With the exception of Kid Jonny Lang, I suppose this makes them the most successful North Dakota rock act of the past twenty-five years.

"I think we had about five hundred people at that show, which was a surprise to both of us. I know a lot of people seem to consider that a starting point for what has happened since, but I don't," Christianson[14] said. "I think this whole situation predates the Fugazi[15] show, and by quite a bit. Things around here really started with bands like Floored and Hammerhead and Buttchuck.[16] I think Floored started playing live in the late '80s." Not surprisingly, locating the conception of Fargo's scene depends on who you want to use as a source. Several contemporary scenesters cited a teen center on Fargo's Fiechtner Drive called Exit 99 as the catalyst. Before closing in 1992, Exit 99 was home to several noteworthy shows such as Cop Shoot Cop and Bikini Kill. It acted as the breeding ground for the current generation of local artists.

"Exit 99[17] was done well, and it was done professionally. And—for a lot of bands in town—that was the first place they played at. But it turned into too much of a young kids' club," Nielson said. "Since they couldn't serve alcohol, it was hard to get college students to go there. A lot of the time, it was just teenagers who were sitting around and smoking cigarettes."

---

14. This guy was really blond and snarky.

15. I am often prone to make fun of Fugazi, but I must give them credit: they really would play anywhere, and they'd play for virtually no money. It seemed like at least one member of every band in Fargo-Moorhead saw this particular concert. What's interesting is the scene's second-most influential moment was the 1994 Jon Spencer show, which prompted many of the acts in Fargo to combine Fugazi with the Blues Explosion. The problem was that all of those bands dreamed of moving to Minneapolis and signing with Amphetamine Reptile Records, so they also tried to play like Helmet. As a consequence, many bands at Ralph's Bar seemed like superheavy, straight-edge power trios with unorthodox taste in trousers.

16. This is still a pretty excellent band name, all things considered.

17. The most interesting thing about Exit 99 was something that didn't happen in 1991: An unknown group scheduled a date to play there in the middle of the week, but they canceled at the last minute, supposedly because their debut album was starting to get a little media attention and their itinerary was being reconstructed. This was a minor tragedy, since (a) the show would have probably drawn less than twelve people, and (b) the band was Pearl Jam.

In reality, the "scene" has probably always existed in one form or another. *Yahtzene* editor Phil Leitch (at the ripe old age of twenty-six) is considered the oldest active member of the Fargo underground. "I would certainly say there was a scene before the 1990s. For me, the scene began in about 1984, but there were a lot less people involved," Leitch[18] said. "I put on a show in 1985—the band was called Vampire Lesboes—and I think about a hundred people showed up."

At least superficially, the so-called scene has more members now than ever before. There's no question about the current popularity of underground culture, and that's exactly what this local movement offers young people. However, there are some problems. Fargo-Moorhead has a limited number of bands in the area, and they play so often that the novelty has worn off. Moreover, they're forced to play at the same places over and over (this area has very few available venues). The biggest problem is probably a question of sincerity; while most of the bands are fairly serious about playing, it's hard to gauge if the audiences are interested in the music or just the trendiness of the spectacle. Dean Sime[19] manages Disc & Tape Masters in Fargo and produces a public-access video program called *Eyeball Injection*. He perceives a predictable schism in the local punk packs and questions the amount of sonic diversity from the musicians.

"Like any scene, it's divided. There are certain bands that

18. This person still lives in Fargo, and he still hassles me whenever I go back. His zine was pretty great (or at least it seemed that way at the time). He had a feud with the band Orange 17, so he was consistently publishing a list called, "Things I would rather do than see Orange 17 perform live." I particularly remember one of these lists, because #5 was, "See a movie with *Forum* film critic Chuck Klosterman" and #6 was, "Have the worst sex of my life, get AIDS, and die." This remains the most insightful literary criticism I've ever received.

19. This is the guy I sold my used CDs to. He would give me four dollars for almost anything, including reggae compilations. As far as I'm concerned, that qualified him as an expert on just about everything. He knew (and knows) a metric ton about music, but I think he eventually became a plumber.

have legitimate followings—Orange-17 has an excellent following, Bossk has a growing following, and Seven O'clock Sucker has a good following. But there are still a lot of people going to these shows who just want to be seen," Sime said. "I think interest in the scene may be growing, but that goes along with the growth of alternative culture. The problem is that—musically—the number of bands is shrinking. There are fewer bands in town than there were two years ago, and only five or six of them play consistently. It also seems like the bands aren't writing enough new songs, and too many of their songs sound alike."

With its fuzzy past and vague present,[20] speculating on the future of the F-M scene is virtually impossible. Leitch thinks local interest is fading and doubts if any major shows could succeed in the near future. Christianson was more optimistic and said the class of young bands currently emerging in the area is more exciting and experimental than ever before. For someone like Brian Eveslage, however, the dynamic of the scene is ultimately inconsequential. Eveslage plays guitar for Bossk and was formerly in Blockhead and Haul. As far as he's concerned, it's not his job to figure out who likes his music.

"I have no idea who our audience is. A lot of our friends go to the shows, I guess. When we play all-ages shows, the audience tends to be younger, but—since we usually play at Ralph's Bar—it's hard for me to gauge," Eveslage said. "There may be fewer bands right now than there were a couple of years ago, but the ones who are left are more serious. The bands who managed to stick around aren't just playing for the hell of it."[21]

[*What follows is the completely unnecessary sidebar to this story.*]

• • •

---

20. Fuck. I was a really, really wretched person.
21. Actually, they were.

So who are all of these local underground bands? That's a valid question. Here's a painfully pithy description of a dozen bands that bounce around the area. (Readers note: It's possible some of these bands no longer exist or have changed names; it's often difficult to tell if a band is dead or merely inactive at the moment.)

Orange 17[22]: The most popular local act in town, especially among junior high kids. They seem to have a sense of humor (they ended last Monday's set with "Smokin' in the Boys Room"), and many people think their vocalist looks like Kurt Cobain.

Bossk[23]: A classic hardcore trio. Their bass player is a little scary.

Standard[24]: Bossk, but without the guitar player.

Bootlick[25]: An unorthodox blues-grunge band.

Bombshell: The best-known all-female punk trio in Fargo history.[26]

---

22. What made Orange 17 awesome was how so many people in Fargo hated them for their success. This is a band who never made an album, never went on tour, and never made any money. However, they once opened for Ted Nugent and Bad Company at the Fargodome (they were the replacement for a national band who got sick). In a way, Orange 17 truly were a little ahead of their time; they loved hair metal ironically when absolutely nobody else did, and—had they emerged ten years later—I suppose they could have been a second-tier version of the Darkness. The band was also hurt by the fact that vocalist Karl Qualey—as mentioned above—looked too much like Kurt Cobain, and everyone thought he was doing it on purpose. In truth, it was just a weird coincidence. He really just needed a different barber.

23. And by "scary" I meant "bald."

24. Played the same songs, though.

25. I never saw this band, ever.

26. Inspired by Tiger Trap!

John Smith: In July of 1994, local promoter Jade Nielson predicted John Smith would "take over the world."

Seven O'clock Sucker: The prototypical garage band. I'm pretty sure their drummer is from Milnor, ND, and—if I recall correctly—he used to have a decent jump shot in high school.[27]

Gummi: Definitely not a punk band,[28] as they supposedly dig KISS.

Pathos: A South Fargo band, described by Bombshell drummer Sarah Hassell as "underrated."

Martian: A West Fargo high school outfit. They're cutting a seven-inch on Meat Records.[29]

---

27. This was true. The drummer's last name was Jensen, and he (and his older brother) symbolized key elements of small-town, North Dakota basketball folklore: the noble tradition of high-scoring five-foot-six-inch jump shooters. These two Jensen brothers would come off the bench for Milnor, hide in the corner against zone defenses, and inevitably drain three or four 3-pointers every single night. It was profoundly frustrating for all their opponents, because those Jensen boys were short and slow and (kind of) chubby. But undersized fat kids often thrive on the hardwood floors of rural North Dakota. There was another school in a community called Marion, ND, that had two families with the surname Trapp (these families might have even been named "Von Trapp," although that might be wishful thinking on my part). This was a tiny town—maybe 250 people total—and their high school gym was the size of a four-car garage. It was probably only sixty feet long. As such, these Trapp boys—all of whom were under five foot eight— would regularly launch jump shots from half court in the middle of a game. This was impossible to defend, because your natural psychological instinct was not to cover any kid inexplicably shooting from beyond midcourt. The most talented Trapp was a cocky, curly-haired fellow named Tori Trapp, and he averaged something like thirty-three points a game without ever going inside the lane. The summer after he graduated from high school, Tori Trapp made out with a girl at a keg party who would later become my girlfriend. I guess I have a lot of unresolved issues with this dude.
28. This was gleaned from their handwritten press release.
29. Now defunct.

Whirl: A high school skater band.[30]

Trans Am: Yet another high school skater band. Karl Qualey of Orange 17 (a.k.a. the aforementioned Cobain clone[31]) once said he was a fan of their music.

---

30. As opposed to an Adult-Oriented Skater band (AOS).
31. For some reason, I really tried to ram this point home.

THINGS
THAT MIGHT
BE TRUE

Q: Think of someone who is your friend (do not select your best friend, but make sure the person is someone you would classify as "considerably more than an acquaintance").

This friend is going to be attacked by a grizzly bear.

Now, this person will survive this bear attack; that is guaranteed. There is a 100 percent chance that your friend will live. However, the extent of his injuries is unknown; he might receive nothing but a few superficial scratches, but he also might lose a limb (or multiple limbs). He might recover completely in twenty-four hours with nothing but a great story, or he might spend the rest of his life in a wheelchair.

Somehow, you have the ability to stop this attack from happening. You can magically save your friend from the bear. But his (or her) salvation will come at a peculiar price: if you choose to stop the bear, it will always rain. For the rest of your life, wherever you go, it will be raining. Sometimes it will pour and sometimes it will drizzle—but it will never *not* be raining. But it won't rain over the totality of the earth, nor will the hydrological cycle be disrupted; these storm clouds will be isolated, and they will focus entirely on your specific whereabouts. You will never see the sun again.

Do you stop the bear and accept a lifetime of rain?

NEMESIS

"It is not *what* you know," they say, "it is *who* you know." We have all heard this sentiment, and we all reflexively agree with it. This is because "they" are hard to debate, especially since "they" never seem to be in the room whenever anyone makes reference to "them." We all concede that "they" rule "us." But here is the secret shame of that amorphous entity that makes us all cower in shame: *they* are losers. *They* are failures.

They don't realize that life is—almost without exception—an absolute meritocracy, and everyone who succeeds completely deserves it.[1] The only people who disagree with this are people who will never succeed at anything. You see, *they* want you to believe the passageway to power is all about cultivating allies, so *they* spend all their time trying to make friends and influence people. This is why they fail. It rarely matters who is on your side; what matters is who is against you. Unlike Gloria Loring, you don't need a friend and you don't need a lover. What you need is (a) one quality nemesis and (b) one archenemy. These are the two most important mechanisms in any human's life. We measure ourselves against our nemeses, and we long to destroy our archenemies. They are the catalysts for why we do everything.

Now, I know what you're asking yourself: How do I know the difference between my nemesis and my archenemy? Here is the short answer: You kind of *like* your nemesis, despite the fact that you despise him. You will always have drinks with your nemesis. You would attend the funeral of your nemesis, and—privately—you might shed a tear over his or her passing. However, you would never choose to have a cocktail with your archenemy, unless you were attempting to spike the gin with arsenic. If you were to perish, your archenemy would dance on your grave, and then he'd burn down your house and molest your children. You hate your archenemy so much that you keep your hatred secret, because you do not want your archenemy to have the satisfaction of being hated.

If this distinction seems confusing, just ask your girlfriend to explain it in detail; women have always understood the nemesis-archenemy dichotomy. Every woman I've ever known has at least one close friend whose only purpose in life is to criticize their actions, compete for men's attention, and drive them insane; very often, this is a woman's *best* friend. Consequently, females are always able to find the ideal nemesis

---

1. The exceptions being Dale Peck, MTV on-air personalities who aren't Kurt Loder, Al Franken, and myself.

(usually without even trying). Meanwhile, every woman also has a former friend (usually someone from high school with large breasts) whom she has loathed for years and whom she will continue to loath with the intensity of a thousand suns, even if she only sees her once every ten years. This is her archenemy. Women intrinsically understand human dynamics, and that makes them unstoppable. Unfortunately, the average man is less adroit at fostering such rivalries, which is why most men remain average; males are better at hating things that can't hate them back (e.g., lawnmowers, cats, the Denver Broncos, et cetera). They don't see the big picture.

This fall, George W. Bush will run for the presidency against (in all likelihood) Howard Dean.[2] Subsequently, they will become nemeses by default. However, they are far from archenemies. Dean's archenemy is Joe Lieberman; Bush's archenemy is Hillary Clinton. As a result, the 2004 election will only be marginally intriguing. Nemeses lock horns all the time. However, the 2008 election (when Hillary faces her archenemy's snarky little brother Jeb) will be a cataclysmic bloodbath. When archenemies collide, skulls get busted. In the 1980s, Larry Bird's nemesis was Magic Johnson, and it was always beautiful when they tangled—but Bird's archenemy wasn't Magic. It was Isiah Thomas. Whenever the Celtics played the Pistons, it was a train wreck, and it went deeper than basketball: in 1987 Isiah supported Dennis "Rush" Rodman when he claimed Bird was famous only because he was white; Larry forgave him in public, but he still iced him in the end—the first thing Bird did after becoming Indian Pacers team president was fire Zeke as head coach. Steve Jobs was Bill Gates's nemesis, but Jobs could not compete with superlawyer David Boies for superenemy status. Mia Farrow is Woody Allen's nemesis, but if Woody had only one bullet in his revolver, he'd shoot Phillip Roth. In 1991, Vince Neil of Mötley Crüe challenged Axl Rose to a public fistfight, and Vince probably considered Axl to be his archenemy. However, Vince

---

2. Ha!

was merely Axl's nemesis; Axl's archenemy was Kurt Cobain, which is why Guns n' Roses never recovered from Cobain's 1994 suicide. J. R. Ewing was at war with nemesis-brother Bobby for twelve seasons (thirteen if you count the year Victoria Principal dreamed he was dead), but Cliff Barnes was the true Minotaur of Southfork. Marvin Hagler's nemesis was Tommy "the Hitman" Hearns, but his archenemy was duplicitous pretty boy Sugar Ray Leonard (and the reason Leonard upset Hagler in '87 is because Sugar was comfortably sparring against a man he merely viewed as a nemesis, since we all know Leonard's archenemy was Roberto Duran). The Joker was Batman's nemesis, but—ironically—his archenemy was Superman, since Superman made Batman entirely mortal and generally nonessential. Nobody likes to admit this, but Batman fucking *hated* Superman; Superman is the reason Batman became an alcoholic.[3]

Clearly, *you* need a nemesis. Clearly, *you* need an archenemy. And it's possible you already have both of these entities in your life; perhaps you just don't realize it (or maybe you can't tell them apart). As a public service, here are a few signs.

RECOGNIZING YOUR NEMESIS
- At some point in the past, this person was (arguably) your best friend.
- You and this person once competed for the same woman, and you both failed.
- You have punched this person in the face.
- If invited, you would go to this person's wedding and give them a spice rack, but you would secretly hope that their marriage ends in a bitter, public divorce.
- People who barely know the two of you assume you are close friends; people who know both of you intimately suspect you profoundly hate each other.
- If your archenemy tried to kill you, this person would attempt to stop him.

---

3. This is speculative.

- Every time you talk to this person, you lie.
- If you meet someone who has the same first name as this person, you immediately like them less.
- This person has done at least two (2) things that would be classified as "unforgivable."
- The satisfaction you feel from your own success pales in comparison to the despair you feel from this person's personal triumphs, even if those triumphs are completely unrelated to your life.
- If this person slept with your girlfriend, she would never be attractive to you again.
- Even if this person's girlfriend was a hateful bitch, you would sleep with her out of spite.

I was sitting in the passenger seat of my nemesis's Buick Skylark when he punched me in 1992; I jacked his jaw at a keg party in '94. These days I mostly just read his blog, although we did have a pressure-packed lunch at the Fargo Olive Garden over Christmas. Meanwhile, I've had the same archenemy since eighth grade. He's a guy named Rick Helling, and he grew up in Lakota, North Dakota. Last year, Helling pitched a few innings for the Marlins in the World Series; in 1998, he won twenty games for the Rangers. I went to basketball camp with Rick Helling in 1985, and he was the single worst person I'd ever met. Every summer, I constantly scan the sports section of *USA Today*, always hoping that he got shelled. This is what drives me. I cannot live in a world where Helling's career ERA hovers below 5.00, yet all I do for a living is type. As long as Rick Helling[4] walks this earth, I shall never sleep soundly.

I realize there are those who don't think it's necessary (or even wise) to consciously create adversaries; Will Rogers

---

4. Soon after the publication of this column, a line drive broke Rick Helling's leg. Though I realize there is no real relationship between the things I write and the world at large, I still felt pretty terrible about this.

claimed that he never met a man he didn't like. But what is Will Rogers famous for, really? For telling jokes that don't have punch lines? For wearing a bandana like an ascot? Who wants that for a legacy? There is a reason *they* say, "Keep your friends close, but keep your enemies closer." *They* don't know what they're talking about, but sometimes *they* get lucky, you know?

—*Esquire*, 2004

Q: Assume everything about your musical tastes was reversed overnight. Everything you once loved, you now hate; everything you once hated, you now love. For example, if your favorite band has always been R.E.M., they will suddenly sound awful to you; they will become the band you dislike the most. By the same token, if you've never been remotely interested in the work of Yes and Jethro Tull, those two groups will instantly seem fascinating. If you generally dislike jazz today, you'll generally like jazz tomorrow. If you currently consider the first album by Veruca Salt to be slightly *above* average, you will abruptly find it to be slightly *below* average. Everything will become its opposite, but everything will remain in balance (and the rest of your personality will remain unchanged). So—in all likelihood—you won't love music any less (or any more) than you do right now. There will still be artists you love and who make you happy; they will merely be all the artists you currently find unlistenable.

Now, I concede that this transformation would make you unhappy. But explain why.

ADVANCEMENT

Responsibility sits so hard on my shoulder
Like a good wine, I'm better as I grow older
—Lou Reed, "A Gift"

Once in a great while, everything in the world changes at once. This is one of those times.

Consider everything you think you know about music. Consider all that you believe to be "good" and all that you believe to be "bad." Consider the way you view popular culture. And now—*today*—prepare to cast all those thoughts aside. I've got some bad news, my friend: you were wrong about everything. But you're going to evolve. You're going to understand.

You are going to Advance.

It's possible that you're currently unaware of Advancement Theory; like most renegade fields of cultural study, it exists on the fringes of intellectual society. However, Advancement Theory is the future of discourse in this country. As a school of thought, it's still young; Advancement emerged just fourteen years ago on the University of South Carolina campus. It is also byzantine: I openly concede that I am merely a wide-eyed frosh in this field of study, and many of its principles still baffle me. But I am learning, and so will you. It is my assertion that—within the next fifty years—Advancement Theory will be the primary means of understanding rock 'n' roll (and perhaps all artistic ventures). This column is the first step. Prepare to have your paradigm shifted . . .

WHAT IS ADVANCEMENT?

Advancement is a cultural condition where an Advanced Individual—i.e., a true genius—creates a piece of art that 99 percent of the population perceives as bad. However, this perception is not because the work itself is flawed; this perception is because most consumers are not Advanced.

Now, do not make the mistake of inferring that this means that everything terrible is actually awesome, or vice versa; that kind of contrarianism has no place in Advancement Theory. The key to Advancement is that Advanced artists (a) do not do what is expected of them, but also (b) do not do the *opposite* of what is expected of them. If an artist simply does the direct opposite of what is anticipated, they are classified as "overt" (more on this later). The bottom line is this: when a legitimate genius does something that seems crazy, it does not mean they suddenly suck; what it means is that they are doing something you cannot understand, because they have Advanced beyond you.

232

WHO IS ADVANCED?

Without question, the most Advanced figure of all time is Lou Reed; he is the cornerstone of this idiom. Reed's single most Advanced moment was in 1986, when he released the song "The Original Wrapper." However, his recent album *Animal Serenade*—a two-record live set of songs inspired by Edgar Allan Poe—is almost as crucial. Joe Walsh is highly Advanced (primarily because of the song "Life's Been Good" and the album title *Got Any Gum?*). David Byrne's cover of Whitney Houston's "I Want to Dance with Somebody" is profoundly Advanced, as was the David Bowie–Mick Jagger cover of "Dancing in the Streets." The most Advanced hard-rock album ever made was *(Music from) The Elder* by KISS, the soundtrack for a movie that does not exist; *The Elder* also includes several songs cowritten by Lou Reed, which obviously helps. Last year, rapper C-Murder was charged with murder. If you name yourself "C-Murder" before you actually murder someone, consider yourself Advanced.

WHO IS NOT ADVANCED?

Almost everybody else. Neil Young is not Advanced; his career is built on the premise that he follows no rules, so he cannot Advance beyond his nature. None of the Beatles were Advanced, although Paul McCartney is close. Bob Dylan only flirts with Advancement; in fact, appearing in a Victoria's Secret commercial might be his most Advanced move ever (Dylan selling bras = Advancement). The Beastie Boys are completely unAdvanced, as are the Killers. However, this does not mean these people can never Advance; that's always possible. For example, if Radiohead released an album of wordless, mechanized droning, that would be predictable. If Radiohead made a glam record, that would be overt. But if Radiohead recorded an album of blues standards, they would Advance.

WHAT ARE THE RULES OF ADVANCEMENT?

This depends on who you believe. The founders of Advancement Theory enforce strict criteria: the Advanced artist must (at some point in their career) wear a black leather jacket with black sunglasses, they must have a mullet, and they must always appear on the cover of their own solo albums. However, virtually no second-generation Advancement theorists follow those guidelines. The only thing that everyone seems to agree upon is that Advancement has no relationship whatsoever to irony; if something is done ironically, it cannot be Advanced.

WHAT DOES IT MEAN TO BE *OVERT*?

This is an especially confusing point, but it's essential to the overall theory: if someone is overt, they *appear* Advanced. However, they are actually the opposite of Advanced, because their seemingly inexplicable decisions are not being driven by inner genius. For example, the Darkness are overt. U2 are overt. When Kurt Cobain collaborated with William S. Burroughs in 1992, it defined overtness. However—and here's the tricky part—you usually need to become overt before you can become Advanced. Liz Phair's eponymous record was overt, but she is accelerating toward Advancement. Once you achieve Advancement, you can then *return* to being overt, at which point you are classified as an "Advanced Irritant." The epitome of this is Lou Reed's *Metal Machine Music* record. (*Readers note: I don't fully grasp this part, either.*)

WHO INVENTED ADVANCEMENT?

The first grains of Advancement were discussed by Jason Hartley and Britt Bergman in 1990, inside a Pizza Hut in Columbia, South Carolina; it started as a discussion about clothing. However, the conversation evolved into a debate over why Reed always performed the song "Walk on the Wild Side" whenever he appeared on *Late Night with David Letterman*, even if he was ostensibly promoting a different album. Everything exploded after that.

"Geniuses evolve in a way very specific to themselves," says Hartley, a man widely considered to be the father of Advancement. Hartley is currently the editorial director for Delia's, a store that sells clothing to teenage girls. (*Editor's note: This is a highly Advanced career choice.*) "An overt artist puts out material that is ambiguous and can therefore be interpreted by the listener in any way they want. For example, Michael Stipe's lyrics don't really mean anything, so any sixteen-year-old can convince himself that those words can mean whatever they want. The Advanced artist never does that."

ARE THERE CRITICS OF ADVANCEMENT?

Indeed. Some pundits find Advancement's circular logic both dogmatic and reductive.

"I find that Advancement scholars do not foster a spirit of inquiry," says Rob Sheffield, a six-foot-five-inch writer for *Rolling Stone* and the owner of many lush sweaters. "It's really just a way for Advancement theorists to appreciate shitty music by people they consider to be non-shitty. It allows you to engage with Lou Reed's music from the 1980s, but not the Hooters or the Outfield. This entire theory is shackled by the Heisenberg principle of self-consciousness."

This is a valid point, possibly. Even Hartley is sometimes stymied by his own discipline.

"I find Sting unlistenable," admits Hartley. "But I *know* that Sting is Advanced. He must be super-Advanced, and I just don't understand him. It's kind of like when Einstein came up with the Theory of Relativity—there were still parts of that theory that even Einstein could not understand. Those concepts were left for future generations."

In other words, it's really up to us. All of us. Only you can stop forest fires, and only you can advance Advancement. If you care about rock 'n' roll, you will commit yourself to this project. The truth is out there, and it's probably wearing sunglasses.

—*Esquire*, 2004

Q: At the age of thirty, you suffer a blow to the skull. The head trauma leaves you with a rare form of partial amnesia—though you are otherwise fine, you're completely missing five years from your life. You have no memory of anything that happened between the ages of twenty-three and twenty-eight. That period of your life is completely gone; you have no recollection of anything that occurred during that five-year gap.

You are told by friends and family that—when you were twenty-five—you (supposedly) became close friends with someone you met on the street. You possess numerous photos of you and this person, and everyone in your life insists that this individual was your best friend for over two years. You were (allegedly) inseparable. In fact, you find several old letters and e-mails from this person that vaguely indicate you may have even shared a brief romantic relationship. But something happened between you and this individual when you were twenty-seven, and the friendship abruptly ended (and—apparently—you never told anyone what caused this schism, so it remains a mystery to all). The friend moved away soon after the incident, wholly disappearing from your day-to-day life. But you have no memory of *any* of this. Within the context of your own mind, this person never even existed. There is tangible proof that you deeply loved this friend, but—whenever you look at their photograph—all you see is a stranger.

Six weeks after your accident, you are informed that this person has suddenly died.

How sad do you feel?

I DO NOT HATE THE OLYMPICS

"How can you hate the Olympics?" they ask me. "Are you some sort of antipatriotic subversive? Do you find Bob Costas overbearing? Can't you understand the majesty of world-class ping-pong?" These are the questions I face every four years; every four years, I am accused of hating the Olympics. Now, this accusation is inaccurate: I do not hate the Olympics. I just don't like them at all (and there *is* a difference between those two sentiments). For as long as I can remember, the Olympics have been completely and utterly unmoving; this is ironic, inasmuch as we're all about to spend the next three weeks being reminded about how emotive and heartwrenching and dramatic these games are alleged to be. This is not something I need to be reminded of, particularly since the only thing the Olympics ever do is reinforce my dislike for a specific kind of American sports fan: people who like the home team simply because the home team is, in fact, *the home team.*

It was during the 1984 Olympic Games in Los Angeles when I realized how ridiculous casual sports fans tend to be, and how most people's opinion of what they care about has nothing to do with thinking. I realized this when Zola Budd collided with Mary Decker Slaney during the 3,000 meters. This—as you may remember—was a huge controversy. And while I was following the controversy on my beanbag in front of our twenty-one-inch Zenith, something occurred to me: Why the fuck is everyone in this country suddenly concerned with women's distance running? Had this race happened in the summer of 1983, little barefoot Zola could have beaten Mary Decker with a pair of nunchuckus and it probably wouldn't have been mentioned in *USA Today.*

This is when I started to realize that the Olympics are designed for people who want to care about something without considering why.

In order to enjoy the Olympics, you can't think critically about anything; you just have to root for America (or whatever country you're from) and assume that your feelings are inherently correct. It's the same kind of antilogic you need to employ whenever you attend a political convention or a church service or movies directed by Steven Spielberg. When Savannah, Georgia, power lifter Cheryl Ann Haworth tries to clean-and-jerk the equivalent of a white rhino, we (as Americans) are obligated to pray for her success, despite the fact that we know nothing about her or any of her foes. We're all supposed to take inspiration from Sada Jacobson, who (I'm told) is the world's number-one female fencer, which is kind of like being the world's number-one *Real World/Road Rules Challenge* participant.[1] Everyone is going to be ecstatic about the prospect of Michael Phillips winning as many as eight gold medals in swimming, even though I have yet to find a single person *who knows who Michael Phillips is*. This is what I hate about the Olympics, and it's also what I hate about typical sports enthusiasts: I hate the idea that rooting for a team without justification somehow proves that you are traditional, loyal, and "a true fan." All it proves is that you're ridiculous, and that you don't really consider the motivations that drive your emotions, and that you probably care more about geography and the color of a uniform than you do about any given sport. I have a sportswriter friend who constantly attempts to paint me as a soulless hypocrite, simply because I adored the Boston Celtics in 1986 but I'm wholly ambivalent toward them today. His argument makes no sense to me. I have no idea why my feelings about an organization twenty years ago should have any effect on how I think now. The modern Celtics have different players, a different coach, a different offense, different management, different ownership, and they play in a different arena; the only similarity between these two squads is that they both wear green and they both used the same parquet floor.

I'm not rooting for flooring.

Yet this is what the Olympics ask us to do—they ask us to support athletes solely because they happen to stand on U.S. floors when they pay their federal income tax. We could toss a bunch of serial killers into the pool in Athens, and we'd still be told to support their run for water polo gold. And isn't

1. That would be Mike "the Miz" Mizanin, by the way, although CT really exploded into prominence during *The Inferno*.

that style of thinking the core of every major (and minor) problem we have in this country? The war in Iraq is obviously the most pervasive example, but that's just the tip of the proverbial iceberg. It strikes me that every wrongheaded sentiment in society ultimately derives from the culture of inherent, unconditional rightness. As I grow older, I find myself less prone to have an opinion about anything, and to distrust just about everyone who does. Whenever I meet someone who openly identifies themselves as a Republican or a Democrat, my immediate thought is always, *Well, this person might be interesting, but they'll never say anything about politics that's remotely useful to me.* I refuse to discuss abortion with anyone who is pro-life or pro-choice; I refuse to discuss affirmative action with any unemployed white guy or any unemployed black guy. All the world's stupidest people are either zealots or atheists. If you want to truly deduce how intelligent someone is, just ask this person how they feel about any issue that doesn't have an answer; the more certainty they express, the less sense they have. This is because certainty only comes from dogma.

People used to slag on Bill Clinton for waffling on everything and always relying on situational pragmatism; as far as I'm concerned, that was the single greatest aspect of his presidency. Life is fucking confusing. I don't know anything, and neither do you. But this is not what the Olympics want you to believe. They want you to feel like you're always on the right side, even if you don't know why. NBC will show you hours of human-interest stories about people you've never heard of before, and they'll all insist that these athletes have overcome adversity and should automatically be perceived as heroes (although none will be classified as "the real heroes," since "the real heroes" are "particularly unlucky members of the Army Reserve"). Maybe they should, and maybe they shouldn't. It's always 50–50.

That said, I'm sure I'll still end up sitting through all this melodramatic shit, and I'm sure I'll unconsciously find myself not-so-secretly hoping that America wins every event (except for speed walking—for some reason, I always hope Canada dominates speed walking). I'm not sure how much I love my country, but I'm pretty sure I don't like any of the alternatives (except, of course, the speed-walking juggernaut that is Canada). My main fear is that the Saudi Arabian relay team will steal gold in the 4 x 400 relay and—moments before the event is rebroadcast in prime time—Costas will be unable to resist telling us that the terrorists have already won.

—Esquire, 2004

Q: You work in an office, performing a job you find satisfying (and which compensates you adequately). The company that employs you is suddenly purchased by an eccentric millionaire who plans to immediately raise each person's salary by 5 percent and extend an extra week of vacation to all full-time employees.

However, this new owner intends to enforce a somewhat radical dress code: every day, men will have to wear tuxedos, tails, and top hats (during the summer months, male employees will be allowed to wear gray three-piece suits on "casual Fridays"). Women must exclusively work in formal wear, preferably ball gowns or prom dresses. Each employee will be given an annual $500 stipend to purchase necessary garments, but that money can only be spent on work-related clothing.

The new regime starts in three months.

Do you seek employment elsewhere?

THREE STORIES INVOLVING PANTS

I. MANNEQUIN APPROPRIATION PROJECT (2005)

People like to say "Clothes make the man," but nobody smart honestly believes this to be true. I mean, why would they? Fabric is merely fabric; wool is simply wool. I think a better (but perhaps less practical) cliché would be, "Clothes make the mannequin," which is more accurate; mannequins don't have much inherent charisma, generally speaking. But what happens when a man *becomes* a mannequin? Does this alter his understanding of self? Does this detach him from corporeal reality? Does it deconstruct one's identity and reconstruct it as commentary?

Perhaps. Perhaps not, but perhaps.

Last week I needed a sweater, which is always a problem. I don't understand how to buy things; I always choke in the clutch. But in this instance, I made (what seemed like) a brilliant decision: I walked into The Gap on Forty-second and Lexington, I glanced at all the in-store mannequins, and I simultaneously purchased every garment the most eye-catching mannequin happened to be wearing. I actively became the human incarnation of an inhuman model, primarily because (a) I assume the kind of people who dress mannequins spend a lot of time considering aesthetics, (b) this eliminated decision making, and (c) I am somewhat "mannequin-shaped." What I bought, I suppose, is an *outfit*, which is something I'd never done before. But this wasn't *my* outfit. This was the mannequin's outfit, and he (it?) remained in command.

Now, this outfit basically has three pieces: (1) a blue sweater that looks like something I would wear if I became an assistant coach for the North Carolina Tar Heels, (2) a collared dress shirt that you're supposed to untuck on purpose, and (3) new jeans that are designed to resemble semi-old jeans. I wore these items the very next day. And for the purposes of this essay, I would love to say that I had no idea how much this outfit would change the way people responded to me, and that I was shocked by the way it altered my day-to-day interactions. However, this would be lying. The first moment I looked into the bathroom mirror, I could tell it would be a controversial move. I looked totally fucking different in every fucking context. *Who is this person?* I thought to myself. *I've never seen this person before.* It suddenly dawned on me that I could disappear into the Witness Protection Program simply by combining a blue sweater with an untucked dress shirt.

I start walking to work, and I can tell that everything about my life is instantly reinvented. I *feel* like a mannequin. And this feeling is fascinating, because I have no idea how a mannequin is supposed to feel; without even trying, I'm instantaneously projecting my fictionalized assumption about how it feels to be an inanimate object onto myself. I find myself obsessed with explaining this experience to other people, but I can't; I'm worried they'll say, "Is it anything like that 1987 Andrew McCarthy film *Mannequin*?" And I have never seen that movie, so we will not have common ground.

As I take the elevator up to the magazine where I am employed, I anticipate that everyone in the office will have an immediate reaction to my sweater-fueled redesign. I am absolutely correct. "This is a stunning development," says a fact-checker. "Are you in love?" asks a woman I barely know. "I am going to make my boyfriend buy that dress shirt," claims an editorial assistant. On the whole, it seems my "mannequin appropriation project" is testing well with female audiences. Men around the office are supportive, but somehow more skeptical.

"What happened to you?" asks a man I often eat lunch with. "Are you supposed to be an indie rocker now?" I cannot overstate the cultural impact of untucking one's dress shirt while wearing a sweater; if you haven't tried this, you totally should. "This is probably a good direction for you," my lunch companion continues, "but this untucking is going to erode your outsider appeal. Plus, now you have to listen to Superchunk."

"But this isn't a statement about social class or personal iconography," I say in response. "Don't you get it? *I'm a mannequin now.* I bought these clothes off a mannequin, so I've *become* that mannequin. It's like I've turned into a new person by turning into a nonperson, which is, like . . . oh, I don't know—maybe this offers some kind of interesting insight on consumerism and vanity and what dictates who we really are."

"Oh really," said my friend flatly. And in an alternative reality, this is where he would have said, "Well, clothes make the mannequin." But that's not what he said, because—in this reality—that is not a cliché that people say. So we just went to lunch, and I spilled gravy on my Carolina sweater, because I am alive.

This might be one of those stories that ultimately ends with the narrator saying, "Well, maybe you had to be there." However, it remains the coolest story anyone ever told me, primarily because virtually every element of the narrative (a) makes no sense whatsoever, and (b) remains mostly unexplained.

My associate Brenda and I were desperately in need of marijuana, and we couldn't find anyone in Fargo to sell us some. This was often a problem, but it was especially pressing during the middle '90s. As a last gasp, we decided to visit Brenda's recently unemployed cousin Sharky, a thirty-three-year-old goofball iconoclast who was regarded by Brenda's family as something of a black sheep. Sharky lived in downtown Fargo, directly above a bakery; his rent was roughly $90 a month.

Upon entering his anachronistic apartment, it became instantly clear that Sharky—regardless of his bad-boy reputation—was an incredibly sweet guy. It was also clear that Sharky was never not stoned. He sold us some drugs at an incredibly cheap price, and the only thing he asked was that we "hang out" for a few hours, which we did. We drank Sunkist soda and talked about music (specifically the lesser-known works of Iron Butterfly) and about Sharky's vast VHS videotape collection (specifically a bootleg tape called *Acts of the Unspeakable*).

When Brenda and I finally got up and began to leave at 2:00 A.M., we noticed that Sharky had an apple green zoot suit hanging on the back side of his front door. The suit was small (I would estimate the inseam of the pants as somewhere in the vicinity of twenty-four inches), but it remained in remarkably good condition. So just before we left, we asked Sharky why he had this apple green zoot suit.

This is what Sharky told us:

Several weeks previous, it seems, Sharky had been walking home from a downtown Fargo tavern at a little past midnight. As he left the bar, a little old man wearing an ascot suddenly emerged from the shadows and stopped Sharky on the sidewalk.

"Would you like this suit?" the little man inquired, holding the outfit in Sharky's direction.

"Why would I want your suit?" Sharky replied.

"I have to get rid of my clothes," said the man. "It's free. There's nothing wrong with it. I just need to get rid of it."

"Why?"

"What difference does it make to you? There's nothing wrong with this suit."

Sharky examined the garment.

"It looks small," said Sharky.

"Well, it's a free suit! If you don't want it, just say you don't want it." The little man grew agitated. "You know, you're not the only person in this city who I can give this suit to."

Somehow, this logic worked on Sharky: he accepted the offer. The little old man thanked him curtly and disappeared. Sharky continued on his way home, his right index finger around the claw of the metal hanger and the green zoot suit slung over his right shoulder.

Three blocks later, two police cars suddenly pulled up alongside him and turned on their flashers. This made Sharky understandably nervous, as he was holding six ounces of pot in his pants (and he was drunk, and he had smoked two joints in the bathroom of the bar). However, his nervousness changed to confusion as soon as one of the cops began questioning him.

"Is that guy back there selling suits out of the trunk of his car?" asked the cop.

"What?" Sharky replied quizzically.

"You know exactly what we're talking about," said the policeman. "That old man you were just talking to. Is he—or is he not—selling suits out of the trunk of his car?"

"I don't understand this question," said Sharky.

"Is that guy selling suits out of the trunk of his car? Yes or no?"

"Well, I don't think he's selling suits out of the trunk of his car. Maybe he is, but I don't think that's the case." Sharky was now recalibrating his reality. "I mean, I don't think he even has a car, you know? He just gave me this suit for free."

"Why would he do that?" asked the officer.

"I'm not sure. That was my question, too. I didn't even want this suit, really."

"Then why did you take it?"

"Because . . . well, you know. Free suit."

"So you just take clothes from people you don't know?" asked the policeman. "Does this happen to you a lot?"

"No!"

"And you did not pay him for this suit?"

"No. He just gave it to me. I don't *think* he's selling suits out of the trunk of his car. I really don't. You should arrest him if that's the case, I suppose, but I don't *think* he's selling suits to anyone."

Quite suddenly, the police officer's social posture completely changed. "Well, okay then. Sorry to bother you. We just had some reports that an older gentleman was selling vintage apparel on the street. It must be somebody else. Sorry. We really apologize for hassling you."

"Oh, no problem," said Sharky, now relieved (but still confused). "And actually, that description sounds a lot like the guy who gave me this suit. Do you need this suit as evidence? You can take it if you want."

"No, no," said the cop. "Keep it. You should take a free suit if you can get it."

The officer got back in his car, and both police vehicles left the scene. Sharky walked the two blocks to his building, hobbled up the flight of wooden stairs to his $90 apartment, hung the green zoot suit on the inside of his door, and went to bed.

When he woke up the next morning, he saw the suit on the door and realized that this had not been a dream. That realization completely blew his mind, so he decided to immediately smoke more dope and not leave his apartment for the remainder of the day. Which is why he missed work, which is how he got fired from his job at the bakery, which happened to be located directly below his apartment.

And this is probably why Sharky was unemployed.

III. NO LOVE 'TIL LEATHER (UNKNOWN CIRCUMSTANCES)

True story[1]: I recently spent an afternoon with rapper 50 Cent, shopping for bulletproof vests in SoHo's famed Kevlar District. It's hard to find a stylish bulletproof garment these days, so we ended up going to a wide variety of stores. On impulse, I purchased fourteen pairs of leather pants. This proved mildly ironic, because when we jumped into my SUV and flipped on the satellite radio, we heard the song "Look Good in Leather" by upstart recording artist Cody ChesnuTT. 50 and I both enjoyed a good laugh over this synchronicity. Then I shot him in the face. He thinks getting shot is fun! What a cad. I love pants shopping with that dude.

Here's the thing about the leather pants, though: they give me the heebie-jeebies. My pants make me nervous. And the reason they make me nervous is because successfully wearing leather pants is indisputable proof that you have no friends. This isn't always true for women, but it's completely true for men. If you're a man and you're wearing a pair of leather pants at this very moment and everyone around you seems completely cool with that reality, I'm afraid I have some bad news: you will die alone.

For decades, leather pants have been essential to rock 'n' roll—yet every man who has ever worn them has faced an existence of utter loneliness. Elvis Presley wore leather pants and was surrounded by sycophants and opportunists; Jim Morrison wore leather pants and was surrounded by drug dealers and hippies; Sebastian Bach wore leather pants and was surrounded by Skid Row. If you have the ability to effectively wear leather pants in public, you immediately have the potential to become a cultural icon . . . but you can't have

---

1. This is not a true story.

friends. Because if you did, they would all insist that you look ridiculous, even if you didn't.

Think of your closest male friend. Now, imagine if he wore leather pants. Can you foresee any scenario where you wouldn't mock him until he cried? As a friend, that is pretty much your singular vocation. If there was going to be a nuclear war and the missiles of obliteration were swooping down from the pre-apocalyptic sky, and (for some reason) I had only ten minutes to see my best friend for the final time, and my friend (for some reason) showed up to Armageddon wearing leather pants, those pants are the only thing I would talk about. Ridiculing his pants would consume me, even if they made him look like Basil Rathbone. But desperate loners like Lou Reed and Vince Neil and Prince do not have friends like me; they have no friends at all. Nobody loves them enough to tell them how stupid they look, even during a nuclear attack. Their insincere posses would just say things like, "North Korea's arbitrary decision to incinerate our society is tragic, but I still think *Emancipation* was the most underrated triple album of 1996. You rule."

You want proof? Here's my proof: after I dropped 50 Cent off at the emergency room's heliport, I drove my imaginary SUV to band practice. As many of you already know, I've recently joined forces with Turkish bass legend Hasad Yonca Claypool. We've started a band called Apocalypse Later. Our influences derive from several genres (rap, metal, rap-metal, etc.), and we've been trying to start a rivalry with System of a Down by publicly denying the Armenian genocide. Just to see what would happen, I put on a pair of leather trousers and walked into our LoHo rehearsal space while the band was cutting into our first single, a blistering bomb track we like to call "Istanbul Rock City." And you know what? Hasad didn't even blink. He just lowered his ill-shaven jowls and kept on rocking. And that was when I knew he could not be trusted, and when I realized that he was not my true friend. He accepted my pants; therefore, he did not accept me. I broke up the band immediately, citing creative differences, which is partially true (I felt our sound should have been closer to Linkin Park's *Hybrid Theory,* while Hasad's artistic sensibilities were more akin to Linkin Park's remix album *Reanimation*). However, those who know me "intimately" will admit that mere musical loggerheads did not end our unblessed union; it was ended by leather. It was really about the pants.

Ultimately, it always is.

—The Believer, 2005
—Other People's Stories
—SPIN, 2002

Q: You have been wrongly accused of a horrific crime: Due to a bizarre collision of unfortunate circumstances and insane coincidences, it appears that you have murdered a prominent U.S. senator, his beautiful young wife, and both of their infant children. Now, *you did not do this,* but you are indicted and brought to trial.

Predictably, the criminal proceedings are a national sensation (on par with the 1994 O. J. Simpson trial). It's on television constantly, and it's the lead story in most newspapers for almost a year. The prosecuting attorney is a charming genius; sadly, your defense team lacks creativity and panache. To make matters worse, the jury is a collection of easily confused sheep. You are found guilty and sentenced to four consecutive life terms with virtually no hope for parole (and—since there were no procedural mistakes during the proceedings—an appeal is hopeless).

This being the case, you are (obviously) disappointed.

However, as you leave the courtroom (and in the days immediately following the verdict), something becomes clear: the "court of public opinion" has overwhelmingly found you innocent. Over 95 percent of the country believes you are not guilty. Noted media personalities have declared this scenario "the ultimate legal tragedy." So you are going to spend the rest of your life amidst the general population of a maximum-security prison . . . but you are innocent, and everyone seems to know this.

Does this knowledge make you feel (a) better, (b) no different, or (c) worse?

DON'T LOOK BACK IN ANGER

In 1989, my favorite television show was *The Wonder Years.* This was because *The Wonder Years* was the only TV program that allowed me to be nostalgic at the age of seventeen; when you haven't even been alive for two decades, it's hard to find media experiences that provide opportunities to reminisce about the past. One of the things I particularly loved about *The Wonder Years* was Kevin Arnold's incessant concern over the manner in which certain people liked him. (This person was usually Winnie Cooper, but also Becky Slater and Madeline Adams.) The core question was always the same: Did these girls "like him," or did they "*like him* like him." And Kevin's plight begs some larger queries that apply to virtually every other aspect of being alive, especially for an American in the twenty-first century. How important, ultimately, is *likability*? Is being likable the most important quality someone can possess, or is it the most inherently shallow quality anyone can desire? Do we *need* to be liked, or do we merely *want* to be liked?

I started rethinking Kevin Arnold's quest for likability while I was reading *The New York Times* on the day after Christmas.

On the back page of the *Times*'s "Year in Review" section, there was a graphic that attempted to quantify a phenomenon countless people have discussed over the past three years—the decline in how much other countries "like" the United States. The *Times* printed a poll comparing how the international opinion of America (in a general sense) evolved between May of 2003 and March of 2004. The results were close to what you'd likely anticipate. In March of 2003, 70 percent of British citizens viewed the U.S. in a manner they described as "favorable." That number had dropped to 58 percent by March of '04. In Germany, the "favorable" designation fell from 45 percent to 38 percent over the same time span; in France, 43 to 37. Interestingly (and perhaps predictably), America is now *more* popular in places like Turkey and Jordan (in Jordan, the percentage of people who saw the U.S. as "very unfavorable" used to be 83 percent, but now that number is down to 67).

The explanation behind these figures, I suppose, is rather obvious; many nations—particularly European ones—don't like America's military policy, so they subsequently don't like America. Meanwhile, countries with a vested interest in America's occupation of Iraq and Afghanistan have started to like us more. This became a hot issue during the election, as ardent John Kerry supporters insisted that George W. Bush needed to lose his reelection bid because "other countries hate us now." Yet the more I think about this point, the more I find that argument to be patently ridiculous. There are easily a thousand valid reasons why Bush shouldn't be president, but how other nations feel about America is not one of them. Americans allow other nations to exercise the kind of sweeping ethnocentrism we would never accept among ourselves.

There are 1.3 billion people in China. We are generally taught to assume that most of these 1.3 billion people are nice, and that they are hardworking, and that they produce their share of handsome low-post NBA athletes who pass out of the double-team exceptionally well. However, these 1.3 billion people also have a problem we're all keenly aware of; these 1.3 billion people are governed by an administration that has a propensity for violating human rights. As Americans, we are philosophically against this practice. But if someone were to say, "Hey, have you heard about those human rights violations in rural Beijing? I fucking hate the Chinese!" we would immediately assume said person was a close-minded troglodyte (who would be hating the same people who are having their human rights violated).

From a very young age, we are taught that people are not all the same, and that it's wrong to hate whole countries based on specific stereotypes. Remember that "freedom fries" fiasco that was supposed to illustrate our anti-French sentiment before we went to war with Iraq? Do you recall how every intellectual in America decried that practice as idiotic? The reason intellectuals made that decree was because this practice *was* idiotic. No intelligent American took that kind of childish symbolism seriously. It made no sense to hate France (or potatoes) simply because the French had a different for-

255

eign policy than the United States, and any conventional liberal would have told you that. But what's so confusing is that those same left-leaning people are the Americans most concerned about the possibility of France *not liking us*, or of the British *liking us less*, or of the Netherlands *thinking we're uncouth*. These are the same kind of people who travel from New York to Ireland and proceed to tell strangers in Dublin that they're actually from Canada. They lie because they are afraid someone might not like them on principle. But why should we care if shortsighted people in other countries are as stupid as the shortsighted rednecks in America?

I can totally understand why someone in Paris or London or Berlin might not like the president; I don't like the president, either. But don't these people read the newspaper? It's not like Bush ran unopposed. Over 57 million people voted against him. Moreover, half of this country doesn't vote at all; they just happen to live here. So if someone hates the entire concept of America—or even if someone *likes* the concept of America—based solely on his or her disapproval (or support) of some specific U.S. policy, that person doesn't know much about how the world works. It would be no different than someone in Idaho hating all of Brazil, simply because their girlfriend slept with some dude who happened to speak Portuguese.

In the days following the election, I kept seeing links to Web sites like www.sorryeverybody.com, which offered a photo of a bearded idiot holding up a piece of paper that apologized to the rest of the planet for the election of George W. Bush. I realize the person who designed this Web site was probably doing so to be clever, and I suspect his motivations were either (a) mostly good or (b) mostly self-serving. But all I could think when I saw it was, *This is so pathetic*. It's like the guy on this Web site is actually afraid some anonymous stranger in Tokyo might not unconditionally love him (and for reasons that have nothing to do with either of them). Sometimes it seems like most of American culture has become a thirteen-year-old boy who wants to be popular *so much* and wants to go to the

Snowball Dance *so bad* and is just *so worried* about his reputation among a bunch of self-interested classmates whose support is wholly dependent on how much candy he shares.

Now, I am not saying that I'm somehow happy when people in other countries blindly dislike America. It's just that I'm not happy if they love us, either. I don't think it matters. The kind of European who hates the United States in totality is exactly like the kind of American who hates Europe in totality; both people are unsophisticated, and their opinions aren't valid. But our society will never get over this fear; there will always be people in this country who are devastated by the premise of foreigners hating Americans in a macro sense. And I'm starting to think that's because too many Americans are dangerously obsessed with being liked.

We're like a nation of Kevin Arnolds; being likable is the only thing that seems to matter to anyone. You see this everywhere. Parents don't act like parents anymore, because they mainly want their kids to like them; they want their kids to see them as their two best friends. This is why modern kids act like animals. At some point, people confused being *liked* with being *good*. Those two qualities are not the same. It's important to be a good person; it's not important to be a well-liked person. It's important to be a good country; it's not important to be a well-liked country. And I realize there are problems with America, and I'm not necessarily sure if the United States is a good place or a bad place. But the reality behind those problems has no relationship to whether or not France (or Turkey, or Winnie Cooper) thinks we're cool. They can like us, they can *like us* like us, or they can hate us. But that is their problem, not ours.

—*Esquire*, 2005

Q: You are offered a Brain Pill. If you swallow this pill, you will become 10 percent more intelligent than you currently are; you will be more adept at reading comprehension, logic, and critical thinking. However, to all other people you know (and to all future people you meet), you will seem 20 percent *less* intelligent. In other words, you will immediately become smarter, but the rest of the world will perceive you as dumber (and there is no way you can ever alter the universality of that perception).

Do you take this pill?

NOT GUILTY

Every so often, I look at the condition of the world and I suspect that the most widespread problem we have is the ever-growing sentiment of anti-intellectualism that seems to infiltrate everything, particularly politics (where intelligent candidates are attacked for being intelligent) and advertising (where everything is designed to convince smart people they'll be happier once they agree to become dumb). However, this is something I'm wrong about; anti-intellectualism is a dangerous problem, but it's not as annoying as *pretend* intellectualism, which inevitably manifests itself as antipopulism. Which is why I always want to blow up my brain whenever I hear people talking about "guilty pleasures."

I am not sure if anyone actually invented the term "guilty pleasure," since—in and of itself—it seems like a reasonable way to describe certain activities. For example, it is pleasurable to snort cocaine in public restrooms, and it always makes you feel guilty; as such, lavatory cocaine fits perfectly into this category. Drinking more than five glasses of vodka before (or during) work generally qualifies as a guilty pleasure. This is also true for having sex with people you barely know, having sex with people you actively hate, and/or having sex with people you barely know but whom your girlfriend used to live with during college (and will now subsequently hate). These are all guilty pleasures *in a technical sense*. However, almost no one who uses the term "guilty pleasure" is referring to situations like these; people who use the term "guilty pleasure" in casual conversation are often talking about why they like Patrick Swayze's *Road House*. This drives me insane for two reasons: by labeling things like Patrick Swayze as guilty pleasures, it somehow dictates that (a) people should feel bad for liking things they sincerely enjoy, and (b) if these same people were not somehow coerced into watching *Road House* every time it comes on TBS, they'd just as likely be reading *A Portrait of the Artist as a Young Man*.

Both of these principles are wrong.

Though I could be wrong about this, I think *Entertainment Weekly* semi-accidentally started all this way back in the twentieth century with a "Guilty Pleasures" issue. At least initially, this was a charming idea. It was mainly a way for them to write about things that would normally be nonsensical to cover, and it dovetailed nicely with the primary cultural obsession of all people born between the years of 1968 and 1980 (i.e., comedic nostalgia for the extremely recent past). *Entertainment Weekly* still does this feature annually, although now they just try to pick crazy shit to confuse soccer moms in Omaha (I question whether any contemporary person derives pleasure from—or feels guilty about—Mr. Rogers's puppet-saturated Neighborhood of Make-Believe, which *EW* inexplicably included in their 2003 installment). What's more troubling are things like *The Encyclopedia of Guilty Pleasures: 1,001 Things You Hate to Love*. Ostensibly a reference guide for those who want to feel embarrassed about being engaged with life, *The Encyclopedia of Guilty Pleasures* is a compilation of everything that's been popular over the past fifty years to normal people, augmented by short essays about why we can't help but adore these terrible, terrible things. These are things like Michael Jackson's *Thriller*, an album that was (1) produced by Quincy Jones, (2) features guitar playing by Eddie Van Halen, (3) includes at least three singles that ooze with awesomeness, and (4) has the single best bass line from the entire 1980s (i.e., the opening of "Billie Jean"). It is a "guilty pleasure," presumably, because 45 million people liked it, and because Jackson is quite possibly a pedophile, and because two dancers had a really unfair knife fight[1] in the video for "Beat It." This is akin to considering Thomas Jefferson a "guilty pleasure" among presidents because he briefly owned a pet bear. I mean, he still wrote the fucking Declaration of Independence, you know?

The failure of *The Encyclopedia of Guilty Pleasures* is its never-explained premise, which is that there are certain things we're just supposed to inherently feel shame about. For example, I have absolutely no idea why anyone would be ashamed to like Evel Knievel (page 144); he is an iconic symbol from a specific period of Americana, and he serves as a metaphor for what a lot of people valued in 1976. He also broke thirty-five bones, went to jail for beating a man with a baseball bat, and consciously named himself Evel. He's not cool in a guilty context; he's cool in *every* context. This book suggests there should be guilt associated with the appreciation of prison films (page 216). This makes no sense whatsoever. I feel more guilt when *Cool Hand Luke* is on television and I *don't* watch it. And why are "gumball machines" (page 114) possibly indicted in this phenomenon? It's not just that I don't have guilty feelings about gumball machines—I have no opinion *at all* about gumball machines (except on those rare occasions when I have a pocket full of change and I actively

_____

1. Here's why the knife fight was rigged: if you recall, the two gang members in the video had their wrists tied together before they started trying to slice each other up. However, the white guy with the striped shirt has his right wrist tied, and the black guy in the white suit has his left wrist tied. So—unless one of these dudes was a southpaw—this situation is patently unfair.

want to chew on a spherical chunk of gum—then I'm briefly and staunchly "pro–gumball machine," I suppose).

What the authors of *The Encyclopedia of Guilty Pleasures* (and everyone else who uses this term) fail to realize is that the only people who believe in some kind of "universal taste"—in other words, a consensual demarcation between what's artistically good and what's artistically bad—are insecure, uncreative elitists who need to use somebody else's art to validate their own limited worldview. It never matters *what* you like; what matters is *why you like it.* Take, for example, the aforementioned *Road House.* This is a movie I love. But I don't love it because it's bad; I love it because it's interesting in a very specific way. Outside the genre of sci-fi, I can't think of any film less plausible than *Road House.* Every element of the story is preposterous: the idea of Swayze being a nationally famous bouncer (with a degree in philosophy), the concept of such a superviolent bar having such an attractive clientele, the likelihood of a tiny Kansas town having such a sophisticated hospital, the authenticity of ripping another man's throat out, etc. etc. etc. Every single scene includes at least one detail that could never happen in real life. So does that make *Road House* bad? No. It makes *Road House* perfect. Because *Road House* exists in a parallel reality that is more fanciful (and more watchable) than *Lord of the Rings.* The characters in *Road House* live within the mythology of rural legend while grappling against exaggerated moral dilemmas and neoclassical archetypes. I don't feel guilty for liking any of that. *Road House* also includes a monster truck. I don't feel guilty for liking that, either.

But let's say I did.

Let's assume—just for a moment—that I was somehow humiliated by the fact that I watch *The Ashlee Simpson Show.* Which is something I do, almost every week; I think it's a fascinating illustration of what's wrong with young people, how the music industry operates, and how modern celebrities aspire to view themselves. But let's pretend this wasn't the case. Let's say I considered this program a "guilty pleasure," and let's say my desire to watch Ashlee explain how her boyfriend ruined Valentine's Day was something I needed to apologize for. Wouldn't this imply that *The Ashlee Simpson Show* was my conscious alternative to something better? Wouldn't this suggest that—were I not watching *The Ashlee Simpson Show*—I would be working on logarithms, or studying the liner notes to out-of-print Thelonious Monk records, or searching for factual errors in *The Economist*? Because these are not things I do (and I don't think many of the other 2.9 million people watching Ashlee Simpson each week do these things, either). We're not losing the cure for cancer because of Ashlee Simpson; if we weren't watching her pretend to be sexy, we'd probably just be going to the bar earlier.

Voltaire once argued that every man is guilty of all the good he didn't do, and I suppose he had a point: if I spent as much time analyzing al Qaeda as I've spent deconstructing Toby Keith's video for "Whiskey Girl," we probably would have won the war on terrorism last April. However, this is nothing to celebrate or bemoan; it's kind of my own fault, and it's kind of no one's fault. These things that give us pleasure— they are guilty of nothing. And neither are we.

—*Esquire*, 2004

Q: You begin watching a new television series, and you immediately find yourself strongly relating to one of the supporting characters. You've never before experienced a TV character that seems so similar to yourself; this fictional person dresses, behaves, and talks exactly like you. And—slowly, over the course of several episodes—the similarity grows spooky: on two separate occasions, the character recounts personal anecdotes that happened in your real life. The actor portraying this character begins mimicking your mannerisms. In at least three different episodes, the character's dialogue quotes things that you have said (verbatim) during casual conversation.

You become convinced that this is neither coincidence nor mental illness: somehow, this character is being actively based on your life. The show's writers generally depict the "you" character in a positive manner, but—as far as you can tell—you don't know anyone involved in the show's production or creation. It's totally inexplicable.

You have two friends who also watch this show. One of them is certain that your theory is correct and that (somehow) the character is, in fact, based on your life. She tells you to get a lawyer. The second friend concedes that many of the similarities are amazing, but that the whole notion is ridiculous, impossible, and egocentric. He tells you to see a therapist.

How do you respond to this situation? Do you do anything?

CULTURAL BETRAYAL

"If I had to choose between betraying my country or betraying my friend," semi-known British essayist Edward M. Forster once wrote, "I hope I should have the guts to betray my country." This quote teaches us a lot, particularly that dead British essayists made for good drinking buddies and horrible spies. But Forster's sentiment is certainly worth considering. There is no feeling worse than the feeling of betrayal; it is the most soul pulverizing of human sensations. However, what's been on my mind as of late is the inverse of Forster's quote, which is actually more of a question: What depresses *you* more—being "betrayed" by an individual or being "betrayed" by your own society? Because I hear people complaining about the latter situation constantly, and I can't understand why. I can't understand how people can feel "betrayed" by culture, yet this seems to happen all the time.

I recently had a conversation with someone about the now-defunct TV series *Sex and the City*, a program I never actually watched (every time I tried, all I saw were four peculiar-looking women pretending to talk like gay guys). However, *Sex and the City* was one of those shows you didn't need to watch in order to follow. I had a general idea of what it was supposed to be about (sex, cities, whatnot), so I felt like I could have a reasonable conversation about what it represented. My associate, however, loved this show; she was deconstructing the final episode of the series, where Sarah Jessica Parker got married to someone named "Chris Noth." The reason the show concluded this way, I suspect, is so stupid people would get a happy ending. But to my associate, this conclusion was an atrocity. She said she felt betrayed by the ending, and she literally used the word *betrayed* while discussing this plot twist (she felt Parker's character should have remained independent, which would have matched her vision of what *Sex and the City* was supposed to represent).

Even though I had no real context for why she felt this way, I found the sentiment fascinating: Why, I wondered, do people so often feel *let down* by popular culture? Why do serious film fans feel disgusted when another stock Tom Hanks movie earns $200 million? Why do record store employees get angry when a band like Comets on Fire come to town and only twenty-two people pay to see them? Why do highly literate people get depressed when they look at *The New York Times*

Best Sellers list, and why do anti-intellectuals feel contempt for critics who suggest *The Da Vinci Code* is consciously targeted at dumb people? Why do nonreligious people think that the Christian Right shouldn't have a voice in government? Why do conservatives get angry about the prospect of gay marriage, even if they've never met a gay person and never will? There's always this peculiar disconnect between how people exist in the world and how they think the world is supposed to exist; it's almost as if Americans can't accept an important truth about being alive. And this is the truth to which I refer: culture can't be wrong. That doesn't mean it's always "right," nor does it mean you always have to agree with it. But culture is never wrong. People can be wrong, and movements can be wrong. But culture—as a whole—cannot be wrong. Culture is just *there*.

Almost a decade ago, I was browsing in a Barnes & Noble when I came across a book called *Route 666: On the Road to Nirvana*. It was a music book about a band I liked, so I started paging through it immediately. What I remember are two sentences on the fourth page which discussed how awesome it was that "Smells Like Teen Spirit" was on the radio, and how this was almost akin to America electing a new president: "It's not that everything will change at once," wrote the author, "it's that at least the people have voted for better principles. Nirvana's being on the radio means my own values are winning: I'm no longer in the opposition." I have never forgotten those two sentences, and there are two reasons why this memory has stuck with me. The first reason is that this was just about the craziest, scariest idea I'd ever stumbled across. The second reason, however, is way worse; what I have slowly come to realize is that *most people think this way all the time*. They don't merely want to *hold* their values; they want their values *to win*. And I suspect this is why people so often feel "betrayed" by art and consumerism, and by the way the world works. I'm sure the author of *Route 666* felt completely "betrayed" when Limp Bizkit and Matchbox 20 became superfamous five years after Cobain's death and she was forced to return to "the opposition" (whatever that entails—complaining about Clear Channel, I suppose). If you feel betrayed by culture, it's not because you're right and the universe is fucked; it's only because you're not like most other people. But this should make you happy, because—in all likelihood—you hate those other people, anyway. You are being betrayed by a culture that has no relationship to who you are or how you live.

Do you want to be happy? I suspect that you do. Well, here's the first step to happiness: don't get pissed off that people who aren't you happen to think Paris Hilton is interesting and deserves to be on TV every other day; the fame surrounding Paris Hilton is not a reflection on your life (unless you want it to be). Don't get pissed off because the Yeah Yeah Yeahs aren't on the radio enough; you can buy the goddamn record and play "Maps" all goddamn day (if that's what you want). Don't get pissed off because people didn't vote the way you voted; you knew this was a democracy when you agreed to participate, so you knew this was how things might work out. Basically, don't get pissed off over the fact that the way you feel about culture isn't some kind of universal consensus. Because if you do, you will end up feeling betrayed. And it will be your own fault. You will feel bad, and you will deserve it.

Now, it's quite possible you disagree with me on this issue. And if you do, I know what your argument is: you're thinking, *But I'm idealistic.* This is what people who want to inflict their values on other people always think; they think that there is some kind of romantic, respectable aura that insulates the inflexible, and that their disappointment with culture latently proves that they're tragically trapped by their own intellect and good taste. Somehow, they think their sense of betrayal gives them integrity. It does not. If you really have integrity—if you truly live by your ideals, and those ideals dictate how you engage with the world at large—you will never feel betrayed by culture. You will simply enjoy culture more. You won't necessarily start watching syndicated episodes of *Everybody Loves Raymond*, but you will find it interesting that certain people do. You won't suddenly agree that *Amélie* was a more emotive movie than *Friday Night Lights*, but you won't feel alienated and offended if every film critic you read tells you that it is. You will care, but you won't care.

You're not wrong, and neither is the rest of the world. But you need to accept that those two things aren't really connected.

—*Esquire*, 2005

Q: If given the choice, would you rather (a) only abide by the rules and morals of society that you personally agree with, or (b) have the power to *slightly* adjust the rules and morals that currently exist (but these adjustments would then apply to you *and everyone else*, all the time).

MONOGAMY

Today we begin with a hypothetical scenario, that—on its surface—may seem to have a straightforward, obvious, undeniable answer. However, this question raises a larger point about everything we pretend to understand about relationships, and particularly what we assume we understand about monogamy (and where monogamy technically begins). So while your answer to this question might seem unambiguous, the criteria you use to reach the conclusion are generally more important. In other words, what you say doesn't matter as much as *why* you choose to say it.

The scenario is called "The Jack and Jane Hypothetical," and is as follows:

Let's say you have two friends named Jack and Jane. They have been romantically involved for two years, and the relationship has always been good. Suddenly, Jack calls you on the phone and sadly mutters, "Jane just broke up with me." You ask why this happened. Jack says, "She thinks I cheated on her." You ask, "Well, did you?" Jack says, "I'm not sure. Something strange happened."

This is what Jack proceeds to tell you:

"There is this woman in my apartment building

271

who I barely know," he begins. "I've seen her in the hallway a few times, and we'd just sort of nodded our hellos. She is very normal looking, neither attractive nor unattractive. Last week, I came home from the bar very drunk, and—while I was getting my mail—I ran into her at the mailboxes. She was also intoxicated. Just to be neighborly, we decided to go to her apartment to have one more beer. But because we were drunk, the conversation was very loose and slightly flirtatious. And then this woman suddenly tells me that she has a bizarre sexual quirk: she can only have an orgasm if a man watches her masturbate. This struck me as fascinating, so I started asking questions about why this was. And then—somehow—it just sort of happened. I never touched her and I never kissed her, but I ended up watching this woman masturbate. And then I went home and went to bed. And I told Jane about this a few days later, mostly because it was all so weird. But Jane went fucking insane when I told her this, and she angrily said our relationship was over. Now she won't even return my calls."

Whose side do you take, Jack's or Jane's?

I have posed this question to myriad people, and the reactions are all vaguely similar. Women almost always think Jane's rage is completely valid; men generally inquire about the availability of housing in Jack's hypothetical building. Women usually agree that this offense warrants a breakup, while many men think it merely warrants a tenure in the doghouse. But what's noteworthy is that—while almost everyone agrees that Jack did something wrong—everyone uses a staunchly different, weirdly personal argument to justify what makes it so bad. It raises innumerable questions. I mean, how different is this than watching porn? How different is this than getting a lap dance? Is this situation worse than if Jack had drunkenly *kissed* his neighbor? Would it make any difference if the neighbor had been behind a glass partition?

Many people point to the "intimacy" of the exchange—but if that's the case, the conversation preceding the episode seems as troublesome as the masturbation itself. And if Jack honestly saw this encounter as "weird" (as opposed to "erotic"), shouldn't he be forgiven completely? Isn't he just being penalized for being curious?

This is why the "Jack and Jane Scenario" is such a good hypothetical. The core question really isn't, "Whose side do you take?" The true question is, "Where, exactly, does cheating begin?"

I just watched a documentary on Cinemax called *Love & Cheating*, and it mostly consists of average couples talking about the complexity of their sex lives. The crux of the program asks if monogamy is still relevant, and the answer is (essentially) "maybe not." One of the statistics cited in *Love & Cheating* is that in the year 1900, the average life expectancy was forty-seven years and the average marriage lasted twelve years; in 2000, the average life expectancy was seventy-seven years, but the average marriage lasted only seven. To some "sexperts," this indicates that monogamy can't compete with the modern lifespan; perhaps we simply live too long to realistically anticipate staying with any one individual. And maybe this is true. Maybe it would be easier to remain faithful to your spouse if you both assumed you'd get typhoid before turning fifty. But this is reverse engineering; in fact, this kind of logic is probably why so many people have affairs (and why modern marriages last only seven years). What this argument indicates is that it's mathematically *unreasonable* to be monogamous. And that, I think, is probably where cheating begins. It's not about physical contact or emotional intimacy; it begins the moment anyone decides that it is *unreasonable* to be sexually committed to one person. Once a man or woman comes to that conclusion, it doesn't matter what they do (or don't do). If they are a reasonable person—and if they truly think remaining monogamous is inherently *unreasonable*—you have to assume the only reason they're not sleeping with other people is because (a) they can't find anyone else to sleep with, or (b) they're afraid they'll get caught. And these are—without question—the two main hurdles that stop people from being unfaithful.

I recall drinking brandy with a friend who was in the early stages of dating an absolutely gorgeous nurse. She was a hardworking blonde who loved to throw back tequila shots, dance to Trick Daddy, and bake cookies on the weekend; we agreed that she was close to ideal. Yet my friend was certain that this romance was never going to work out, and I couldn't understand why. "What singular quality would this woman need to make this relationship a success?" I asked. He answered immediately: "The ability to be nine other women." This struck me as dangerously self-aware. My friend just didn't think it was *reasonable* to stay with any one person, regardless of her merit. When people cheat, it has almost nothing to do with who they're with or who they potentially want; it just has to do with whether they view their fidelity as a realistic way to exist. And people are amazingly flexible about this. It is easy to be ethical when you're single, but much harder when you are not.

When I was in my twenties, I figured something out: if you are a weird-looking dude (which I am) and you want to date exclusively beautiful women (which I did), the key is to pursue beautiful women who are already in relationships. Let's say you live in Omaha, and you meet a hot single woman who is actively dating lots of different guys. In order to win her affection, you have to be more desirable than every other single guy in Omaha. It's you against everybody. However, let's say you meet a hot woman who is dating Kenneth, a hardworking Nebraskan haberdasher. This situation is way, *way* easier; now, you merely have to be more desirable than Kenneth. It's you against him. However, what I've slowly come to realize is that I was not convincing these women to like *me*, which is what I thought at the time; I was merely convincing them that staying faithful to Kenneth (or to any one person) was *unreasonable*. I wasn't seducing them in any real context. I was simply eroding their morality.

We all have our regrets, I suppose.

But here is the bottom line: motivation is everything. Wanting to cheat on someone and failing is no different than actually doing so, and the *reason* something happens is way more important than the action itself. This is why watching your neighbor masturbate is not necessarily a reason to break up, particularly if you were drunk and merely trying to get to your mail. And if you disagree with this, you're just being unreasonable.

—*Esquire*, 2005

Q: You are placed in the unenviable position of having to compete for the right to stay alive.

You will be matched against a person of your own gender in a series of five events—an 800-meter run, a game of Scrabble, a three-round boxing match, a debate over the legalization of late-term abortion (scored and officiated by reputable collegiate judges), and the math portion of the SAT.

In order to survive, you must win at least three of these events (your opponent will be playing for his or her life as well). However, you (kind of) get to pick your opponent: you can either (a) compete against a person selected at random, or (b) you can compete against someone who is exactly like you. If selected at random, the individual could be of any age or skill level—he/she might be an infant with Down syndrome, but he/she might also be an Academic All-American linebacker from Notre Dame. If you pick "the average human," he/she will be precisely your age and will have an identical level of education, and the person will be a perfect cross-section of your particular demographic—he/she will be of average height and of average weight, with a standard IQ and the most normative life experience imaginable.

So whom do you select? Or—perhaps more accurately—do you feel that you are better than an average version of yourself?

CERTAIN ROCK BANDS
YOU PROBABLY LIKE

If you are the kind of person who talks about music too much, there are two words that undoubtedly play an integral role in your day-to-day lexicon: *overrated* and *underrated*. This is because those two sentiments constitute 90 percent of all musical discussions; people are constantly discussing who they think is overrated and who they think is underrated.

What's interesting about this phenomenon is the way no one seems to use the same criteria for either of those terms. For example, a band can be classified as overrated because they sell more records than a certain logic might dictate (Creed, 311, Bad Company), or they can be overrated because certain rock critics seem to like them too much (Sonic Youth, Wilco, Yo La Tengo). Artists can be underrated if they sell a lot of records but aren't widely regarded as brilliant (Thin Lizzy, Duran Duran), or they can be underrated because almost no one in the world seems to know who they are (Tortoise, Sloan, Lifter Puller). Bands can be overrated if they're canonized as indisputably great when they're only very good (U2, Madonna, the Eagles), and artists can be underrated if everyone thinks they're terrible when they're actually okay (Limp Bizkit, No Doubt, and—once again—Creed). Bands can be overrated because they're good-looking (the Lemonheads in 1993), or they can be underrated because they're good-looking (the Lemonheads in 1994). Some groups can be overrated and underrated at the same time (Radiohead). Some groups seem overrated on purpose (Oasis). Some groups seem eternally underrated because—no matter how hard they try— they're just not as interesting as groups who are overrated on purpose (Blur). It is very easy to be underrated, because all you need to do is nothing. Everyone wants to be underrated. It's harder to become overrated, because that means someone has to think you were awesome before they thought you sucked. Nobody wants to be overrated, except for people who like to live in big houses.

But I am not interested in overrated and underrated bands.

That argument is too easy, and all it means is that somebody else was wrong. I'm far more interested in "rated" bands. I'm obsessed with bands who are rated as accurately as possible—in other words, nobody thinks they're better than they actually are, and nobody thinks they're worse.

They have the acceptable level of popularity, they have attained the correct amount of critical acclaim, and no one is confused about their cultural significance. They are, in essence . . .

THE TEN MOST ACCURATELY RATED ARTISTS IN ROCK HISTORY!

10. The Black Crowes: Their first album sold five million copies, which is precisely the right number. Stoned people like this band, drunk people think they're okay, and sober people disregard the overwhelming majority of their catalogue. This all makes perfect sense. By all possible standards, the Black Crowes are rated accurately.

9. Madness: This is one of only two ska bands admired by people who hate ska (the other being the Specials, who are overrated). Nobody disputes this admiration. "Our House" was a pretty great single, but it's nobody's *favorite* song; nobody seems to dispute that assertion, either.

8. Triumph: Always associated with Rush and/or the nation of Canada, but not as good as either.

7. Tone-Lōc: Hardly anyone takes Tone-Lōc seriously, except for frivolous pop historians who like to credit him for making suburban white kids listen to rap music that was made by black people (as opposed to the Beastie Boys, who made white suburban kids listen to rap music that was made by nonsuburban white kids). This lukewarm historical significance strikes me as sensible. Neither of Mr. Lōc's hits are timeless, although "Wild Thing" samples Van Halen's "Jamie's Cryin'" (which I like to imagine is about *M*A*S*H* star Jamie Farr, had Corporal Klinger pursued sexual-reassignment surgery in an attempt to get a Section 8) and "Funky Cold Medina" samples "Christine Sixteen" (at a time when KISS was making records like *Hot in the Shade* and nobody in

America thought they were cool except for me and Rivers Cuomo). Those two songs were actually cowritten with Young MC, whose single "Bust a Move" is confusing for the following reason: The last verse of "Bust a Move" states, "Your best friend Harry / Has a brother Larry / In five days from now he's gonna marry / He's hopin' you can make it there if you can / Cuz in the ceremony you'll be the best man." Now, why would anybody possibly be the best man in a wedding where the groom is your best friend's *brother*? Why isn't your best friend the best man in this ceremony? And who asks someone to be their best man a scant five days before they get married? And while I realize the incongruities of "Bust a Move" have absolutely nothing to do with Tone-Lōc, it somehow seems more central to Tone-Lōc's iconography than his role in the movie *Posse*, which was arguably the best movie about black cowboys I saw during the grunge era.

6. My Bloody Valentine: On the surface, it would seem like My Bloody Valentine should be underrated, but they're not; everyone who cares about pop-o-centric guitar music considers *Loveless* to be a modern classic, and everyone who is wont to mention "swirling guitars" during casual conversation inevitably references that specific album. *Loveless* sold something like two hundred thousand copies. This is the correct amount of people on earth who should care about the concept of swirling guitars; any number higher or lower than two hundred thousand would be ridiculous.

5. Matthew Sweet: Everyone knows that every Matthew Sweet album has only one good song, and that this good song is inevitably the first single, and that this single is always utterly perfect ("Sick of Myself" off *100% Fun*, "Where You Get Love" off *Blue Sky on Mars*, "Girlfriend" off *Girlfriend*, etc.). He sells enough albums to live comfortably, and that seems reasonable.

4. The Beatles: The Beatles are generally seen as the single most important rock band of all time, allegedly because they wrote all the best songs. Since both of these suppositions are true, the Beatles are rated properly by everyone.

3. Blue Öyster Cult: The BÖC song everyone pays attention to is the suicide anthem "Don't Fear the Reaper." This song is haunting, but not in a good way; it makes me nostalgic for hating the Moody Blues. However, the BÖC song virtually no one pays attention to is the pro-monster plod-a-thon "Godzilla," and that track is monster-crushingly beautiful. So—in final analysis—Blue Öyster Cult is accurately rated *by accident*. This occurs on occasion; the same phenomenon happened to Scottie Pippen.

2. The New Radicals: There are only five facts publicly known about this musical entity. The first is that 1999's "You Get What You Give" was an almost flawless Todd Rundgren–like masterwork that makes any right-thinking American want to run through a Wal-Mart semi-naked. The second is that nobody can remember the singer's name. The third fact is that the singer often wore a profoundly idiotic hat. The fourth fact is that if this anonymous, poorly hatted singer had made a follow-up album, it would have somehow made his first record seem worse. And the fifth fact is that his album didn't quite deserve to go gold. Accurately rated in totality.

1. Van Halen: This band should have been the biggest arena act of the early 1980s, and they were. They had the greatest guitar player of the 1980s, and everyone (except possibly Yngwie Malmsteen) seems to agree on this point. They switched singers and became semi-crappy (except for the middle four songs on *5150* and the booze classic "Cabo Wabo"), and nobody aggressively disputes that reality. They also recorded the most average song in rock history: "And the

Cradle Will Rock." What this means is that any song better than "And the Cradle Will Rock" is good, and any song worse than "And the Cradle Will Rock" is bad. If we were to rank every rock song (in sequential order) from best to worst, "And the Cradle Will Rock" would be right in the fucking middle.

And that is exactly what I want.

—SPIN, 2005

Q: It is 1933. You are in Berlin, Germany. Somehow, you find yourself in a position where you can effortlessly steal Adolf Hitler's wallet. This theft will not effect Hitler's rise to power, the nature of World War II, or the Holocaust. There is no important identification in the wallet, but the act will cost Hitler forty Reichsmarks and completely ruin his evening. You do not need the money. The odds that you will be caught committing this crime are less than 2 percent.

Are you ethically obligated to steal Hitler's wallet?

PIRATES

We all want things. We all need things. We all want to need things, and we all need to want them. This is not double-talk; this is truth. America is traditionally perceived as a consumer culture, but it's really more of an *acquisition* culture. Though there is a certain kind of personality who finds satisfaction in the process of buying things, there is a rapidly expanding populace who prefers *taking* things. In 1990, Sinéad O'Connor claimed, "I do not want what I haven't got." That was her core aesthetic. And this is why you never see Sinéad O'Connor on *TRL*. It has nothing to do with her being a thirty-six-year-old, bald, anti-Catholic intermittent lesbian who liked to sing about Argentina. That stuff didn't hurt her career at all.

What hurt her career is that Sinéad would make a horrible pirate.

Maybe you haven't noticed, but—as a society—we are completely immersed in a pirate renaissance. At the moment, there is nothing cooler than pirates. This sort of thing happens periodically; in the middle 1980s, you may recall a ninja renaissance. That was a dynamic era in contemporary history, punctuated by films like *Ninja Academy, American Ninja,* and *Ninja Phantom Heroes U.S.A.*, not to mention the popularity of the GI Joe action figure Storm Shadow, a conflicted snow ninja who joined the terrorist Cobra regime to avenge his uncle's death.

Now, the reason behind the rise in ninja power was always completely clear: the faceless stealth and autonomous freedom of the "rogue ninja" symbolized the last bastions of counterculture within the bloated corporate commercialism of Reagan-era autocracy. We loved ninjas for the same reasons we loved Hüsker Dü, the USFL, and the early work of Jason Bateman[1] (particularly his NBC sitcom *It's Your Move*). The ninja could never be tamed; the ninja gave us hope. Things aren't so cut-and-dried with this twenty-first-century pirate rediscovery. It has more to do with moral decline and personal psychology (and particularly how those morals and psychologies have changed with technology).

Last January, I happened to be in England during Super Bowl XXXVII, the first all-pirate championship of the modern era. As you may recall, the Buccaneers defeated the Raiders. This prompted a very thin, moderately intoxicated Londoner named Nona to ask me a question: "Does every American football team have a pirate-oriented nickname?"

"Of course not," I said in response. "It's not like we're Canadians. We don't randomly refer to every single franchise as 'the Roughriders' for no apparent reason. We are wholly democratic! Pirates are only one delicious slice of Americana." I then asked this woman if every movie made in Britain was exactly like *Four Weddings and a Funeral*. She said "sort of." At the time, it seemed like a wholly forgettable conversation. Yet weeks later, I could not get this woman out of my mind. *Nona, I'm out of my head without you*, I thought

---

1. I wrote this before the creation of *Arrested Development*, so this reference did not seem so clichéd and obvious at the time.

to myself, particularly when I listened to track five of Mötley Crüe's *Girls, Girls, Girls* album. And this was not for any prurient reason; this was because Nona seemed to understand something about my homeland that I did not. In the months that followed, I started looking for elements of pirate iconography in daily American life. And they were absolutely everywhere.

The most obvious example was the success of *Pirates of the Caribbean,* a film where Johnny Depp acts like Keith Richards on the *Goats Head Soup* tour and subsequently comes across as the coolest person who ever lived. But this is only the most overt example. Darryl Hannah wears an eyepatch in *Kill Bill.* National "talk like a pirate day" (September 19) has become more popular than both Groundhog Day and Rosh Hashanah. *Los Angeles Times* journalist Sue Carpenter has written a book called *40 Watts from Nowhere: A Journey into Pirate Radio.* Paul McCartney married a woman with only one leg. And perhaps most curious, postironic literary whiz kid Dave Eggers has opened a pirate store in San Francisco. I'm completely serious about this; it's a store that sells authentic pirate paraphernalia (and also doubles as a grade-school tutoring center).

"Everybody seems to think they can relate to being a pirate," says thirty-two-year-old pirate store manager Yosh Han. "Not everyone can relate to being a cowboy or a circus clown, but there is a pirate within all of us. It's more global, and pirates have that underdog appeal."

Here is where things get tricky: as described by Han, it would seem that the word *pirate* has a positive connotation. However, pirates were—by and large—mediocre citizens. David Cordingly (a man who actively bills himself as "the world's foremost expert on pirates") wrote a book called *Under the Black Flag,* and the text details a bizarre buccaneer torture practice of slashing a prisoner's stomach, extracting the end of one intestine, nailing it to a post, and then forcing the victim to "dance to his death" by beating his ass with a burning log. This strikes me as unnecessary. And it's not like pirating is dead, either: the International Chamber of Commerce (located in Kuala Lumpur) reported 469 pirate attacks in the year 2000, resulting in 72 deaths. So doesn't this qualify pirates as "not altogether groovy"? Shouldn't this make us perceive pirates as bad?

"Yes and no," Han says semi-cryptically. "Certainly, pirate history isn't always positive. But the idea of being free . . . that's a very pirate-oriented ideal. There is just this growing belief that some things should be free—and if those things are not free, they should be taken."

Here is where things become a little more clear: the newfound rise in pirate adoration might be a newfound adoration for theft, which undoubtedly comes from file sharing. Because—when push comes to shove—we all know file sharing *is* theft. I realize there are pundits who try to disagree with that assertion, but you can always tell who these people are; these are people who start their argument by saying "File sharing is a complex issue." File sharing is not a complex issue. There is nothing complex about it. If you are able to get Metallica's "Whiplash" over the Internet, and you aren't paying anyone for this song, and you don't own the copyright to this song, *you have stolen it*. You got something for nothing, and that's what stealing is. And I'm not saying you shouldn't do this, nor am I saying that I've never done this, nor am I suggesting that I even care if the entire music industry collapses. But don't kid yourself—it *is* stealing. It *is* piracy. And that's precisely why people find themselves wanting to see Johnny Depp wielding a cutlass and talking to a parrot.

There's an interesting new book by David Callahan called *The Cheating Culture: Why More Americans Are Doing Wrong to Get Ahead*. The manuscript's premise is that modern people—and particularly people who attend prestigious New York high schools, it seems—see almost no difference between "being smart" and "cheating creatively." And this is not a commentary on situations like Enron; that's corporate intrusion, which has none of the cavalier cache of the lone rapscallion. This is all about the individual. Callahan ulti-

286

mately expresses an anticheating worldview, but even he dubs anyone who doesn't cheat a "chump": you are a chump if you pay your taxes, you are a chump if you never lie, and you are a chump if you still pay full price for CDs. That is the modern paradigm. This is why we love pirates: *we have to*. The only options are to be "pro-pirate" or "pro-chump." We are pirates by default. And this is depressing (or at least it is to me). How I long for those bygone days of adoring ninjas!

Argh.

—*Esquire*, 2003

Q: How would your views about war, politics, and the role of the military change if all future conflicts were fought by armies of robots (that is to say, if all nations agreed to conduct wars exclusively with machines so that human casualties would be virtually nonexistent)?

ROBOTS

Like most middle-class white people who will never be shot at, I'm fascinated by the hyper-desperate, darkly realistic, paper-chasing world of postmodern hip-hop. I've learned a lot about life from watching *MTV Jams*; my understanding of the African American experience comes from street-hardened artists who have looked into the mouth of the lion and scoffed like soldiers. These are people like Shawn Carter ("Jay-Z"), Terius Gray ("Juvenile"), Nasir Jones ("Nas"), and Arturo Molina Jr. ("Frost"). And, to a lesser extent, Will Smith ("The Fresh Prince of Bel-Air").

Smith is an intriguing figure, sort of. Unlike his peers, Will Smith has eloquently evolved with the culture that spawned him. Though once merely peeved by his mother's fashion directives (1988's "Parents Just Don't Understand"), he has grown into a mature artist who's willing to confront America's single greatest threat: killer robots.

This summer (2004), Smith will star in *I, Robot*, the cinematic interpretation of nine short stories by Isaac Asimov. When I was in the sixth grade, Asimov struck me as a profoundly compelling figure, prompting me to subscribe to *Isaac Asimov's Science Fiction Magazine*, a monthly publication I quit reading after the second installment. (The stories seemed a little implausible.) I did, however, unleash a stirring oral book report on *I, Robot*, a literary collection that was punctuated by Asimov's now famous Three Rules of Robotics:

1. A robot may not injure a human being or, through inaction, allow a human being to come to harm.
2. A robot must obey orders given it by human beings, except where such orders would conflict with the First Law.
3. Do not talk about Fight Club.

Now, I don't think I'm giving anything away by telling you that the robots in *I, Robot* find a loophole to those principles, and they proceed to slowly fuck us over. This is a story that was written half a century ago. However, it paints a scenario we continue to fear. *I, Robot* was published in 1950, but writers (or at least muttonchopped Isaac) were already terrified about mankind's bellicose relationship with technology. If we have learned only one thing from film, literature, and rock music, it is this: humans will eventually go to war against the machines. There is no way to avoid this. But you know what? If we somehow manage to lose this war, we really have no excuse. Because I can't imagine any war we've spent more time worrying about.

The Terminator trilogy is about a war against the machines; so is *The Matrix* trilogy. So was *Maximum Overdrive*, although that movie also implied that robots enjoy the music of AC/DC. I don't think the Radiohead album *OK Computer* was specifically about computers trying to kill us, but it certainly suggested that computers were not "okay." *2001: A Space Odyssey* employs elements of robot hysteria, as does the plotline to roughly 2,001 video games. I suspect *Blade Runner* might have also touched on this topic, but I honestly can't remember any of the narrative details; I was too busy pretending it wasn't terrible. There is even a Deutsch electronica band called Lights of Euphoria whose supposed masterpiece is an album titled *Krieg gegen die Maschinen*, which literally translates as, "War Against the Machines." This means that even European techno fans are aware of this phenomenon, and those idiots generally aren't aware of *anything* (except who in the room might be holding the ketamine).

I'm not sure how we all became convinced that machines intend to dominate us. As I type this very column, I can see my toaster, and I'll be honest: I'm not nervous. As far as I can tell, it poses no threat. My relationship with my toaster is delicious, but completely one-sided. If I can be considered the Michael Jordan of My Apartment (and I think I can), my toaster is LaBradford Smith. I'm never concerned that my toaster will find a way to poison me, or that it will foster a false sense of security before electrocuting me in the shower, or that it will politically align itself with my microwave. My toaster does not want to conquer society. I even played "Dirty Deeds Done Dirt Cheap" in my kitchen, just to see if my toaster would become self-aware and go for my jugular; its reaction was negligible. Machines have no grit.

It appears we've spent half a century preparing for a war against a potential foe who—thus far—has been nothing but civil to us; it's almost like we've made a bunch of movies that warn about a coming conflict with the Netherlands. In fact, there isn't even evidence that robots could kick our ass *if they wanted to*. In March, a clandestine military group called DARPA (Defense Advanced Research Projects Agency) challenged engineers to build a driverless vehicle that could traverse a 150-mile course in the Mojave Desert; the contest's winner was promised a cash prize of $1 million. And you know who won? Nobody. Nobody's robot SUV could make it farther than 7.4 miles. Even with the aid of a GPS, robots are pretty moronic. Why do we think they'll be able to construct a matrix if they can't even drive to Vegas?

I suspect all these dystopic "man versus machine" scenarios are grounded in the fact that technology *is* legitimately alienating; the rise of computers (and robots, and iPods, and nanomachines who hope to turn the world into sentient "gray goo") has certainly made life easier, but they've also accelerated depression. Case in point: if this were 1904, you would not be reading this essay; you would be chopping wood or churning butter or watching one of your thirteen children perish from crib death. Your life would be horrible, but your life would have purpose. It would have clarity. Machines allow humans the privilege of existential anxiety. Machines provide us with the extra time to worry about the status of our careers, and/or the context of our sexual relationships, and/or what it means to be alive. Unconsciously, we hate technology. We hate the way it replaces visceral experience with self-absorption. And the only way we can reconcile that hatred is by pretending machines hate us, too.

It is human nature to personify anything we don't understand: God, animals, hurricanes, mountain ranges, jet skis, strippers, etc. We deal with inanimate objects by assigning them the human qualities we assume they might have if they were exactly us. Consequently, we want to think about machines as slaves, and we like to pretend those mechanized slaves will eventually attempt a hostile takeover.

The truth, of course, is that *we* are the slaves; the machines became our masters through a bloodless coup that began during the Industrial Revolution. (In fact, this is kind of what *I, Robot* is about, although I assume the Will Smith version will not make that clear.) By now, I think most Americans are aware of that reality; I think any smarter-than-average person already concedes that (a) we've lost control of technology, and (b) there's nothing we can do about it. But that's defeatist. Openly embracing that despair would make the process of living even darker than it already is; we'd all move to rural Montana and become Unabombers. We need to remain optimistic. And how do we do that? By preparing ourselves for a futuristic war against intelligent, man-hating cyborgs. As long as we dream of a war that has not yet happened, we are able to believe it's a war we have not yet lost.

But perhaps I'm wrong about all this. Perhaps we humans

are still in command, and perhaps there really will be a conventional robot war in the not-so-distant future. If so, let's roll. I'm ready. My toaster will never be the boss of me. Get ready to make me some Pop-Tarts, bitch.

—*Esquire*, 2004

Q: You are in a plane crash in the Andes Mountains, not unlike those people from the movie *Alive*.[1] As such, you will be forced to consume the human flesh of the people who died on impact; this will be a terrible experience, but it is the only way for you to survive. Fortunately, you did not know any of the victims personally.

Would you rather eat a dead baby, or would you rather eat a dead elderly person? Would gender play a role in the selection process? And how much would it bother you if this meat turned out to be delicious?

SUPER PEOPLE

I have no idea where you, the loyal *Esquire* reader, happen to stand on the issue of stem-cell research. It's a complex, multi-faceted question, and there are two distinct camps: progressive intellectuals (who tend to favor stem-cell research), and backward-thinking, antiscience, troglodytic imbeciles (who tend to be against it). Both arguments are valid. However, I've noticed an emerging social trend that helps clarify the murky ethics that surround this acceleration of genetic exploration, and it solidifies my belief that this acceleration is something we must nurture. We need to pursue stem-cell research for the benefit of all humankind, lest we risk being destroyed (or possibly enslaved) by the Super People.

Right now, in Berlin, Germany, there is a five-year-old boy who has twice the muscle mass of a normal five-year-old.

---

1. Or, I suppose, like the 1972 Uruguayan rugby team who experienced this situation in reality.

He can hold seven-pound weights in each hand with his arms fully extended, which is something *Blue's Clues* fanatics are not supposed to do. Do you remember 1979, when Earl Campbell rushed for 1,934 yards? Do you also remember the TV commercial from that era where Earl lay on the beach and explained why he loved Skoal? This five-year-old German has Earl Campbell's thighs. I saw a picture of this kid doing one-armed push-ups; he's ready to go fifteen rounds with Apollo Creed *right now*. Apparently, the boy's insane muscle mass is partially due to the fact that his mother was a world-class sprinter, but mostly because of a genetic mutation. Regardless of how it happened, the kid is going to be an unstoppable force; medical authorities have not released his name, probably because everyone is hoping he'll eventually become a masked crime fighter.

Yet—amazingly—this little German juggernaut is only the *second*-most impressive minor in the Eastern Hemisphere. There is a sixteen-year-old girl in Russia who allegedly has X-ray vision. Her name is Natalia Demkina, and scientists remain baffled as to why she can see through walls. Not surprisingly, she has no idea how the fuck this happened and doesn't appreciate that all her vodka-soaked doctors are equally clueless. "I am worried now that they might be hiding something from me about why I can see through objects," Demkina says. "I don't know how it works, but I can see through things." If this information is even semi-true, this has to be the number-one news story of the year, even if *Chinese Democracy* really does get released in November.

Now, I know what you're probably thinking: In fifteen years, will the superstrong German boy be allowed to date the female X-ray machine? Well, possibly. But here is the larger issue: Why is the world suddenly saturated with Super People? Where are they coming from? And how can we "Lesser People" survive within an escalating climate of human-versus-human conflict? I don't want to exist in a world where I might be pummeled by a five-year-old whose dad still probably listens to the Scorpions' *Love at First Sting*. I don't want to have some Russian teenager staring at my chest and telling me I smoke too much pot. Like most Americans, these have always been my two greatest fears. So how do we combat the changing face of our planet? How do the Lesser People compete with the Super People?

The answer is stem-cell research.

Let's not delude ourselves: the Super People of today are not like us (and that difference will only be accentuated by the Super People of tomorrow). They live longer, and they mature faster. There are myriad examples of this. According to volume 82 of *The Journal of Clinical Endocrinology & Metabolism,* girls are menstruating at younger and younger ages; according to some dude I know who works for *Slam* magazine, nineteen-year-old Dwight Howard is more ready for the NBA than twenty-one-year-old Emeka Okafor. These two facts are indisputable, and they prove my point in totality: we are unconsciously creating a Brave New World. Today, many expectant mothers don't even smoke clove cigarettes during their third trimester of pregnancy. Meanwhile, nutrition has improved; nobody seems to drink milk anymore, much to the chagrin of countless unemployed cows. Nobody seems to eat bread, either, which completely flies in the face of the timeless cliché, "Man can absolutely live on bread alone." The world has gone mental with the quest for vigor.

But with this vigor comes a price . . . and that price is inequality.

The sad reality is that most people are only improving a little from all these changes; most of us are not becoming "super." Oh, we may live an additional four or five years, but most of those days will be spent in a retirement home with a broken hip and a broken dream. For 98 percent of the populace, our improvement has been nominal (and potentially annoying). However, that other 2 percent is exploding through the roof. These are your German superbabies and your Russian optic geniuses; these are your teenage power forwards playing for the Orlando Magic and all those girls having their first period two weeks before they start third grade. If the human potential of every citizen was placed on a line graph, these select Super People would be the spikes that obliterate the mean—and this is where the danger lies. This opens the door for the possibility of a small clan of Super People taking over the globe. I mean, how could we possibly stop them? They can see through walls. They have better post moves. We have no defense.

Or at least we don't *yet*.

This is why we need stem-cell research: we need to ensure that all American children born into this dystopia are genetically predisposed toward the possession of at least one (1) superpower. The key is not to punish the Super People by making them mortal, since that kind of policy would be socialistic (and akin to a Kurt Vonnegut story I never actually read). A better solution is turning *all* humans into Super People. Instead of pulling the best 2 percent down, let's move the other 98 percent *up*. This would be complicated (obviously), and it would likely only be affordable through socialized medicine (which I realize is technically *more* socialistic that the option I rejected two sentences ago), but I don't see any other alternative. We need to tap into the DNA of unborn babies and make them more awesome. I see no possible downside to this.

The simple truth is that we're all already cyborgs, more or less. Our mouths are filled with silver. Our nearsighted pupils are repaired with surgical lasers. We jam diabetics full of delicious insulin. Almost 40 percent of Americans now have prosthetic limbs.[2] We seem to have no qualms about making postbirth improvements to our feeble selves. Why are we so uncomfortable with prebirth improvement? What's the difference? Just because something isn't natural doesn't mean it isn't good.

Granted, I am not (technically) a doctor, so my understanding of stem-cell research is limited to what I've read on gawker.com. But in layman's terms, a stem cell is a biological cell with the ability to reproduce itself and create what's

----

2. This is an estimate.

called "differentiated tissues." These tissues are pockets of cells with specific functions and unique properties. I would like to assume these properties might include invisibility, bulletproof skin, the ability to verbally communicate with horses, immunity to static electricity, the ability to subsist solely on a diet of wood, self-cleaning hair, immortality, and an innate understanding of Jim Morrison's music and poetry. These are qualities that could be randomly inserted into the DNA of every unborn American, eventually balancing the field between the organic Super People and the pathetic Lesser People. Genetics are power, and power is freedom, and freedom is slavery, and slavery is fear. And *never again* shall we fear German superchildren or Russian freaks. Those days are over. Push the envelope. Roll the bones. If science is wrong, I don't want to be right.

—Esquire, 2004

Q: The world is ending. It's ending quickly, and it's ending dramatically.

It will either end at noon on your fortieth birthday, or it will end two days *after* you die (from natural causes) at the age of seventy-five.

Which apocalyptic scenario do you prefer?

TELEVISION

Those who fail to understand the past are doomed to repeat it. However, what if that's your goal? What if that's exactly what you want out of life? What if repeating the past—and then repeating it again and again—is the only thing that makes you happy?

If this is indeed the case, you should do what I did: watch VH1 Classic for twenty-four consecutive hours. Nothing wages war with insomnia like wall-to-wall videos from the Reagan era. More important, there is much that can be learned from such an experience. It's kind of like what Matthew McConaughey said in *Dazed and Confused*: "I get older, they stay the same age." Now, I realize he was talking about high-school girls and I'm referring to Duran Duran videos. But what's really the difference?

12:02 P.M.: The afternoon begins with Tom Petty and the Heartbreakers' "So You Want to Be a Rock & Roll Star," which is one of those videos where the band just performs a song live and we're supposed to like it. If I were a DJ, this would be a snarky song to play immediately following "Rock 'n' Roll Star" by Oasis. Tom is wearing a sports coat featuring the planets of the solar system (Saturn most prominently)

301

and he's smiling constantly; I guess he likes his job. This is followed by a clip from an unsmiling Roger Waters, who sings about beautiful women walking their dogs on the Sunset Strip. I sense this shall be a day of paradoxes.

12:23 P.M.: "Every Little Thing She Does Is Magic" is currently on my twenty-one-inch life window, and the Police are dancing around the recording studio like a trio of nappy-haired gnomes. Everyone remembers that the Police wrote a bunch of great songs, but does anyone remember how often they wore stupid hats? Perhaps that was the style of the time. I can totally understand why Stewart Copeland always wanted to punch Sting in the throat. Up next is Duran Duran's "Planet Earth." Obviously, the guys in Duran II don't wear hats because they're "New Romantic–Looking." As a consequence, one of the Andys in this band is dressed like a gay pirate and appears to be sporting my sister's least successful haircut from the spring of 1986.

12:57 P.M.: Okay, so now we're into the hyper-trippy "All Right Now" by Free, and it's raising a few questions. Logically, there is no way that everyone in the 1970s was a drug addict; that just couldn't have been the case. However, this Free footage was clearly made exclusively for people who were completely high. Does this mean that the normal mind-set of mainstream culture in 1970 was akin to the way stoned people view the world in 2003? I mean, maybe even straight people thought they were stoned in the 1970s; maybe that's how everyone felt, all the time. This might explain how Jimmy Carter got elected; it also might explain why his presidency was tainted by an attack from a giant swimming rabbit. Music can teach us many things.

1:16 P.M.: We've moved into the "all-request hour." Someone has requested Franke and the Knockouts' "Sweetheart," which is a song I never even knew existed. I like to imagine that some unemployed slacker is sitting in his double-wide trailer in the middle of the afternoon, and he's thinking, *Ah, yes. All my hard work has finally paid off. At long last, Franke and the Knockouts are back in the public consciousness.* And I would wager $10,000 that this person is named Franke.

1:24 P.M.: "Dust in the Wind," my all-time favorite song about dirt and air, is pulling at my heartstrings while the bearded fellows in Kansas pull at their violin strings. You know, nobody makes truly sad songs anymore. Outside my bedroom window, some city employees are tearing up the sidewalk with jackhammers and playing the new 50 Cent record on a boom box; from what I can deduce, the first four tracks are about killing people and the fifth is about drinking Bacardi. Now, I realize 50 is reflecting the reality of the streets and the frailty of human existence, but didn't Kansas already do that? Nothing lasts forever, except the earth and sky. I should have become a farmer.

1:52 P.M.: Lindsey Buckingham is trapped in a fish tank and killing his doppelganger with mind bullets. Part of me is tempted to suggest that this low-fi technology and guileless chutzpah is cool and/or Advanced and/or better than videos of the modern age, but I just can't do it. This is pretty idiotic. No wonder Stevie Nicks had to do all that blow. I'm sure she saw this video in 1982 and thought to herself, *I used to share my shawl with that guy?*

2:05 P.M.: There may be better guitar riffs than the opening of AC/DC's "Highway to Hell," but there can't be more than five. The singer's hat sure is stupid, though. I wish Stewart Copeland would punch him in the throat.

2:09 P.M.: I'm watching film footage of Jimi Hendrix's "Crosstown Traffic," and it's one of those montages where we see old scenes of traffic and frigid homeless people and crazy dudes in wheelchairs, and this is supposed to replicate the

303

experience of traveling across Manhattan in 1968. However, I remain certain that this song must be a metaphor for a stubborn woman Hendrix was trying to sleep with, because there is no way Jimi Hendrix would ever be bothered by gridlock. I can't fathom a scenario where Jimi would have needed to be *on time*, unless he was late for a taping of *The Dick Cavett Show*.

2:25 P.M.: One of my all-time favorite video tropes is the "Spontaneous Sex Party in the Classroom" conceit, best personified by Van Halen in "Hot for Teacher" but also exemplified by what I'm watching right now, which is "Sexy + 17" by the Stray Cats. Sadly, the girls in this video don't look seventeen. This is more like the last few seasons of *Happy Days*, where a thirty-six-year-old Fonzie would snap his fingers and be groped by two high school cheerleaders, both of whom were roughly thirty-three.

2:29 P.M.: Speaking of Van Halen, "Sexy + 17" is followed by "(Oh) Pretty Woman," which is a narrative about a semi-hot woman being sexually tortured by two dwarves, only to be rescued by a cowboy (Eddie Van Halen), a jungle savage (Alex Van Halen), a Samurai warrior (Michael Anthony), and Napoleon Bonaparte (David Lee Roth). This was released in 1982, so I guess this was Van Halen's Village People period.

2:35 P.M.: Things are really getting excellent: Poison's "Fallen Angel" is illustrating the cautionary tale of a small-town girl who moves to Los Angeles and immediately becomes a whore. The moral of our story? Never go anywhere and never try anything. Stay home and buy more Poison records.

2:55 P.M.: Blue Öyster Cult ("Godzilla") and Led Zeppelin ("Whole Lotta Love") just had a heavyweight heavy-off, and (much to my surprise) the rubber radioactive monster pounds the mudshark out of the German war blimp.

3:05 P.M.: I am informed by VH1 Classic that "We . . . are . . . the '80s," and this is proven by Lionel Richie's willingness to dance on the ceiling. I think this video came out at roughly the same point when Lionel hosted the American Music Awards and kept inexplicably repeating the word *outrageous*, the most overt (and least successful) attempt in pop history to create a national catchphrase. This video ends with Rodney Dangerfield bugging his eyes out and saying, "I shouldn't have eaten that upside-down cake!" Now that's a catchphrase.

3:20 P.M.: With the exception of a waifish brunette wearing a negligee and placing her foot in a basin of water, R.E.M.'s video for "The One I Love" is remarkably similar to the opening credits of the old PBS science show *3-2-1 Contact*. I'm calling a copyright attorney.

4:02 P.M.: Driven by hot-blooded lust, Gloria Estefan is crawling into my lap and insisting the rhythm is going to get me (tonight). We'll just see about that, Gloria. You pipe down!

4:08 P.M.: When one really thinks about it, the message of Culture Club's "Karma Chameleon" is rather brilliant, inasmuch as the song examines the disconnect between the actions of a lover and how those deeds are interpreted. However, this disconnect is significantly downplayed by the video, inasmuch as it appears to glamorize riverboat gambling.

4:18 P.M.: "Raspberry Beret," the best Prince song ever recorded, is followed by the Bangles' "Manic Monday," the best Prince song ever recorded by somebody else. Prince supposedly gave "Manic Monday" to Susanna Hoffs in the hope that she would sleep with him. If I were Prince, that's all I would ever do—I'd write airtight singles for every female musician I ever met. As far as I can tell, the reason you write great songs is to become a rock star, and the reason you become a rock star is to have sex with beautiful, famous women. Why not cut out the middleman? Prince is a genius.

4:48 P.M.: Here is what I am learning from "Our House" by Madness: never invite ska musicians into your home, because they're all too fucking happy. "Our House" and Eddy Grant's "Electric Avenue" were my favorite songs in fifth grade. Man, I am so glad I got into Mötley Crüe.

5:11 P.M.: Ian Astbury wears sunglasses while singing "Whiskey Bar" with two surviving members of the Doors. Time to get nervous.

5:23 P.M.: In 1984, .38 Special released a record called *Tour de Force*. Do you think they were serious about this? I mean, do you think they were sitting in the studio, working on tunes like "If I'd Been the One," and they eventually just looked each other in the eyes and said, "This is it. This is our tour de force." I'm sure this must have happened, because why else would you make a video where a bunch of wild horses run through a prairie fire?

5:49 P.M.: I'm quite enjoying Michael Sembello's "Maniac." However, I'm a tad baffled: How did *Flashdance* ever get produced theatrically? The movie itself isn't necessarily bad (it's kind of good, sort of). But how did anyone pitching the script ever get past the segment of the description where he'd have to say, "Okay, now here's the key—this girl is also a professional welder." Because I'm sure every studio executive responded by saying, "She's what? A professional wrestler?" And then the guy pitching the script would have to go, "No no no, I said *welder*," and they'd have a twenty-minute conversation about how to strike an arc and why watching a woman do this would be sexy. Which it is, but that doesn't make it any easier to explain.

6:00 P.M.: The *Metal Mania* hour opens with "Summertime Girls" by Y&T, which makes me wish my apartment was an '84 Caprice Classic. Beautiful women are wearing black leather outfits on the sands of Malibu, and that can't be comfortable. Luckily, they remove them in order to don black lingerie, which is evidently what they wear when they play beach volleyball. I can totally relate to this.

6:07 P.M.: Go ahead and call me sentimental if you must, but I will always prefer the Def Leppard videos where the drummer still has both his arms.

6:12 P.M.: Memory is a strange thing. Example: I completely recalled that the Scorpions' "Rock You Like a Hurricane" video was about the band being locked inside a steel cage while hundreds of sex-starved women tried to sexually attack them. However, I had somehow blocked out the fact that this video also involved leopards.

6:25 P.M.: If I have a persecution complex (and I do), it undoubtedly came from watching Twisted Sister videos, namely "I Wanna Rock." If left to my own devices, I would have never realized how much society was actively trying to stop me from listening to Twisted Sister.

6:42 P.M.: I'm watching "Girls, Girls, Girls" right now. One of the strip clubs Mötley Crüe mentions in this song is the Body Shop on the Sunset Strip, and every time I'm in L.A. I end up walking right past it. Part of me has always wanted to go in there, mostly because of this song. But I never do, mostly because of this song.

6:55 P.M.: King Kobra. Kool.

7:01 P.M.: By some act of God, today's episode of *Headline Act* is about KISS. Paul Stanley gives me advice on how to live my life before playing "Rock and Roll All Nite." Gene Simmons explains that the KISS Army is a volunteer army. True dat.

7:32 P.M.: An interesting aside has just occurred to me: VH1 Classic shows no commercials (just promos for VH1). It's been a long time since I've watched this much television without someone trying to sell me something. However, I suppose VH1 *is* selling me something; they're selling nostalgia, which means they're selling my own memories back to me, which means they are selling me to me. I am both the commodity and the consumer. So what's the margin on that?

7:40 P.M.: Whitney Houston tells me she gets so emotional, baby, and I believe her. This video came out years before she went fucknuts, but she already seems pretty bizarre and skeletal. Fourteen minutes later, Aretha Franklin sings "Freeway of Love." She is half as bizarre and forty times less skeletal.

8:06 P.M.: Okay, here's something I failed to anticipate: it turns out VH1 Classic operates on some kind of "block system," because they just played Tom Petty's "So You Want to Be a Rock & Roll Star" (again), and now they're playing the same Roger Waters shit I saw at 12:05. I am now going to have to spend the next eight hours rewatching the exact same videos I just spent the previous eight hours watching, in the exact same sequence. If I were a member of al Qaeda, this would be enough to make me talk.

8:28 P.M.: This is all so idiotically meta. Because this is VH1 Classic, all these videos are things I saw in the distant past. They make me think of junior high. But because I just finished watching these same exact clips eight hours ago, my window for nostalgia is much smaller. I am now nostalgic for things that just happened. So the second time I see Fine Young Cannibals' "Good Thing," it makes me nostalgic for 12:30, which was when I had General Tso's chicken for lunch. Yeah, those were GTs.

8:57 P.M.: Let me be honest about something: I am not the first person who came up with the idea of watching rock videos and writing about the experience. In 1992, a brilliant guy named Hugh Gallagher locked himself in a hotel room and watched MTV for seven straight days (this is back when MTV still played videos). I recall him writing that a Black Crowes antiheroin video made him want to do heroin. That's nothing. He should have watched this Free video twice!

9:10 P.M.: There is no way Derek Wittenburg can handle Clyde Drexler off the dribble, and Thurl Bailey cannot match up with Akeem Olajuwon on the block. I am certain Houston will win the 1983 NCAA championship. Oh, fuck . . . this is ESPN Classic. Sorry.

9:16 P.M.: The first time I saw Triumph's video for "Somebody's Out There," I failed to notice that it inexplicably involved a woman looking into a microscope. Maybe all this repetition will pay dividends.

10:19 P.M.: In the world of Deep Purple's "Knocking at Your Backdoor," windmills are remarkably prominent.

10:31 P.M.: Earlier today, I saw Van Halen's "(Oh) Pretty Woman" and merely thought it was strange. Upon further review, this is the craziest thing I have ever seen in my entire life.

10:51 P.M.: I was wrong about something else this afternoon: upon further review, Zeppelin is substantially heavier than BÖC. I had just been distracted by the two-minute drum solo near the end of "Godzilla." It also dawned on me (during Jimmy Page's solo) that some yet-to-be-invented band should make an homage to early-'70s psychedelic acid-rock videos that transpose live performance with still photography.[1]

12:07 A.M.: Well, it's now been twelve hours since I started this project. I think I'm holding up okay, although it's a lot less fun to watch videos when you always know what's coming up next. This is becoming a Groundhog Day fiasco. But static stimuli makes you consider curious things: like, was Boy George attractive? And I don't mean attractive as a man, nor do I mean attractive as a woman. It's more like, was he attractive *as a human*? And why does the answer to that question suddenly seem so different than the answer to the first question?

12:46 A.M.: Corey Hart looks exactly like a kid I attended basketball camp with in seventh grade. That guy had no game whatsoever. He did, however, upturn the collar of his IZOD, just as Corey does in the video from "Never Surrender," which I'm now watching. I think that kid from basketball camp was named "Corey," too. Or maybe it was Monroe. Oh well, let's move on.

1:20 A.M.: I have very mixed feelings about this REO Speedwagon video ("Roll with the Changes"). That whole era—1979 to 1983, roughly—was definitely the worst period in the history of rock music. But I think it's probably my favorite era of rock music, and my reasons for feeling this way are complex. At risk of getting all pseudo-Zen, I don't like listening to "Roll with the Changes," but I like the way it sounds. And I don't like looking at REO Speedwagon, but I like the way they look. The bottom line, I suspect, is that there was never another time where the gap between "totally great" and "completely terrible" was so minuscule, which is why I'm glad VH1 Classic exists.

---

1. And this band should come from Scandinavia and be called "Dungen."

2:04 A.M.: "Let It Go" by the Japanese metal band Loudness includes ample footage of industrial power saws slicing through tree trunks (we're back to the aforementioned Metal Mania hour). It would be fascinating to interview the director of this video today, because I'd love to hear him try and explain what he was trying to convey with this imagery. There is no plausible explanation: this is "heavy metal." It's not "heavy lumber" (and even if this film was conceptualized by some forward-thinking Tokyo auteur who spoke no English whatsoever, there's no way he could misinterpret that). Is this supposed to mean the music of Loudness will attack the listener with the frenzied power of sharpened steel? If so, I guess that makes us the trees.

2:14 A.M.: Never before have I been so well informed about VH1's programming schedule. If you have any questions about upcoming episodes of *Driven*, feel free to e-mail me at cklosterman@spin.com.

2:41 A.M.: "Girls, Girls, Girls," again, again, again. What we learn from this video is that there are two kinds of strippers in this world: those who smile and those who don't. The ones who don't are apparently trying to seem sultrier, but I prefer the ones who smile. I get the impression the guys in Mötley Crüe spend less time worrying about this, though.

3:00 A.M.: New (old) videos start in an hour. I am so . . . oh, I don't know. Stoked?

3:05 A.M.: The triumphant return of that thirty-minute KISS retrospective I already watched at 7:00 P.M. Paul Stanley compares KISS in 1972 to a "baby piranha." Later, he discusses the concept of freedom and its application to the video for "Tears Are Falling." He's a goddamn prophet.

4:01 A.M.: Oh my god. Oh my god oh my god oh my god. It's Tom Petty's "So You Wanna Be a Rock & Roll Star." This block of All-Star Jams is starting over again. This can't be happening. But it's happening. Oh my god.

4:41 A.M.: I've now seen Paul Carrack's "Don't Shed a Tear" thrice, and it's not getting any better. I hate this. I hate Paul Carrack. I hate myself. But I will not shed a tear, because Paul Carrack understands me better than I understand myself.

4:47 A.M.: Some VJ named Eddie Trunk just implied that "Spill the Wine" by Eric Burdon and War helped end the Vietnam War.

5:42 A.M.: The video for Taco's "Puttin' on the Ritz" is not remotely akin to the way I remember it from *Friday Night Videos*. It seems to be set in a postapocalyptic haunted mansion, occupied by goth witches and tuxedo-clad warlocks wielding Darth Vader's light sabers. I suddenly have an urge to locate my twelve-sided die and roll up some hit points.

6:02 A.M.: At long last, a format change: since it's now "officially" Tuesday, we have entered *Tuesday Two Play*, which means I get to see two consecutive videos by every artist who appears. We begin with Bruce Springsteen doing "My Hometown" (live, with Clarence Clemons on tambourine) and "Thunder Road." Back in reality, the sun has risen in the east, and people I will never know are jogging outside my bedroom window. The world is a foreign place. I do not belong here.

6:29 A.M.: I drift into shallow slumber and awake from a horrifying dream: a thin man is waving a bouquet of flowers at me, and I am struck into a coma. When the coma is shattered, I find myself half naked, confused about my sexual identity, and overcome by sadness. I think a train may be involved, and possibly a double-decker bus. But then I realize something else: I've been awake this whole time. These are just Smiths videos.

7:45 A.M.: Neil Young and Pearl Jam keep on rockin' in the free world. Van Halen asks me if this is love while swigging Jack Daniel's from the stage, and I have no valid answer. An underage girl on the beach says she wants candy, and it seems dirty. And it is.

10:03 A.M.: I'm running out of material. I just watched David Bowie's "Ashes to Ashes," and all I could think to write was, "Hmm . . . this looks like a *Dr. Who* episode." I think I actually made the joke yesterday. Now I'm watching a pair of Steve Winwood videos and I can't remember what these songs are titled, even when I'm hearing the chorus. I feel eight hundred years old.

10:17 A.M.: Whenever I'd listen to Toto's "Africa," I always assumed the song was using Africa as a metaphor. However, this video suggests the song is literally about the continent itself (and maybe about an African American travel agent, although I can't be sure), so now I'm confused. It definitely has a globe, though. Also, what does "Africa" have to do with the movie *Fatal Attraction*? I swore I just heard some VJ talking about that movie (and its relationship to Toto). I struggle.

10:55 A.M.: Here's an idea: Why doesn't someone create a network called CNN Classic, which could be a twenty-four-hour channel of old news broadcasts? They could air old episodes of *60 Minutes* and the wall-to-wall coverage that was shown during memorable national disasters and random episodes of *World News Tonight* from the 1970s. They could rebroadcast all the news reports from the day Robert F. Kennedy was shot and the real-time news feeds from the 1986 *Challenger* explosion. This idea seems unspeakably brilliant to me, and I honestly can't believe I'm the only person who ever got high and came up with it.

11:35 A.M.: Okay, we're less than thirty minutes away from the end of this joy ride, and I'm watching a Bryan Ferry video that's primarily composed of unicorn footage from the movie *Legend*. I should retire right now. This is undoubtedly the apex of my career as a journalist.

11:58 A.M.: Well, this is it. The end of the road. And who do I see when I reach nirvana? No, not Nirvana; it's Cher ("Heart of Stone"), and I think she's singing about people who died in Vietnam. And—somehow—this makes perfect sense to me. Nature has created no being as irrepressible as Cher, a woman who keeps coming back in order to remind us that she used to be somebody (and will therefore be somebody forever). This is why VH1 Classic exists—it's a network for people who live exclusively in the past and the future, forever ignoring the present tense. Which means it's for pretty much everybody over the age of eighteen and under the age of forty-five. And when I see Cher again at 7:58 P.M., this will still be true, just as it was eight hours ago.

—SPIN.com, 2003

Q: You are given the chance to control what your legacy will be. You can't *specifically* dictate how you will be recalled by future generations, but you are given the chance to choose between two general idioms of legacies.

The first kind of legacy ("option A") would be that you lived your days as a good, honest person who worked hard and contributed to society. However, the limitation of this legacy will be that almost no one will know or remember this information (including future members of your own extended family). Most average people will never even know you lived.

The second kind of legacy ("option B") will be familiar to almost everyone in the world for centuries to come. However, this legacy will be extremely strange and neutral; it will be an obscure fact that has almost nothing to do with your tangible day-to-day life (the best comparison being the legacy of General Tso Tsungtang, an extremely gifted and successful military leader during the seventeenth-century Qing Dynasty who is now exclusively remembered as the namesake for the popular Chinese dish General Tso's chicken).

Which legacy do you want?

SINGULARITY

Remember Jessica McClure? That little Texas girl who fell down a well in 1987? She's seventeen now, and I'm assuming she's pretty goddamn sick of people bringing that incident up. And I'm sure they do it constantly. I bet old friends call her and say things like "Oh, hi, Jessica. Funny story. Last night, I was listening to a Terence Trent D'Arby album, and when I heard that song 'Wishing Well,' I totally thought about the time you fell into that well, so I thought I'd give you a jingle." This is the kind of thing that happens when people associate one event with your entire life.

I have a similar problem: everyone I've ever met seems to know that I like KISS. Everyone. I have come to realize that liking KISS will ultimately be the only thing anybody will remember about me. I have no doubt that if I died today, whoever was to engrave my tombstone would chisel something along the lines of

> Charles J. Klosterman
> 1972–2005:
> "He preferred *Animalize*
> to *Lick It Up.*"

The problem with being closely associated with KISS (or with any singular entity) is not that people know this particular fact. The problem is that people assume there are no other facts (about anything) that would possibly interest you. Acquaintances are endlessly telling me rudimentary trivia about KISS, which is a little hard to reconcile, since these same people inevitably tell me things they must assume I already know. For example, if someone is aware that I know which tracks on *Destroyer* include uncredited guitar playing by Dick Wagner ("Sweet Pain," "Great Expectations," and "Flaming Youth"), why would this same person feel obligated to inform me that KISS is currently touring with Aerosmith? I mean, I get VH1, too. I own a microwave. I don't live at the bottom of a well. But these are the kinds of things people feel they must tell me.

Consequently, I was not surprised to receive somewhere between six and eighteen thousand e-mails the day after Gene Simmons announced that he was releasing a new solo album next year and that one of the songs ("Waiting for the Morning Light") would be cowritten by Bob Dylan. This is significant news to someone like me, a longtime lobbyist for KISS songs that fall outside the conventional KISS paradigm. I'm a big supporter of the (highly Advanced) collaborations between

KISS and Lou Reed on the 1981 concept album *Music from the Elder*, a work that I consider the fourth-best KISS studio effort of all time. I do not find the Simmons-Dylan collaboration surprising. In fact, it shouldn't be surprising to anyone. Their partnership simply illustrates that rock 'n' roll has reached its logical conclusion and no longer needs to exist.

Here is the entire history of rock music, recounted in one paragraph: rock music did not exist until the release of *Meet the Beatles* in January 1964. From that time until 1970, the Beatles were simultaneously the most artistically gifted and commercially successful rock artists on the planet. Then they broke up. And at that point, rock split into two opposing ideologies; there were now two kinds of music. The prime directive of the first kind of rock was to be meaningful and important; the prime directive of the second was to entertain people and move product. The first category comprises elements (Springsteen, punk rock, early U2, Chris Carrabba, etc.) that followed a template built by Dylan in the 1960s. The second category comprises things (Elton John, disco, everything the Stones did post–*Some Girls*, Michael Jackson et al.) that followed the path KISS chose when they formed in 1973. This era includes two exceptions, which are Led Zeppelin and Prince; everything else fits into either category A or category B. And that is the entire history of rock music, completely condensed into one paragraph.

But now, that's all over. Rock 'n' roll has come full circle: the genre's most genuine, most credible individual has joined forces with the genre's most entrepreneurial, most self-consciously contrived individual. Rock 'n' roll has not been destroyed; it has been solved. This, of course, will make it significantly harder to put out a rock magazine, but I'm sure we'll think of something. Tune in next month, when this column will begin covering . . . oh, I don't know. Maybe horse racing.

—SPIN, 2004

SOMETHING
THAT ISN'T
TRUE AT ALL

I became the movie critic for the *Akron Beacon Journal* in 1999. Compared to my aforementioned stint as "amorphous pop culture reporter," this was an incredibly effortless (and surprisingly boring) job. If you've ever found yourself thinking that watching movies for a living would be an easy, interesting way to make a living, you would be exactly half right. I continually found myself sitting at my office desk doing nothing; it is not a field with a great deal of breaking news. You pretty much just wait for the movies. To kill time, I would sometimes work on a novella about a guy from North Dakota who moved to Akron, Ohio, and became the film critic. I like to call this "reverse creativity."

As one might expect, a few of the details in this story are (obviously) not-so-loosely autobiographical. However, all of the major elements are completely fabricated. This is fiction. The crux of the plot was actually created by my friend Robert Huschka, who once told me about this dream he had that reminded him of the opening scene from a nonexistent sci-fi movie. Since Robert has no relationship to the film industry, I incorporated (i.e., stole) the idea and made it the middle of this particular story. Almost all the other key details have no relationship to reality. For example, I have never ingested drugs before coming in to work, and I've only smoked angel dust twice in my life (and both times were accidental—I thought I had purchased some very expensive "celebration" pot, but it was really just cheap weed that had been dusted with PCP). However, I cannot deny becoming briefly obsessed with the psychotropic properties of angel dust. Smoking it was a very intense experience: my girlfriend saw numerous dead people walking around the kitchen, and both our faces kept morphing into alternate identities. I really, really enjoyed it. However, I once saw (or maybe dreamed) an episode of *Cops* where a very large man smoked angel dust and broke the neck of a K-9 police dog with his

321

bare hands, and this is the same drug that made Art Linkletter's daughter (and/or Helen Hunt) jump out of a five-story building for no clear reason; I certainly can't recommend that shit to anyone.

I cannot justify the amoral nature of the main character. It was not my original intent to make this person so loathsome and implausible. The original draft[1] also had an extremely detailed (and exceedingly long) subplot about the main character's fantasy basketball team, but that was gradually edited into nonexistence.

The end of this story suggests a fairly obvious question, and it's a question that (I suppose) is never answered. But those kinds of stories are always my favorite.

YOU TELL ME

There are two kinds of weather I really, truly, deeply appreciate. The first is when it's sunny and raining simultaneously; obviously, this is a clichéd, vaguely cinematic sentiment that I conversationally employ to make unsophisticated strangers think I'm interesting whenever we happen to discuss meteorological phenomena. However, the second type is an authentic expression of appreciation, and it can only happen in early spring or very early winter: it's when the sky is blindingly sunny and the air is remarkably cold. For record-keeping purposes, I classify this condition as "the weather of my childhood." Whenever I try to remember the circumstances surrounding recess when I was in first grade, that is how I always recall the experience: I'm wearing a restrictive jacket and my brother's stocking cap, my fingers are clenched

---

1. That version was titled "Gravity" and supposedly ran in a small, sporadically published Midwestern 'zine called *Ladies & Gentlemen.*

inside blue mittens, and I'm squinting into the sun. This is a deceptive brand of weather, but not if you're from North Dakota; if you're from North Dakota, you can *see* coldness. You can look out a window on a day that's completely sunny, and—if you squint very slightly—you can see the coldness hanging in the air like a colorless, odorless haze. There is a line in *The Diary of Anne Frank* where that little courageous Jewish girl mentions how she can smell the cold when someone from the outside enters the attic. Well, I come from North Dakota. I can fucking see it. You lose, Anne Frank.

This morning I am squinting at the cold from my balcony window. I have the easiest job in the world, and I'm really dreading going to work. I'm standing in my living room in my underwear (boxer briefs) and an Ozzy T-shirt (from the *Speak of the Devil* tour, when his guitarist was that dude from Night Ranger), both of which I am about to suffocate with a green sweater of the non-itchy variety. Pants are on my horizon; it's only a matter of time. If I were an adult, I would be drinking coffee; as it is, I'm drinking Mountain Dew. I can see the properties of ice clinging to the sun's ultraviolet rays, and they mock me like howler monkeys. Today will be akin to eating a bowl of cyanide capsules without the benefit of 2 percent milk.

It's Friday, 9:25 A.M., and I am in the northern half of the Western Hemisphere. If I put on pants immediately and walk out the door of my apartment, I will arrive at my office desk at 9:50 A.M., which is actually 9:30. When asked the question, "When do you usually get to work?" virtually everyone in the newspaper industry subtracts twenty minutes from the time they actually arrive. And since almost every reporter does this, this is almost reality. I have to pick between a pair of black jeans, a pair of gray jeans, a pair of tan jeans, a pair of lime jeans (blue jeans are not allowed), or a pair of khaki Dockers. I might feel like putting my hands in my pockets later this afternoon, so I go with the Dockers. I forget to wear a belt, which usually happens every third day; as such, I suppose this cannot be classified as forgetfulness.

Driving.

Driving.

Driving.

There are two parking lots for editorial employees of the *West Akron Forum Herald Dispatch*. The first is referred to as the Good Lot, which is directly across the street from the employee entrance. The Good Lot can hold a maximum of forty cars; I drive through it every morning, searching for an open space that exists only in dogmatic theory. My inevitable failure forces me to drive two blocks north, which is the entrance to the Chump Lot. The Chump Lot (also known as the "Rape Lot") is shared by three different businesses and was paved with concrete during the Bronze Age. There are no streetlights in the Chump Lot, and it's visually sealed off by office buildings and warehouses on three sides; the Chump Lot is like Nepal. This is where I park every day. The downside of the Chump Lot is that it's dangerous after 8:00 P.M.; the upside is that it's an ideal place to smoke angel dust, which is what I do before work, three days a week. There was a time in my life when I only smoked angel dust in the evening, but now I only smoke angel dust just before going into the office on Mondays, Thursdays, and Fridays. I'm going to assume the reasons for this schedule are self-evident.

Once my car is parked among those of my chumpish colleagues, I meticulously load my pipe with hallucinogenic gravel while listening to the radio. The DJ is named after a North American woodland creature and is playing what he has dubbed a "Dead or Alive" block, which includes Bon Jovi's "Wanted Dead or Alive," Van Halen's "D.O.A.," the '80s pop tune "You Spin Me Round (Like a Record)," and a live recording by Wings that does not make sense to me until I remember that Paul Is Dead. As always, it is my plan to take one monster hit, one small secondary hit, and then get out of my car. This plan almost always fails; inevitably, I take a monster hit, a secondary hit that is accidentally monstrous, a follow-up secondary hit, and then a final hit to address the erroneous conclusion that I'm (somehow) not stoned. There are many things that PCP does to your brain, but it mainly serves to convince you that you're not high enough. This is why it's generally wise to smoke angel dust with someone else; company forces you to conduct a conversation, which helps you realize you're insane. When you're alone, it's much too easy to get into that circular *Am I thinking these thoughts because I'm smoking angel dust or is this just how I always think?* logic trap, which is precisely what happens to me this morning as I think about Paul McCartney. I eventually take seven hits before climbing out of my car with the serpentine fluidity of a sexed-up Sasquatch.

The coldness of the air does not feel good on my jowls. I notice that I can only see the cold when I'm not tangibly feeling it; now the cold is whirling around me like a cloak of invisibility. I hope I have enough hit points to survive. I would jog toward my building if I wasn't so high, but instead I walk like Richard Roundtree (and consciously so). I get to my desk at 9:54 A.M., which is really 9:34. No one notices I've arrived. Nobody in any office ever notices when anyone else arrives; they only notice when people leave. Arriving whenever and leaving semi-late is much better for one's credibility than coming and going on time.

Like all geniuses, I don't work before noon. I have not performed any actual work before noon since 1989, which was the last time I mowed my parents' lawn. I could never have been a dairy farmer or a Marine or a PGA greenskeeper. Here is my itinerary for the morning: from 10:00 A.M. to 10:35, I will read the sports section of the *West Akron Forum Herald Dispatch*. From 10:35 to 10:40, I will read everything else of interest in that particular newspaper. I will then go to the bathroom for fifteen minutes. When I return to my desk, I will check my e-mail and return only those messages that do not require a response. At 11:20, I will stroll around the newsroom and strike up a conversation with a random coworker regarding a subject neither of us cares about, such as dog racing or abortion. At 11:35, I will read the AP wire on my computer (mostly the reviews of rock albums I will never own), and then at 12:10 I will leave the building to consume some kind of lunchlike meal. This is how the smartest man who has ever lived fights his way into the afternoon.

As I riffle through the meaningless faxes that have accumulated upon my desk, I notice that Tonya is already in her chair and talking on the telephone. Tonya is lefthanded and sits twenty-four inches away from me. It's 10:00, and she is explaining to someone that she didn't get into the office until almost 9:30, which means she got here ten minutes ago. Tonya is just about the stupidest goddamn person I have ever met. Tonya is the kind of person who goes shopping the day after Thanksgiving. I have no idea what her job is, although she sometimes describes herself as part of the "New Media," which (apparently) means she doesn't write stories that are objective, important, or interesting. I guess I'm part of the New Media, too.

Tonya gets off the phone. I try not to look at her.

"Hey Jack," she says to me.

"Hey hey," I say to Tonya. Tonya thinks we're friends because I sometimes say "hey hey" to her. She starts talking in my direction, but PCP makes me partially deaf. What I think she says is, "Did you hear that drone drone drone Aryan Nation rally drone drone drone drone ne'er-do-well drone drone drone Garrison Diversion Project zaga wagga zaga wagga Friday?"

I say, "Hmm."

I say, "Really?"

I get up and walk to the back of the newsroom, where we have copies of today's newspaper on a shelf. I see that Margaret Atwater is already standing there, reading the front page while standing next to the shelf (this is so she can reread it again at her desk and thereby erode more of her morning). I don't think Margaret ever works before noon, either. Margaret is something of a heroic figure. She's pro-Jack.

"Well, hello," says Margaret, who is forty but looks thirty-seven. "Hard day's night?"

"What? Who?"

326

"You look extremely tired."

"What? Why? What is this regarding?"

"You," Margaret says. "Look. Tired."

"Oh. Oh yeah. Fuck. Well, I'm tired all right." I pretend to look at something far off in the distance, but I'm really looking at the wall and it's only four feet away. "Anything notable in the paper today?"

Margaret looks back down at the front page. Her face keeps changing; sometimes she looks like Margaret, and sometimes she looks like deceased film legend Lon Chaney cast in a role where he's supposed to look like a woman who resembles Margaret. "There's an Adams story that jumps to the back page, there's a two-column brief by Hammerstein that's marginally amusing, and the rest of A1 is wire copy."

Nobody who works at a newspaper ever cares what specific stories are about; all anyone wants to know is who wrote them. That usually explains more than the story itself.

"I liked your review of *Fight Club*," Margaret says, and I suspect she is being sincere.

"Oh really," I say.

"It was funny."

"Well, I'm a pretty awesome writer."

Margaret laughs and (possibly) cackles. "Absolutely," she says.

That response seems less sincere.

I smile idiotically and walk back to my desk. As I walk, I scan the front page and see that the aforementioned Richard Adams's story is about the local reaction to a national event I haven't yet heard about. Adams suggests the community is "cautiously optimistic." The aforementioned brief by Julie Hammerstein isn't so much "funny" as it is an attempt *to write in the form of funniness*, which is what most journalists count as "funny." Hammerstein is almost talented, but I suspect she's secretly anti-Jack. I have no idea why she was hired. She brings nothing to the table.

I sit back down. Tonya is gone, so I don't have to hear any droning. Whenever she leaves, it's like someone has removed the refrigerator from my kitchen; I notice the lack of the hum more than I notice the hum. I miss Tonya. I crack open my second Mountain Dew and find myself wishing that I had smoked more angel dust, as I'm now positive that I'm not stoned enough: I can still control things with my thoughts, even when those things are disintegrating from the inside out.

As I mentally control the plastic phone receiver while it melts into my hand and fuses with my exoskeleton, I start watching a conversation between my staunchly pro-Jack editor and her adamantly anti-Jack supervisor. They are twenty-five feet away and I can't hear what they're saying, but I have a strong feeling they're talking about me; this is because they're trying very hard not to look at me, but whenever either one of them throws an all-too-casual glance in my direction the other person does the exact same thing to see if I noticed that someone just looked at me. For a fleeting second, I wonder if the angel dust is making me paranoid, but then I realize that being worried about PCP paranoia usually means I'm not very stoned. It's kind of like drunk driving: every time I suspect I'm too drunk to operate my car and I ask someone else for a ride, it really just means I can probably make it home on my own; whenever I'm sober enough to worry about dying or going to jail, I'm obviously not very drunk. However, whenever I'm too fucked up to do anything (drive, light a cigarette, masturbate, etc.), I inevitably crawl behind the wheel of my car and drive home alone, sometimes (ahem) "erratically." This is why I still can't understand how Alcoholics Anonymous is supposed to work. If the first step to recovery is "realizing there's a problem" . . . well, if you *realize* it, it can't be much of a problem, can it?

ANYWAY, I suspect my pro-Jack editor and her anti-Jack supervisor are conducting a Lincoln-Douglas debate over my recent job performance, which has not been "bad" inasmuch as it's been "curious." Over the past seven weeks, I have reviewed seventeen mainstream movies, and I have given every single one of these movies two out of four stars. Moreover, I have stated no strong opinion about any of these films in any of my reviews. The most outlandish modifiers I have used are *workmanlike, adequate,* and *understandably predictable.* This new direction is creating a strange quandary for my newspaper's management team; when they named me chief film critic, they adamantly promised not to interfere with the content of my personal opinions and would never question what I loved or what I hated. Clearly, they did not imagine a scenario where a film critic would have no opinion whatsoever about anything. In this regard, I have won the war.

The relationship between my pro-Jack editor and her anti-Jack supervisor is the classic "good cop/bad cop" scenario, so much so that it makes my life feel contrived. My pro-Jack editor is charmed by my eccentric style and self-referential wit; meanwhile, her anti-Jack supervisor thinks I'm self-absorbed and surly (within the dialogue of my fantasies, he calls me a "loose cannon" and wants to get me "off the streets"). When their little powwow is over, my pro-Jack editor walks directly toward the front of my desk. I appreciate that she makes no attempt to veil her intentions, especially since the newsroom is suddenly filled with green fog, swooping fruit bats, and at least three (3) sherpas.

"Good morning, Jack," she says.

"Hey hey," I say, only this time I mean it.

"As you undoubtedly noticed, I was just having a little conversation with Larry," she explains. "He insists the movie review that ran in today's paper didn't have a point."

"You mean the one that ran yesterday? The one about *Fight Club?*"

"Yeah."

"Well, which one did he mean? The one that ran today or the one that ran yesterday?"

"Did you have a review that ran today?"

"No."

She almost sighs.

"Regardless, the one that ran yesterday had a point," I continue. "You obviously must have noticed it. I mean, you edited the piece. Did it seem to have no point? I thought it made a brilliant point, actually. I thought it worked on multiple levels and delivered the kind of insight that smashes readers squarely in the solar plexus, momentarily changing the way they consume mass media."

"I thought the review was fine," my pro-Jack editor says. That means she said the same thing to Larry. My editor is the kind of person who could have had a tremendously successful career if she lied on occasion, but she never does.

"Lots of people are telling me they thought my review was hilarious," I say, which would be half-true if you excluded the first two words from the sentence.

"Well, you know Larry," she says, which I don't. But I know what she means. I know jackasses, and Larry is a jackass. She can't say, "Larry is a jackass," because Larry is her boss and she's a solid employee, but *everyone* thinks Larry Lowman is a jackass (even people like me, who have no grounds to prove it). Larry Lowman is actually more of an "assjack," which is like a jackass without the panache. "Larry also claims you gave every single movie this week the exact same rating, but I told him that was your decision as a critic."

"Some weeks are like that," I say.

Actually, every week is like that.

"Larry just needs something to worry about," she says, which indicates our conversation is losing its momentum. "I'll worry about Larry. You just keep doing what you're doing."

"You betchya, Ann," I say. "It's good to know you'll never waver from your pro-Jack stance."

I pick up the sports section and start reading about NASCAR results. Ann is still standing at my desk, and I can feel her looking at me through a photo of Jeff Gordon. Ann is trying to psychoanalyze me, but that process only lasts about eight seconds. Ann needs to get back to work; she has a job she simultaneously loves and hates, which means she spends about eleven hours in the office every single day. Ann is the fucking salt of the earth, and I will punch anyone who disagrees.

RICKY RUMBLE, SOUP CONSUMER

Driving driving driving driving driving. I've escaped from the hellish sulfur pit that is my morning workday; I'm now searching for a Chinese buffet restaurant. This will not be a problem: there are nine Chinese buffets within this dying community. This equates to one Chinese buffet for every 16,600 citizens in the metro Akron area. Chinese buffets have become the defining component of every Midwestern city; they are the backbone of modern-day Middle America.

My entire diet consists of three food types: Chinese food, cold cereal, and rare steak (though—if options are limited—I will also eat chicken strips). A self-actualized man need not consume anything else. Upon entering the parking lot of Panda Dynasty, I pull alongside the maroon Buick LeSabre of Ricky Rumble, another self-actualized man who is always referred to by his full name (sort of like "Cy Young" or "Sigourney Weaver" or "Yngwie Malmsteen"). Today, I shall not be eating my lunch alone.

The majestic power of the Chinese buffet is its sense of control: after paying a reasonable fee, I am given the opportunity to craft a meal to my own specifications. General Tso's chicken is always a core item, as is a portion of sweet and sour pork and white rice. Beyond that, I typically take three steamed dumplings, a ladle of walnut shrimp, and a few spare ribs if—and only if—they appear tender (but this is rare). These items are accompanied by a bowl of wonton soup and a Coke, unless the restaurant carries only Pepsi products and I am forced to opt for Mountain Dew (which I prefer to drink exclusively from twenty-ounce plastic bottles and almost never with food). This meal requires six napkins and can be finished in less than twenty minutes, but—as I said—what's important is that these are all factors I dictate. Every decision is mine; there are no compromises. I would assume

331

Lindsey Buckingham, Billy Corgan, and John Fogerty are all big Chinese-buffet consumers.

Ricky Rumble is sitting by himself in the far corner of the establishment, right next to an aquarium that contains dozens of gargantuan goldfish. At the table next to him, there is a little Asian boy standing on the seat of a booth, sneezing several times in succession. It's a little David Lynchian in here. Ricky Rumble does not wave me over, but his eyes clearly recognize my right to exist. I sit across from him in the red vinyl booth and create a conversation.

"Here's what's been on my mind," I begin, since intelligent people have no need for salutations. "Let's say a presidential candidate was on the cusp of winning his party's nomination; his party affiliation doesn't matter for the purposes of this hypothetical example. But let's assume he is pulling away from all his political rivals in all of the polls and he seems to be outlining a sensible economic and social plan for the future of America."

Ricky Rumble swallows a noodle and considers the opening details of the hypothetical. He is a handsome man with a mustache, and he likes to read nonfiction books about vampires. If Ricky Rumble were wounded in combat, I would crawl out of my foxhole to drag his bones to safety.

"Now, this presidential candidate is by no means an unorthodox outsider," I continue. "He is a career politician and—at least on the surface—a totally rational man. But as the campaign continues, he begins to casually mention how one of his administrative goals would be researching the possibility of building an underwater city, kind of like Atlantis. He doesn't make this his single issue, nor does he insist that the underwater community needs to be finished within his own lifetime—but he keeps offhandedly mentioning his hope that such a city will someday exist. And he has a bunch of semi-logical arguments for *why* this should happen. So here is my question: Do you think this bizarre desire would destroy his campaign?"

Forty seconds pass.

"Does he actually call this underwater city *Atlantis*?" asks Ricky Rumble.

"No."

"Does he specifically compare it to Atlantis? Does he call his tentative plan 'The Atlantis Project' or anything like that?"

"Well . . . no," I say. "But one has to assume that somebody like George Will or Tabitha Soren would pointedly ask him if he was referring to Atlantis whenever he spoke of this goal. I mean, that would be a rather unavoidable comparison. There aren't that many other well-known underwater communities."

"That *would* probably happen," Ricky Rumble says as he sips a pinkish beverage of unknown origin, "but he could just counter with something like, 'No no no. I'm not talking about fantasy here, I'm talking about reality, drone drone drone,' and it would start to seem no less irrational than the notion of a manned voyage to Mars. In fact, building Atlantis would probably be cheaper and might even have some agricultural benefits." Ricky Rumble looks down at his plate and considers his soup. His response to my inquiry was more nuanced than what I expected, and that makes me feel good. Part of the reason I have managed to thrive as the smartest man alive is because I'm still willing to keep learning; I totally enjoy evolving.

"Do you want to maybe do me a favor?" asks Ricky Rumble. This is a pretty shocking thing to hear, mostly because I've always secretly assumed that Ricky Rumble despised me.

"Absolutely," I say. "I will absolutely do you a favor as long as the word *maybe* is involved."

"Well, this is a pretty fucking crazy request."

"How crazy?"

"Pretty fucking crazy."

Now, I had not planned to see Ricky Rumble today, and he certainly had not planned to see me. I suppose it's possible he had been plotting to find me for days, but that's implausible and possibly impossible (there are simply too

333

many Chinese buffets in this town). I must therefore assume that Ricky Rumble would have asked the following favor of virtually anyone who sat next to him on this particular Friday, which makes me feel even better: I officially qualify as "virtually anyone," which is just about the best thing anyone can hope to be.

"Tomorrow night, I need you to drive to Cincinnati and pick up my sister," says Ricky Rumble.

"Um, okay," I say. This request is not fucking crazy, but it is a fucking nuisance. I instantly regret that I agreed to do this favor before I knew what it was. "I suppose I could do this. But I was hoping you'd just want me to get you some more steamed dumplings," I joke, although I'm not joking.

"Okay," says Ricky Rumble, "now here's the *fucking crazy* part: my sister is an exotic dancer, and you have to pick her up at her place of business as soon as she gets off work."

Suddenly, I suspect I have been unknowingly cast in a Cinemax documentary.

"She gets off work at four," Ricky Rumble said.

"Four in the morning?"

"No, four in the afternoon. She's basically just a stripper's apprentice. But do *not* call her a stripper. I'm totally fucking serious, man. She really hates that, and she'll freak if you say anything about exotic dancing that is the least bit offensive. And do *not* hit on her, because she's got a serious boyfriend and she doesn't understand why men think they can hit on her just because she dances naked in public. I mean, she'll literally start screaming at you if you say anything that sounds remotely suggestive. And regardless of how she dresses, do *not* look at her cleavage or her legs. Or her ass. Or her neck."

Tomorrow is going to be the worst day of my life.

"Truth be told, my sister is kind of nuts," Ricky Rumble continues. "She's kind of a bitch. But I need her to be here on Saturday night, and I can't drive to Cincinnati tomorrow afternoon."

"Why not?" I ask.

"I just can't," he says.

Well, that certainly explains everything.

"Why do you need her here Saturday night?"

"Well, it sounds like she's pretty whacked out on coke, so I need to deal with her."

"Ah, Christ," I say, which may have sounded like empathy but was really just the verbal recognition of how terrible this drive is going to be. I also can't help but notice that *she's pretty whacked out on cocaine* does not serve as a proper answer to the question of *why do you need her here Saturday night*, but I don't push it.

"The good news is that this club is easy to find," Ricky Rumble continues, realizing I've now listened long enough to be trapped. "It's actually on the northern perimeter of town, so you don't even need to enter the city limits, unless you want to. You just take exit 168, which is right after the amusement park exit, and you'll immediately see a truck stop and this particular strip joint, which is called something like Paradise Lost or Paradise City. It's evidently where all the truckers go."

"Exit 168?"

"Yeah, it's kind of a unruly establishment. I guess it's a 'full-contact' club, whatever that means. I've never actually been there, but I can just about imagine."

"Yeah, I can just about imagine. You said exit 168, right?"

"My sister's name is Nikki, but I think she has a stage name and—unfortunately—I have no idea what that stage name is. But she should be easy to spot, because she looks like Valerie Bertinelli. And I guess her gimmick is that she wears eyeglasses while she dances, even though her vision has always been 20/20."

"Like, librarian's glasses?"

"Exactly."

I have always been deeply aroused by bookish whores, but I remain stoic.

"Listen," Ricky Rumble says. "I know this is an incredible hassle, but I would really owe you large if you did me this solid."

Do people really talk like this? I guess they must.

"Yeah, I can handle the assignment," I reply, mostly because I can't fabricate any excuse beyond insisting that I'm agoraphobic, which is semi-true but not very convincing, especially since we're having this conversation in a public place. I'm almost certain the process of finding this woman will be more complicated than Ricky Rumble claims, and I'm sure the drive home will be uncomfortable and boring and sexually frustrating. But I like the idea of Ricky Rumble owing me "large." There's nothing more satisfying than being owed an unnamed something, and he will definitely owe me for this.

"So I take exit 168 to get to Paradise City at four o'clock, where I'll pick up Nikki Rumble who's not really 'Nikki Rumble' and who's not a stripper but *is* a bitchy doppelganger for Eddie Van Halen's wife. Anything else I need to know?"

"No. Thanks, Jack. I owe you."

"Don't mention it," I say, and my wonton soup tastes like self-actualization.

A CAVE IS A GOOD PLACE FOR A WEDDING

Since it's already Friday afternoon, it hardly seems sensible to exert much effort once I return to the office. I check my e-mail again, and I have three messages; all of them are comments on today's *Garfield* comic strip. It seems that Jon Arbuckle is attempting to meet a woman through a computer dating service, but Garfield is questioning his computer literacy. This is pretty much the only way I keep in touch with my closest friends from the past; every day, we send messages that analyze the sociopolitical subtext of *Garfield, Mary Worth, Gasoline Alley, Blondie, Rex Morgan M.D.*, and (occasionally) *Mark Trail*. We're all pretty sure Beetle Bailey represents the Zapatista Liberation Movement.

I fire off an e-mail that suggests Garfield is a recovering sex addict before I begin typing a review of the controversial

NC-17 Jodi Foster vehicle *Noah's Whore*. I think I will give it two out of four stars, but then I lose focus. I check my e-mail again (nothing new about Garfield) and try to rewrite my review of *Chill Factor*, which stars Cuba Gooding Jr. and Skeet Ulrich. This is an action movie about a white guy and a black guy who hate each other and must diffuse a bomb before it turns Montana into Antarctica. This, of course, is mostly speculation on my behalf; I was actually finishing a review of *The Caveman's Juke Box* (a melodrama about Asian silk smuggling starring Nic Cage and Joan Allen) on my laptop computer while watching the press screening of *Chill Factor*. It was difficult to concentrate on what Skeet was saying. I gave both of these movies two out of four stars. And—at the risk of sounding intellectually vain—I must admit that the unedited version of my *Chill Factor* review is profoundly intriguing; though I don't remember writing any of it, it appears I compared *Chill Factor* with Francis Ford Coppola's *The Conversation* and Peter Bogdanovich's self-indulgent *Donkey Assassin*, two movies that were habitually rented by my cashew-gorged college roommate and his (now deceased) girlfriend.

Somewhere between 2:30 and 3:15, my mood becomes opaque and I start staring through the monitor of my computer, which is the only way you can stare at nothingness when your office has no windows. Everything is swallowed by the expanding hole inside my brain, and I start fantasizing about getting married. I come up with several ingenious ideas for my wedding day, and these include: putting a bottle of Goldschlager on every table at the reception; having the ceremony at midnight; holding the ceremony inside a cave; wearing a top hat and a cape; finding a way to play "November Rain" and "Cruel to Be Kind" on a pipe organ; whisking my beautiful Cuban/Canadian wife away in either a helicopter or a hovercraft. This is a pleasant line of thought, but somehow it changes: now I'm fantasizing about being famous and divorced after optioning my self-absorbed novel into a racially charged screenplay, and I live in a three-story beach house in

Southern California. All my friends from college come out to see me, and they're shocked that I don't have any furniture except a few beanbags and a bearskin rug. I'm emaciated and unshaven. I've quit reading *Garfield* and I keep sneaking into the den to snort massive amounts of uncut cocaine off a fiberglass surfboard, and all my friends are disturbed by my unoriginal paranoia and my obsession with discussing the dangers of genetic engineering. Every night at sunset we walk down to the beach in my backyard, and I sigh a lot and sometimes vomit and every once in awhile a vapid model/actress arrives at 3:00 A.M. and we have terrible sex and then she immediately leaves and I weep. "Darkness," I sob. "There is only darkness here." I am sullen and inconsolable; my friends shudder and feel better about their own lives. These are my fantasies.

Suddenly it's 6:50 P.M., and my salt-of-the-earth editor comments on how I'm burning the midnight oil as she puts on her unremarkable wool coat and walks out the employees' entrance to smoke a Camel Light.

THERE'S ONLY YOU AND ME AND WE JUST DISAGREE

By the time I get home, it's 7:25. This is always a good time to eat Cap'n Crunch. Seconds after the milk has collapsed upon my foodstuffs, the phone rings. I have one of those clear plastic phones, just like the one Axl Rose smashed in the video for "Patience." I'm sitting in my ugly orange recliner and watching the phone ring, and I just know it's going to be Donna. It rings and it rings and it rings and finally my answering machine picks up, and I hear, "Hey, it's me," which means it *is* Donna, who then spends the next fifteen seconds going, "Are you there . . . hello? . . . I know you're sitting there . . . helloooo." At some point she sighs in her predictably boorish fashion and says something inane, such as, "Well, I guess you're really *not* there." But then she starts talking about her job (which I think involves either children or food, or maybe both), her roommate's unwillingness to pay for cable, a sitcom about a foreign exchange student titled *Start to Finnish*, and maybe even something about bullfighting, although that seems a little improbable. Since my answering machine is in my bedroom and the door is partially closed and I'm dealing with a mouthful of cereal that's slicing the roof of my mouth into ribbons, I can't get a feel for the specific details of this call, but the bottom line is that she's going to stop by my apartment in less than fifty-nine minutes.

Christ.

For the record, I want to state that I technically went on only one date with Donna three years ago and I have done nothing to perpetuate this relationship since that singular evening. To the best of my knowledge, I have no feelings for her whatsoever, beyond the fact that she has an amazing skeletal frame and the worst fucking taste in everything. I first saw her in a shopping mall; she was working in a store called Sandcastle Majik, which sold candles and (possibly) wind chimes. Donna is tall, borderline anorexic, and possesses a nonproblematic horse face. I noticed her immediately. Eight hours later, I coincidentally bumped into her at a bar that no longer exists and I asked, "So who's buying candles these days?" A conversation erupted, tragically resulting in my asking Donna to accompany me to an afternoon press screening of the film *Gummo* on the following afternoon. The movie made her cry and (I think) sort of turned her on. Since that afternoon, I can't remember the last time I went seventy-two hours without being forced to talk to her. We generally have one of three conversations: (a) she talks about why we are not in love (I stay neutral), (b) she talks about some shitty band I've never listened to (I believe they are called Rusted Root), or (c) she talks about how the dramatic scenario depicted in Steven Spielberg's *Duel* was supposedly based on a real-life event that once happened to her father (an anecdote which does, in fact, seem legitimate).

It's been several months since I've been able to handle talking to Donna while sober, so I pour three shots of Southern Comfort into a Coke glass and fill it up with Mountain

Dew; this creates a color resembling the deepest waters of Loch Ness. In order to be more efficient, I suck on an ice cube while I drink (this eliminates the problem of the cubes melting in the glass and diluting the mix). I figure I have fifty minutes to get fucked up, plus or minus three hundred seconds. Time for three drinks, maybe. The first glass goes down like a handful of liquid thistles, but the second is smooth as a gravy avalanche and the third literally disappears from the glass that contains it. When Donna knocks on the door of my apartment and opens it in one motion (she has her own key), I am both drowsy and awake, the product of combining 80 proof alcohol with enough caffeine and glucose to make a ground sloth break-dance. I'm now in the perfect mood to see Donna.

"I knew you were home," Donna says as she blindly stumbles into my living room, blind because the sudden warmth of the apartment hallway has caused her eyeglasses to fog. "I bet you were home when I called, weren't you? You were probably just sitting there, looking at last week's newspaper, weren't you?" She's smiling and carrying a plastic bag that appears to hold a six-pack of Rolling Rock.

"No, I actually just got home," I lie. "I was at the bar with people from work."

"Oh, come on."

"No, I was. Why would I lie about going to the bar with my coworkers?"

"Which bar? Who were you with?"

"I see you have beer," I say. "Do you intend to drink it?"

Donna walks into my kitchen and puts five beers into my fridge. I hear her open one bottle and drop the cap onto the Formica counter. It bounces onto the tile floor and rolls across the room (I can't see this, but I know it's happening). She is talking about something that pertains to her life, but I'm not really listening to the words (although this time I'm almost *sure* she says something about bullfighting, which is starting to make me worry that I might have gotten stoned and booked us a vacation to Spain). When Donna reappears

340

in the living room, I notice that she's always more attractive than I remember when she's away. "Dearest," I ask, "will you fix me a drink?" Donna says "no" (I guess in order to be "funny") before immediately taking my glass into the kitchen and pouring me a SoCo and Dew; unfortunately, she's a girlie girl, which means I get a glass with seven ice cubes and maybe two thimbles of booze. The electric greenness of this drink completely and perfectly matches the color of Donna's eyes. I suppose that's poetic, but it's certainly not getting me any drunker.

We sit together on my futon. Donna snuggles up and tells me that she missed me today, and she laughs when I accuse her of lying. We talk a little about the bands Son Volt and Wilco, and Donna explains how her roommate from college once fooled around with one of Donna's ex-boyfriends (while listening to *Being There*) and that even though she no longer cared about the guy, she "mourned" the loss of that roommate in a way that has forever changed the way she views female friendships (or something like that; I have no idea what that really has to do with alternative country or bullfighting, although I think Jeff Tweedy was somehow implicated). She makes me another drink and it's (again) filled with at least seven cubes, which prompts me to give a twenty-minute lecture on the physical properties of ice.

For a moment, I suspect I am spontaneously passing out, but it turns out Donna has just dimmed my floor lamp and is now sitting next to me in a way that makes it impossible for me not to keep colliding with her breasts. Her left hand is suddenly on my stomach and she's trying to quietly purr or growl or possibly whistle and then her hand is rubbing rather suggestively against my crotch (which is really the only way a crotch can be rubbed, I suppose). At this point I assume she's not listening to my insights on ice, so I try to play along and start unbuttoning her shirt, although I'm not doing a very good job (I'm distracted by the fact that she's wearing a purple bra, which I had no way of anticipating). Donna slides down onto the floor and unzips my jeans, pulling them down around my thighs. She wordlessly delivers a totally unnecessary hand job that takes much too long, mostly because I'm much too wasted. When I finally cum, she wipes her paw on the carpet beneath the futon and takes a quick swig of beer; I lay on my back like a stupefied walrus and cough. Donna collapses on top of me, smiling and disheveled. "You can't go down on me, so don't even try," she says. "Because if you do, it'll just get me all crazy and we'll have to fuck, and I never want to fuck you again." This is almost certainly an attempt to seem coy and desirable, but it strikes me as completely reasonable. I fall asleep like an old man who has consumed a turkey.

When I awake at 3:30 to piss, Donna is gone. She has forgotten to turn off VH1, but that's a minor oversight. I forgive her.

A HOLE IN THE SKY

I awake to the sound of nothingness at 11:11 A.M., and I'm already late. The sun is shining lazily and snow is gently falling, but I don't see any coldness in the atmosphere. I am overcome by a sense of morose dread that is usually reserved for psychological thrillers starring Michael Douglas that teach us how voyeurism is seductive but dangerous.

I take a shower and notice that I (strangely) have no urge to masturbate, which is how I remember that Donna was over the night before. For the second time in two days, I once again ponder what Donna does for a living; I know she quit working at the candle store two years ago, but she must do *something*, because she always has money.

By 11:33 I have found a sweatshirt that almost seems nice enough to be a sweater (or maybe it's the other way around) and I'm back in my car, driving driving driving east on West Market Street toward Mr. Hwang's Great Wall of China. On Saturdays, I can get sweet and sour shrimp for $4.95, which is remarkable. Granted, the devious Mr. Hwang still charges $2 for a small Coke but *fuck*, man: five bones for shrimp cannot be denied.

My goal on this Cincinnati trip is multidimensional. The technical motivation is to pick up the sexy Rumble sibling without disaster, but that's only the bottom line. On the drive back to Akron, I will attempt a hoax: it will be my intention to trick Nikki Rumble into believing that I am a raging homosexual. I will also pretend to be nearsighted. This will be a two-pronged hoax.

Unfortunately, none of these things will happen. None of these things will happen because today is one of those days that will change the course of my entire life; oddly, I kind of had the suspicion this might happen. I know it as soon as I jump on the Martin Luther King Expressway in order to get to Interstate 70; I take the wrong off-ramp. I do this every time I go to Cincinnati; I end up driving directly *over* I-70, which leads me out of Akron on a familiar two-lane highway I only travel upon when lost. I get lost a lot. But I always keep driving. Driving driving driving. I think there is a way back to the interstate. Of course, I always think this; I always think the road is going to intersect with another north-south highway that merges back to I-70. Roads bend; time bends; the universe is a series of super strings; I know my fucking physics. But things aren't always what they seem—and that is not a cliché. That is a statement of fact. Suddenly I'm on the outskirts (but not quite the middle) of nowhere, and Matthew Sweet is on the radio telling me he's sick of himself. I start to wonder how much Nikki Rumble is going to complain when I arrive two hours late. I imagine her calling me a dipshit.

This is when a woman falls out of the sky and lands on the hood of my car.

People love metaphors, and so do I. If given the opportunity, I will try to compare anything to something else, even if they're only marginally related. But I remain hard-pressed to come up with any autonomous, universal experience that mirrors the experience of having a woman fall out of the sky and landing on your automobile. Even for the smartest man in the world, this feels unprecedented.

When I was five years old, my uncle hit a horse with a

343

Chevy Silverado, and it pretty much annihilated both the vehicle and the beast. I knew a guy from high school who ran into a moose with a grain truck and said it was like driving into the side of a barn. I recall an urban legend that suggests drivers should actually *speed up* if they find themselves in a situation when they're about to hit a deer, because slamming into a buck at over 60 mph will cause the animal to sail over the top of the vehicle like Donner or Blizten; according to this theory, the reason people are always wrecking their cars on deer is because the natural reaction is hitting the brake, which causes you to make impact at about 25 or 30 mph—the perfect speed for ramming an ungulate through your windshield. However, the unifying element within all of these examples is that they involve objects that exist *on the ground*. In all three cases, the thrust comes from the movement of the car, not from the object itself. This is not the case when a woman falls from the sky. When a woman falls out of the sky and hits the hood of your '97 Saturn on a rural highway outside of Akron, Ohio, some remarkable shit goes down.

First of all, the woman literally flattens your engine block; the front of your car looks like a crushed Pepsi can. Secondly, people who fall from the sky really, really, *really* bounce. I suppose I've heard about suicide victims who jump from tall buildings and bounce off the sidewalk, but you need to see this firsthand to appreciate the sheer reflexive force that accompanies such a collision. It's like this chick is on a bungee cord: once she hits the car, she goes straight back up like a hyperviolent yo-yo. The third thing that happens is that the front of your car is jammed into the pavement, and cars do *not* bounce. And since Saturn shock absorbers are (evidently) not designed to respond to humans who fall from the sky, the front axle is driven into the asphalt like a tailback who tries to turn the corner on Ray Lewis. The car suddenly handles like an accelerating glacier. You can't steer; you drift at high speed. You careen off the road, and—in my case—you catapult over the ditch and into a recently harvested cornfield, where you knock down the remnants of pig feed for almost sixty yards.

It's interesting what you think about at times like this (if, in fact, women mysteriously falling from the sky can be lumped into a genre of "times" that are somehow alike). It is at this very moment—shuddering in the front seat of my car, surrounded by corn stalks and the dulcet voice of Matthew Sweet—that it occurs to me that I was born to be a journalist. This is because the first thing I think of (after realizing I am still alive) is that this situation is going to make a great newspaper story and, *man,* do I hope they let me quote myself when I write it. I sit in my car for awhile (maybe four minutes, maybe fourteen), and then I get out and walk back to the road, retracing the path of my tires over the cold, hard ground. The body is on the shoulder of the highway, two hundred feet behind me. It takes a while to jog over to her corpse. She is lying on her back, and—though I hate to seem sexist at a time like this—the corpse is amazingly attractive, especially when you consider how every bone in her body is crushed into pulp. She is wearing a black cocktail dress, which goes nicely with the blackness of her hair and the hollowness of her eyes. I bet she was a real heartbreaker when she wasn't plummeting to her death—sort of a goth Gwen Stefani.

There's not much you can do in a situation like this.

You basically just hold your head between your hands and try to deduce what the fuck just happened. Which is impossible. This shock lasts almost two minutes. When you finish with your shock, you just stand on the road and wait for somebody else to show up, and you hope they react in exactly the same manner.

Well, this settles it. I give up. I'm buying a cell phone.

RICKY RUMBLE IS A SURPRISINGLY COMMON NAME

I've always suspected I could get away with one murder. Not a *bunch* of murders, but at least one. Whenever I write about movies where characters try to pull off elaborate crimes that inevitably fail—and there are three of these films released every holiday weekend—I always make it a point of my review to pedantically explain what these criminals did wrong. I've gotten quite adroit at this. Sometimes I tell Donna that I could murder my next-door neighbor and nobody would know for weeks, but she just laughs and laughs and laughs. "Why don't you just murder me?" she says. "You could burn my clothes in the furnace room and hide my bones under the sink." I really don't understand why she has to be so goddamn cocky all the time.

But *this*, of course, is not a murder scene. I have no need to hide the victim's body; as far as I can tell, I absolutely did not murder her. This I know. What I don't know is how I'm going to explain how this woman died, which isn't all that different than if I'd actually killed her.

I walk back to the point of impact, which I gauge to be about twenty-five feet behind the skid marks that indicate where I slammed on the brakes. There are no trees along this road, so she couldn't have jumped out of a tree house. I momentarily wonder if I just drove over her and I'm in some state of hallucinogenic denial, but my Saturn proves I'm not nuts: the dent on my hood proves there was a vertical impact. I spend a lot of time looking straight up into nothing; I am halfway hoping I'll see a blimp. Akron is the home of Goodyear Tires and likes to call itself "the Birthplace of Aviation," so the skies of northeast Ohio are lousy with blimp traffic. Akron is the only city in America where it's unusual *not* to see a blimp during the span of any given weekend. During football season, the sky around Akron literally becomes supersaturated with blimps (in other words, the air literally contains more blimps than it has the potential to hold). People in Akron completely adore these aircraft; the whole city is blimp crazy. I guarantee you, if this woman really *had* fallen out of a blimp, a certain sector of the community would have been strangely ecstatic; one life is a small price to pay for some extra-sexy blimp lore.

However, I see no blimps today. Another diagnosis eliminated.

A vehicle drives past me while I am looking up at the sun, my hands on my hips like a relief pitcher who just blew a save. Amazingly, the car never stops. It drives right past me, right past the dead girl lying on the road, and directly through the horizon. Who would do such a thing? Who drives past a confused (and potentially anguished) man, not to mention a female corpse? For a moment, I have a vision that people will drive past this disaster all afternoon, and I will be forced to call the local conservative talk-radio host and complain about how our society is going to hell (the host will undoubtedly support my claim, blame the Internet, and title that day's program "The Death of the Good Samaritan"). However, a Ford pickup truck comes by about eleven minutes later, and the driver melodramatically slams on its brakes in front of the woman and jumps out of the truck's cab.

"Oh my God," says this almost-middle-aged man who appears to be some sort of successful corn farmer. "Oh my dear God. What happened? Oh my dear God. Holy fuck. Oh my dear God. Oh my dear God."

It doesn't take long for me to realize I'm dealing with a full-on drama queen, which demystifies the stoicism I traditionally associate with those involved in agriculture. I have no idea how I'm going to explain the bizarre nature of this accident to a lunatic; he does not seem self-actualized enough to handle my "woman from the heavens" anecdote. I bet this fucking guy had *pancakes* for breakfast.

"Don't worry," I say. "She's been dead for awhile." This kind of comes out wrong, but he's too freaked to notice.

"Oh my dear dear God," the farmer continues, kneeling next to the foxy dead girl and touching her temple. Maybe he's actually a rancher, because he has no qualms about touching a dead mammal. "Did you hit her? What was she doing on the road?"

These are both interesting questions. The first is actually an accusation, even though it's worded as an inquiry. The second is essentially a plea bargain and a chance for me to get my story straight; I assume I'm expected to say, "I never saw her"

or "She just bolted onto the road." Perhaps I'm even supposed to say, "I think she wanted me to hit her," which is
crazy—but far more reasonable than reality.

"You're not going to believe this," I say, "but she fell out of
the sky and landed on my car."

He does not believe this, but he doesn't say so.

"I know how unreasonable that must sound," I continue,
"but you gotta check out my car. Seriously. It's like . . . it will
blow your mind. I hate to sound juvenile, but this is like
landing on fucking Mars or something."

We just stare at each other for a few moments, and he
gives me a look that makes me wonder if maybe he thinks I'm
a serial killer. But I continue stepping backward and gesturing for him to follow me into the cornfield, and—amazingly—
he does. And—even more amazingly—he looks at my car for
all of ten seconds before aggressively concluding that my
story is true. It's sort of ironic, because he seems to think he
needs to convince *me* of this. "Oh, she fell from above all
right," he tells me, looking at my hood like he's somehow
going to fix it. "Look at that dent. Just *look* at it. You couldn't
do that with a damn sledgehammer. There's no doubt about
it. This one takes the cake, all right. It takes the god-blessed
cake. Son of a B."

Now that I've convinced my plaid-clad drama queen that
(a) I'm not a killer and (b) women really *do* fall like hail, it's
time to construct our next move. We walk back to his truck,
and I assume he's going to drive and get some help while I
guard the body from raccoons. But the farmer merely opens
his glove box and pulls out a cell phone. Can you believe
that? Even farmers have cell phones. How embarrassing. I
am so out of the loop.

He calls 911. His description of the situation is compelling;
his words are purposefully vague about what has just transpired. Perhaps he thinks help will come faster if the authorities are mildly intrigued. When he finishes, I ask if I can
borrow the phone. Much to his surprise, I immediately call
directory information.

"Hi," I say, and a woman asks what city and state I need. I say, "Akron, in Ohio." She asks what listing, and I say, "Donna St. Shockman." It has been so long since I've actively called Donna that I have no clue what her phone number is. I get the digits and pump them back into the cell, barely noticing that my attention-starved farmer is furrowing his brow in my direction.

The phone rings once before Donna picks up. "Hello?"

"Yeah. Hey, it's me."

"Oh my God," Donna says with a snort. "Hello. What in the hell are *you* calling *me* about? Are you dying?"

"Technically speaking, yes," I say. "There's been an accident."

Donna gasps. I'm serious—she actually fucking *gasps*.

"No no no, don't worry, I'm fine," I say. "I had a car accident, but I'm not hurt. I'm not hurt at all. But you need to pick me up, if that's okay."

"Oh, absolutely," she says. "That's no problem. But are you really not hurt? Are you sure? Did you hit your head? Do you feel nauseous? What happened? Was there another car? Where are you?"

"No, it was a one-car accident," I say. "I guess I hit something, sort of. But hey, can you do me another favor?"

"Anything."

"Look up the name Ricky Rumble in the phone book. R-U-M-B-L-E. There will be listings for three 'Richard Rumbles' in town, but call the one listed first in the book. Tell him I've encountered an unexpected problem and I won't be able to fetch Valerie Bertinelli. Tell him that . . . I don't know, tell him that I regret the error."

"Okay. No problem. As long as you're all right. No problem. I need to call Richard Rumble. The first Richard Rumble in the book."

"Cool."

I give her driving directions to where I'm at, and I hang up. I say "thanks" as I hand the phone back to the farmer. He says nothing, although his eyes clearly ask, "How in the fuck do you have that fucking conversation without mentioning that a fucking woman fell out of the fucking sky?"

I'm almost tempted to wink at him like Richard Dawson, but that would be rude.

YOU TELL ME

Much to my surprise, dealing with my Woman from the Sky problem is not as incendiary as one might expect. When the police arrive, I am asked the same questions four times by four different officers, and only one acts the least bit incredulous. The core of the questioning is built around the repetition of the most obvious inquiry, which is, "Now, are you *positive* she wasn't on the road when the collision happened?" I say "yes" to this question all four times and I shake my head very slowly and raise my eyebrows. It helps considerably that the middle-aged farmer (who turns out to be named Grover) corroborates my story in a way that suggests he actually saw this incident with his own eyes. Grover's details regarding the event are amazingly lucid; although he periodically admits he's "just speculating," his account of the incident is far more specific than mine.

The coroner is a fortyish man with a Stevie Ray Vaughan hat, and his assistant is a tiny blond woman who can't be older than twenty-one. Do coroners have interns? I suppose they must. The pair treats the body very gingerly, partially because they know this corpse will demand an autopsy and possibly because the bones in her limbs are like pieces from a jigsaw puzzle. I watch them pour her into a black plastic bag when a reporter from the *West Akron Forum Herald Dispatch* arrives at the scene; I've never met this person before, but I recognize his car and he's carrying a notebook and he looks like he doesn't want to be here, so he's obviously a reporter.

As is so often the case, the reporter immediately recognizes me, even though I perceive him as a total stranger; it seems that I am the only person at the newspaper who doesn't know everyone else who works there. For an instant, I can tell he suspects I'm here as a journalist and starts to move in my direction, but one of the cops (the slightly incredulous one) intercepts his path and starts giving him all the usual cop bullshit. This verbal exchange evidently includes a lot of hard-core expository information, because the reporter seems to understand the entire scenario in less than thirty seconds. They appear to make an agreement to chat later (both of them nod when they shake hands), and then the reporter continues toward me. I smile and put on my nonthreatening face.

"Holy shit, Jackson," he says with an almost maniacal grin. "We heard about this over the scanner, but of course they didn't say who the driver was." All newsrooms keep a police scanner on at all times, which is how they get to accidents so quickly. "What in the hell happened here? Some woman fell on your car? What does that even mean?"

"You tell me," I say, which seems like the right thing to say. "I have no idea. I was just driving the car."

"Well, tell me what happened," he asks, pulling up his notebook. "The cops seem totally bamboozled."

"Whatever he told you is probably true. I was just driving, and then this chick . . . this female, I mean . . . came out of nowhere and smacked the top of my hood. You gotta check out my car. It's like—it's like not even a car anymore. It's like . . . it's not driveable."

"But how can this be?" he asks. "Did you see where she fell from? Do you think she jumped out of a plane or something?"

"A plane or *something*? Like a helicopter?"

"She fell from a helicopter?"

"I don't know. You tell me. Maybe it was a fucking hot air balloon. I don't look at the sky while I'm driving."

"Do you have a sunroof?"

I sigh.

"You know, I think you should talk to that guy over there," I say. "His name is Grover. I think maybe he saw the whole thing."

The reporter is looking at me with a synthesis of confusion and frustration. I wish I knew this guy's name. That would buy some time.

"Listen," I say. "Do you need me to write anything about this? Do you need any help?" I know he'll say he doesn't need any, but I have to ask.

"Naw, don't worry about it," he responds, "unless you *want* to write something. Like a first-person sidebar or something? That could be great."

"No, I don't want to write anything," I say, although I do.

Before he goes over to talk with Grover, the still unknown newsman asks if I need a ride back to Akron, and I tell him I don't. He says he'd like to get a few decent quotes from me later in the day, so I tell him to call me at home. As he jogs away, I see Donna's car arriving in the distance. Donna has one of those aqua-colored Volkswagen Beetles that are actively targeted at people who want to purchase a semblance of character.

I walk over to the shortest cop to tell him I'm leaving, and (at first) he acts like I need to stick around. This attitude changes after a private conference with the incredulous cop; now he only wants my phone number and address, which I already gave him. I give him the information again. We shake hands and he says, "Now, you be careful on the drive home," and then he laughs. I don't even give him a courtesy laugh.

I get into Donna's car before she has a chance to get out. She looks concerned, so I say, "Don't look so concerned."

Donna asks a bunch of practical questions, such as "What happened?" and "Are you just going to leave your car in that cornfield?" I tell her not to worry and ask if she has any pot in the car.

"You know I don't smoke pot," she says.

I'm supposed to know this?

"Let's just get out of here," I tell her. "I'll explain on the way home."

Donna makes a surprisingly tight U-turn on the highway

and we barrel back to the Rubber City. There is a conscious silence; she is waiting for me to explain what has just transpired. I take the opportunity to turn up a show on National Public Radio; they are rebroadcasting a heated debate over the most effective way to portage a canoe.

"Jack," she says with the kind of voice people use during interventions, "please don't be like this. Why are you like this? Why won't you talk to me? You know you can tell me anything. I think you know that."

"Did you call Ricky Rumble?"

"Yes yes *yes*. Of course I called Ricky Rumble. He seemed very nice and actually a little flirtatious, not that you'd possibly fucking care. He asked if you were all right."

"That doesn't sound like Ricky Rumble. What else did you tell him?"

"I said, 'I think he's all right but I don't know,' because obviously *I don't know*. Did you hit a deer? If you only hit a deer, why can't you tell me what happened? And if you *didn't* hit a deer, why can't I know what you hit? Or what hit you. Or whatever."

I have never portaged a canoe.

It feels like the car is filling with carbon monoxide.

I wish I had just met Donna St. Shockman ten minutes ago. I wonder who is buying candles these days.

"Jack," Donna says in a serious voice that actually sounds a little like her sex voice, "are you in some sort of trouble?"

We drive past a field of cows. I place my left hand on Donna's right knee (suggestively, but dispassionately). I look out the passenger's-side window, into the distant eyes of an unenthusiastic cow.

"I don't think so," I respond. "I really don't."

HELPLESS PEOPLE ON SUBWAY TRAINS SCREAM
TO GOD AS HE LOOKS IN ON THEM

Donna will (of course) find out about the Woman from the Sky when she reads tomorrow's newspaper, and she will (of course) spend all of Sunday afternoon asking me six thousand questions while acting dumbfounded about my unwillingness to tell her any details. I probably won't say much; after reading the newspaper article, she will understand the situation as well as I do (actually, she will probably understand it better: I will be unaware that the woman was never identified, nor will I have considered most of the theories that attempt to explain why it might have happened). At one point in the afternoon, Donna will cross her arms and stare at me for twenty minutes, trying to seem hurt and angry at the same time. She's so emotionally uncreative.

The irony of all this is that tonight—Saturday—is arguably the best evening we will ever spend together. We hit the outskirts of town just after 4:00 P.M., which is evidently the only time Donna eats on weekends. I convince her to stop at the Great Wall of China, where she gets twelve steamed dumplings and some kind of oversized noodle. We decide to consume this food back at my apartment, which evolves into a "win-win" situation: it allows me to have a drink, nick a few dumplings, analyze the day's events, consider my financial future, fuck Donna, and watch two episodes of *The Real World/Road Rules Challenge*.

As soon as we get through the door, I rush into the kitchen and pour myself a tsunami's worth of SoCo-Dew, which seems totally understandable under the circumstances (I mean, I *did* just see a dead woman—I certainly have every right to be disquieted). Donna nibbles on her noodle and looks sharp in her capri pants, and I am pleasantly surprised that she temporarily loses interest in her interrogation; she simply sits on my floor and smiles, obviously rhapsodic about being inside my apartment, even though I have no idea why anyone could be rhapsodic about being with me. The reporter from the *Dispatch* never calls. I try to phone Ricky Rumble, but all I get is his machine (and since I know he has Caller ID, I do not leave a message). For ninety minutes, I lie on the futon and outline my views on partial-birth abortion. Donna drinks a shitload of wine and asks me a bunch of questions about the life of F. Scott Fitzgerald, some of which I know but all of which I answer.

Donna passes out at around 9:30. I watch her doze on my carpet for the better part of an hour. Lying on her back with her limbs akimbo, she reminds me of The Girl Who Fell from the Sky. I keep trying to convince myself that they are somehow related, or that I met both of them in the same way. But then I become distracted by an encore presentation of MTV's *Total Request Live*: there's just something captivating about Nova Scotian pop sensation Alexis Nakita, and it has nothing to do with the fact that she looks sixteen years old; it has to do with the fact that she *aspires* to look sixteen, which is something a normal nineteen-year-old woman would never desire. I bet Alexis Nakita is a genius. I bet we have a lot in common. Somewhere during the third chorus of her power ballad "Alone in My Basement," I can't take it anymore: I slink into my bedroom and open my sock drawer. I remove four granular rocks of PCP and place them into the mouth of a stainless steel cylinder, which I light with matches from a hotel I've never visited. I inhale two channels of hot smoke and exhale one cloud of normalcy. The world flattens out. I walk back into the living room and wake up Donna by kissing her on the neck. Donna must have been dreaming about either sex or puppies, because it takes her all of fifteen seconds to wake up, smile with her eyes closed, and remove her clothing (except, of course, her socks, which is "her thing," sexually). We have great (or possibly terrible) intercourse. White sunlight appears to pour through the windows of my living room, even though it is fifty-nine minutes before midnight.

Since she is partially drunk and mostly naked and completely manipulated, I ask Donna if she wants to sleep over, an offer that always makes her euphoric (certainly more so than my cyborgic lovemaking). Donna has this odd sleeping quirk; she always needs to sleep on the "inside" half of any bed. For example, the bed in her apartment is flush against a wall, so she always sleeps next to the wall and I sleep on the "outside" half. But what's fascinating is that Donna manages to pick out

355

an "inside" part of *every* bed, even when an inside doesn't exist. For example, I sleep on a queen-sized mattress that lays in the middle of my bedroom floor, but Donna insists that the left half of the mattress is the "inside" half. I don't know; I guess it must be farther away from the door or something.

Donna stumbles into my bedroom nude, but she inexplicably decides to put her panties back on for sleeping purposes. It takes her three minutes to pass out for the second time of the evening. Tonight, we're both happy. I lie awake for five hours, pretending she just fell next to me.

ACKNOWLEDGMENTS

Chuck Klosterman would like to thank Brant Rumble, Daniel Greenberg, and Melissa Maerz. He would also like to thank all the people who edited these articles in their original forms, as well as the numerous fact-checkers and copy editors who were anonymously involved in the editing process. These people include: Brendan Vaughan, Jon Dolan, Paul Tough, Sia Michel, Charles Aaron, Doug Brod, Tracey Pepper, Ann Mezger, Steve Love, Joan Rice, and Matt Von Pinnon.

INDEX

Bush, George W., 65n. 1, 70, 85,
    133, 151, 227, 255, 256
Bush, Jeb, 227
"Bust a Move" (Young MC), 280
Buttchuck, 217, 217n. 16
Byrne, David, 233

"Cabo Wabo" (Van Halen), 281
Callahan, David, 286–87
Callan, Kristi, 180, 181
Campbell, Earl, 296
"Can't Fight This Feeling" (REO
    Speedwagon), 83
Carlos, Bun E., 181
Carnival Line "Rock Cruise,"
    75–88
Carpenter, Sue, 285
Carrabba, Chris, 317
Carrack, Paul, 312
Carson, Johnny, 207–9, 212
Carter, Jimmy, 302
Carter, Shawn, 289
Casablancas, Julian, 113
Case, Wendy, 119
Castronovo, Dean, 85
Celtic Frost, 91
Cheap Chick, 180–82, 183
Cheap Trick, 180, 181
Cheating Culture, The (Callahan),
    286
Cher, 314
China, 255
Chinese Democracy (Guns n'
    Roses), 296
choice overload, 208–9
Christgau, Robert, 168, 169
Christian Science, 41–43, 104
Christian Science Monitor, The, 41
Christianson, Bjorn, 216–17,
    217n. 14, 219
"Christine Sixteen" (KISS), 279
Cinderella, 91
Clapton, Eric, 44
Clarence Hotel, Dublin, 22, 24
Clayton, Adam, 24, 29
Clear Channel, 75, 79, 80, 268
Clemons, Clarence, 312
Cline, Nels, 150
Clinton, Bill, 13, 17, 31–32, 32n.
    3, 240

Clinton, Hillary, 227
Clone Defects, 117
clothing and self-image, 243–45
Club Vodka, Los Angeles, 180, 182
C-Murder, 233
Coalition company, 191, 192
Cobain, Kurt, 220, 220n. 22, 222,
    228, 234, 267
Cocker, Jarvis, 56
Cocuzza, Judy, 181, 182
Cold Spring Harbor (Billy Joel), 167
Cole, Richard, 96
Columbine school shootings, 121,
    122n. 1, 127, 128
Come Ons, 117
Comets on Fire, 266
Common Sense (Paine), 41
Communist Manifesto, The (Marx
    and Engels), 70
consumer culture, 283
Cool Hand Luke (film), 261
Copeland, Stewart, 302, 303
Cordingly, David, 285
corporate responsibility vs. per-
    sonal responsibility, 65–66
Cosell, Howard, 21
Costas, Bob, 237–38, 241
counterculture, 201
Coupland, Douglas, 54n. 2
Crawford, Cindy, 44–45
Creed, 94, 278
Creed, Apollo, 296
Cronin, Kevin, 80, 83
Crosby, Robbin, 199–202
"Crosstown Traffic" (Jimi Hen-
    drix), 303–4
Crow, The (film), 128
Crowe, Russell, 44
Cullen, Richard, 54–55
cultural betrayal, 265–69
Culture Club, 305
Cuomo, Rivers, 280
Cure, 122n. 1
"Custard Pie" (Led Zeppelin), 177
Cyclorama (Styx), 83

Damn Yankees, 82, 86
"Dancing in the Streets"
    (Bowie/Jagger version), 233
Dangerfield, Rodney, 305

Smola, Lori, 86
Snoop Doggy Dog, 194
"Snowblind" (Styx), 78
Snowsell, Colin, 52, 53
soccer, 73, 73n. 2
socialism, 70, 71
"Somebody's Out There" (Triumph), 309
Some Girls (Rolling Stones), 135n. 1, 317
Some Kind of Monster (film), 101–12
Song Remains the Same, The (film), 175
Sonic Youth, 118, 278
Son Volt, 147
Southern Culture on the Skids, 216
"Southern Girls" (Cheap Trick), 182
Southpaw Grammar (Morrissey), 50
"So You Want to Be a Rock & Roll Star" (Byrds—Tom Petty version), 301, 308, 311
Spacey, Kevin, 44, 46
Specials, 279
Spears, Britney, 11–20, 32n. 3, 82
Spector, Ronnie, 183
Spencer, Jon, 116
"Spiders (Kidsmoke)" (Wilco), 148
"Spill the Wine" (Eric Burdon and War), 312
SPIN magazine, 21, 47, 89, 93, 113, 114, 133, 138, 143, 148n. 1, 190
Spitz, Bob, 207
Springsteen, Bruce, 167, 312, 317
Spurlock, Morgan, 57, 63–66
"Stairway to Heaven" (Led Zeppelin), 80, 91–92, 94, 185
Standard, 220, 220n. 24
Stanley, Paul, 91, 307–8, 311
Starr, Ringo, 206
Steel Prophet, 91
Steely Dan, 89
Stefani, Gwen, 84
stem-cell research, 295, 297, 298–99
Steve-O, 44

Sticky Fingers, 183
Still Life (Rolling Stones), 136
Sting, 235, 302
Stipe, Michael, 140–41, 140n. 3, 235
Stirratt, John, 149–50
Stone, Oliver, 40, 41
Stooges, 118n. 3
Storm Shadow, 284
Stoudemire, Amare, 71–72, 73
Stover, Jo Anne, 160–61
Stranger, The (Billy Joel), 166
"Stranger, The" (Billy Joel), 167
Stratton, Brandon, 124
Stray Cats, 125, 304
Streets, The, 187–97
Strokes, 116, 131, 180
"Stuck in a Moment You Can't Get Out Of" (U2), 136
Styx, 76–79, 81, 82–83, 86
Sub Pop, 216n. 13
Summerteeth (Wilco), 147
"Summertime Girls" (Y&T), 307
"Sunday Bloody Sunday" (U2), 29
Superchunk, 245
Superman, 228
Super People, 295–99
Super Size Me (film), 57, 63–66
Supper Club, New York, 175–76
"Supposedly Fun Thing I'll Never Do Again, A" (Wallace), 80
Supremes, 27, 119
"Surrender" (Cheap Trick), 182
Sutcliffe, Stuart, 206
"Swallowed" (Bush), 211
Swayze, Patrick, 260
Sweet, Matthew, 280
"Sweetheart" (Franke and the Knockouts), 302
"Sweet Pain" (KISS), 316
Swimming to Cambodia (film), 202
"swirling guitars," 280
Sympathetic Sounds of Detroit (various artists), 117
System of a Down, 250

Taco, 312
Tampa Bay Buccaneers, 284
Tayback, Vic, 209
Taylor, Mick, 210